THE BELL WITCH PROJECT
Sean Casteel and Timothy Green Beckley
Additional Material By Shawn Robbins and Paul Eno

THE BELL WITCH PROJECT
Sean Casteel and Timothy Green Beckley
Additional Material By Shawn Robbins and Paul Eno

This edition Copyright © 2015 by Global Communications/Conspiracy Journal

All rights reserved. No part of these manuscripts may be copied or reproduced by any mechanical or digital methods and no exerpts or quotes may be used in any other book or manuscript without permission in writing by the Publisher, Global Communications/Conspiracy Journal, except by a reviewer who may quote brief passages in a review.

Revised Edition

Published in the United States of America By
Global Communications/Conspiracy Journal
Box 753 · New Brunswick, NJ 08903

Staff Members
Timothy G. Beckley, Publisher
Carol Ann Rodriguez, Assistant to the Publisher
Sean Casteel, General Associate Editor
Tim R. Swartz, Graphics and Editorial Consultant
William Kern, Editorial and Art Consultant

Sign Up On The Web For Our Free Weekly Newsletter
and Mail Order Version of Conspiracy Journal
and Bizarre Bazaar
www.ConspiracyJournal.com

Order Hot Line: 1-732-602-3407
PayPal: MrUFO8@hotmail.com

CONTENTS

The Ghostly Portal Of The Bell Witch by Shawn Robbins i

Little Known Spellbinding Facts About the Bell Witch by Sean Casteel vii

Paul Eno's Tales Of Vampires and The Paranormal by Paul Eno And Tim Beckley xix

Native American Ghosts And Monsters by Sean Casteel xixv

Demonic Possession And Witchcraft In Early America by Sean Casteel xliii

Welcome To Sleepy Hollow by Timothy Green Beckley And Circe liii

The Haunted 19th Century Lives On By Sean Casteel lix

The Town Overrun By Ghosts—Jerome, Arizona by Timothy Green Beckley lxvii

The Bell Witch Project—Chapter 1—Introduction 1

Kate And The Bell Family—Chapter 2 5

The Bell Family—Chapter 3 15

Betsy Bell And Her Trials—Chapter 4 21

The Homestead—Chapter 5 25

Kate Batts And The Witch—Chapter 6 29

Witchcraft And The Bible—Chapter 7 35

Family Touble—Chapter 8 49

After John Bell's Death—Chapter 9 87

Negro Stories—Chapter 10 107

General Andrew Jackson—Chapter 11 113

Theny Thorn—Chapter 12 119

Recollections—Chapter 13 127

Testimonials Chapter—14 145

Latest Demonstrations Chapter—15 159

The Mississippi Bell Witch Legend 165

Spooks, Ghosts And Telepathic Hallucinations 182

More Ghosts 187

Telepathy 197

THE GHOSTLY PORTAL OF THE BELL WITCH

By Shawn Robbins

There is no doubt in my mind about the existence of the creepy phenomena long associated with the Bell Witch name. I can say this with certainty as – thanks to the imminent parapsychologist Dr. Hans Holzer – I actually travel to the time and the place when and where the events in this book were actually taking place.

My name is Shawn Robbins, author, psychic and paranormal researcher. I live in two worlds: the real and the unexplained. The real world is much easier to explain because it is constant and never-changing. Since the dawn of time, the sun rises in the east and sets in the west. Just a fact of life, it is what it is, nothing more and nothing less.

The unexplained world is much more dark and mysterious. It is a ghostly portal where time stands still and things go bump in the night. It is a world filled with lost souls and ghostly apparitions that roam the night. Many of these lost souls are seeking help in transitioning from one world to the next so that they can rest in peace, whilst others seek revenge on those living here on Earth who put them in this suspended form of ghastly animation, leaving them caught between two worlds, the living and the dead.

Whether you are a skeptic or believer, someone who has seen a ghost or not, one cannot dispute the fact that ghosts exist. How do I know? I was trained to become a medium by the esteemed ghost hunter, Hans Holzer. I became the voice of the living dead. I was their ghostly advocate, their friend, and – at times – the only person in the world whom they felt understood their agony and pain at being caught between two worlds.

One of my many documented encounters with these unseen beings was back in the 1970s when noted Hans Holzer asked me to investigate a haunted house on Gay Street, in Greenwich Village, New York City. Hans asked me to meet him in front of this old and storied brownstone to see what vibrations I could pick up and help answer the burning question the terrorized occupants of the household had: "Who, what, and why are these ghostly beings here?"

I set out on my task with nothing more than Hans at my side and a flashlight in my hand. I walked around the house, going from room to room, but found nothing unusual, no cold spots, no smell of flowers, no shadows, nothing that would indicate any ghostly beings lived there. I felt dismayed, heartbroken, that I could not help the people who lived there find peace.

I proceeded to put on my coat and was just about to walk out the door when the unexpected happened. The floor underneath me began to shake. I looked at Hans in shock and said, "Did you feel that?" Hans said, "Feel what?" I said, "The floor shaking." At that moment, I knew we were not alone.

It didn't take long after that to pick up that the house was used by bootleggers in the Prohibition days, and, whether it was an argument over money or the sale of these illegal goods, someone was murdered in the basement of that house.

One of the most daunting tasks of a psychic/medium is to try and tell these ghostly apparitions that their time had expired the moment they passed on, something not all ghosts like to hear. And, contrary to what everyone "knows" about ghosts, many of them will not move on and continue to haunt the living for eons to come.

Over the years, many other psychics and mediums have visited the Haunted House on Gay Street, adding to their own impressions of its history and the uninvited guests, hoping, like me, to help them find peace.

But here is one of the more interesting stories I have to tell, something that I have kept hidden up until now and which is bound to send shivers running up and down your spine…

The Bell Witch Project

Hans Holzer, my mentor and best friend, knew I had an interest in witches and pagan beliefs, and, not widely known before the Bell Witch story became famous, Hans also had an interest in this haunted and storied place as well. The Bell Witch poltergeist, as it seems most often to be referred to, has become part of the historical lore of America. One of the earlier accounts was written down, dramatically, by historian Albert Virgil Goodpasture in "A History of Tennessee."

"A remarkable occurrence, which attracted wide-spread interest, was connected with the family of John Bell, who settled near what is now Adams Station about 1804. So great was the excitement that people came from hundreds of miles around to witness the manifestations of what was popularly known as the 'Bell Witch.' This witch was supposed to be some spiritual being having the voice and attributes of a woman. It was invisible to the eye, yet it would hold conversation and even shake hands with certain individuals. The freaks it performed were wonderful and seemingly designed to annoy the family. It would take the sugar from the bowls, spill the milk, take the quilts from the beds, slap and pinch the children, and then laugh at the discomfiture of its victims. At first it was supposed to be a good spirit, but its subsequent acts, together with the curses with which it supplemented its remarks, proved the contrary. A volume might be written concerning the performance of this wonderful being, as they are now described by contemporaries and their descendants. That all this actually occurred will not be disputed, nor will a rational explanation be attempted."

The incidents associated with the demented saga of the Bell Witch become, according to historical books, even creepier when the soon-to-be President, General Andrew Jackson, took a profound interest in the circumstances of the case. A quote from the files of author A.V Ingram shows how the events unfolded:

"Gen. Jackson's party came from Nashville with a wagon loaded with a tent, provisions, etc., bent on a good time and much fun investigating the witch. The men were riding on horseback and were following along in the rear of the wagon as they approached near the place, discussing the matter and planning how they were going to do up the witch. Just then, traveling over a smooth level piece of road, the wagon halted and stuck fast. The driver popped his whip, whooped and shouted to the team, and the horses pulled with all of their might, but could not move the wagon an inch. It was dead stuck as if welded to the earth. Gen. Jackson commanded all men to dismount and put their shoulders to the wheels and give the wagon a push, but all in vain; it was no go. The wheels were then taken off, one at a time, and examined and found to be all right, revolving easily on the axles. Gen. Jackson after a few moments thought, realizing that they were in a fix, threw up his hands exclaiming, "By the eternal, boys, it is the witch." Then came the sound of a sharp metallic voice from the bushes, saying, "All right General, let the wagon move on, I will see you again to-night." The men in bewildered astonishment looked in every direction to see if they could discover from whence came the strange voice, but could find no explanation to the mystery. The horses then started unexpectedly of their own accord, and the wagon rolled along as light and smoothly as ever."

According to a variety of accounts General Jackson spent an unsettling night being rebuffed by the obnoxious spirit..."It is said that Betsy Bell screamed all night from the pinching and slapping she received from the Witch, and Jackson's covers were ripped off as quickly as he could put them back on, and he and his entire party of men were slapped, pinched and had their hair pulled by the witch until morning, when Jackson and his men decided to hightail it out of Adams. Jackson was later quoted as saying, 'I'd rather fight the British in New Orleans than to have to fight the Bell Witch.'"

But for the purposes of my participation in this matter, let me start from the beginning of my involvement with this historical occult affliction.

It was a snowy day in New York City, and the weather outside was frigid and cold. I was lying in bed when suddenly the telephone rang, jarring me out of a deep sleep. "Hello, hello," I said, hoping it was not some sort of family emergency. It was Hans asking me if I could come over to his apartment later on in the day. He had something important he needed to discuss, and it could not be done over the telephone.

I arrived at Hans' apartment at about 3 P.M., took off my coat and wet boots, and followed him into his book filled den. I could tell from the look in Hans' eyes that this meeting was not the usual, but, instead, unusual and strange. Hans asked me if I could use my powers of remote-viewing, transport myself into the Bell Witch House, and give him my impressions.

The answer was yes!

Hans then proceeded to put me in a trancelike state using hypnosis to see if I could give him more information then what was in print about the Bell Witch. Hans' instincts were right.

With my powers of remote-viewing (being able to transport myself mentally to places I had never been before and describe them accurately, down to the furnishings and even the occupants of a house, living or dead), I was able to tell Hans things that have never been revealed before up until now.

In my trancelike state, I felt my physical spirit leaving my body and speeding through space and time until I finally reached my ultimate destination – the Bell House.

I immediately encountered the ethereal spirit, Kate Batts, who had a distraught and distressed look upon her face. She quickly pointed to her belly and said, "It is not my child."

"Who then?" I asked.

"The slave Wilbur," she replied. I asked Kate why this was important. She answered, "I was raped!" At that very moment I knew this was the information that Hans sought and had eluded so many others.

In further conversations with the Bell Witch, Kate revealed to me she carried the child for seven months and gave birth to it prematurely. The male child died a few hours later. When her husband saw the baby was not his, he immediately went into shock and accused Kate of having an affair. Thereafter, Kate and her husband Frederick's relationship was never to be the same. It was filled with a lifetime of tears and unhappiness. Frederick never forgave her, and Kate never forgave herself for never telling Frederick she was raped.

Suddenly, and without warning, I felt my life force being drained from my body. I kept hearing my name, "Shawn, wake up, wake up." It was Hans, awakening me from my trance. He immediately wrote down everything I saw and heard and, subsequently, years later, in one of his many books on haunted houses, Hans talked about the Bell Witch as well as revealing other information he himself discovered.

My name is Shawn Robbins, and everything that I have just told you is true!

Famed medium and psychic Shawn Robbins. An associate of the late Dr. Hans Holzer, Ms. Robbins investigated many hauntings on his behalf, including a spook that is said to have materialized in a dwelling along Gay Street in Manhattan.

Dr. Hans Holzer was the original "ghost-buster," working with Shawn Robbins on numerous occasions.

Contacting spirits became a popular pastime in early America.

Before he became president, General Andrew Jackson tangled with Tennessee's Bell Witch.

The Gay Street apartment where a quarrelsome spook tormented the residents.

An historical marker tells us a bit about the Bell Witch curse

LITTLE KNOWN, SPELLBINDING FACTS ABOUT THE BELL WITCH

A Brief Synopsis of the Bell Witch Story

By Sean Casteel

The term "ghost," intended most often to refer to the disembodied spirit of deceased person, has been in use since the late 1500s and derives from the more ancient term, "gast," in the language that eventually came to be modern German. The original meaning of "gast" was "terrifying rage," and a person who experiences shock and terror can still be described as "aghast," which translates as "frightened by an angry ghost." The fear of angry ghosts is built into the word itself.

In the uniquely American story of the Bell Witch haunting, in which a ghost took up residence in the home of Kentucky family in 1817, the supernatural presence did indeed vent a great deal of anger on the household, but that was only one among the many emotions the unseen spirit expressed.

In the course of one legend told about the ghost, a group of young boys were exploring a cave overlooking the Red River in Tennessee. During the wet months of the year, the cave is made inaccessible by water gushing out of its mouth and forming a spectacular waterfall. But during the dry months, it is possible to crawl into the muddy cavern and squeeze into its numerous nooks and crannies.

One boy in the group ventured too far inside and became stuck in a tiny crawl space. He screamed for help in the darkness, then heard a booming female voice say, "I'll get you out!" The boy felt his legs being pulled as he was dragged backwards through the thick mud back to the cave entrance. They never found out who or what saved him, but the locals believed it must have been the Bell Witch.

THE BELL FAMILY IS TARGETED BY "KATE"

The boys of the cave incident were friends of Betsy Bell, daughter of John Bell, Sr., and Lucy Williams Bell, the owners of the land where the cave was located. The Bells, a happy and industrious farming family, had moved to Adams, a rural community in Robertson County, Tennessee, from North Carolina in 1804. They settled 1,000 acres of land on the Red River, then a major waterway to ports on the Mississippi River. John Bell erected a log cabin for his family, cabins for their slaves and various outbuildings. After 13 years of hard work, the farm became a successful, thriving operation.

Bell was highly respected in the community as farmer, husband and father and was known to be a devoutly religious man. He also had a reputation for being a hard-nosed business man who would turn a profit whenever possible.

The strange events that would soon become legendary began in 1817, when John was walking through his cornfield. He sighted a strange, doglike creature in the distance that suddenly disappeared. Around the same time, Drewry Bell, one of his sons, saw a large, ugly bird, unlike any he had seen before, perched on a fence. On another evening, Drewry and young Betsy were walking through an orchard when they noticed an old woman walking beside them. When Betsy spoke to her, the woman disappeared.

These sightings eventually led to strange, unexplainable noises in and around the Bell house, such as knocking sounds on doors and windows, wings flapping against the roof and animals fighting and scratching. As the noises became more intense, the family tried desperately to find the source but found nothing. Then bed coverings began slipping off the beds as if being pulled by someone. Sometimes one could hear noises like lips smacking and gulping. Evenings in the Bell house became a noisy nightmare.

One night, the spirit began to talk, introducing itself with hysterical, mocking laughter. When questioned repeatedly as to its name was, the spirit answered "Kate." From then on, Kate seldom kept her mouth shut, arguing theology, teasing and tormenting, spreading gossip and singing loudly. She seemed to know intimate details about everyone and took great delight in being able to pester the household at will.

Why had Kate chosen to torment the Bell family? Among many answers that the spirit gave was that she was a witch conjured by Kate Batts, an eccentric woman who had lived nearby with her ailing husband. There are historical records to the effect that John Bell, Sr., had been convicted by the State of Tennessee of the crime of usury, or charging excessive interest, in a slave deal with Kate Batts' husband.

On her deathbed, the old woman swore that she would haunt John Bell and his descendants. The spirit calling itself Kate repeatedly expressed her hatred for Bell, physically abused him and threatened to kill him. She threw furniture and dishes at Bell, pulled his nose, yanked his hair and poked needles into him. She yelled at night to keep him from sleeping and snatched the food from his mouth at mealtime. No one ever saw Kate/the Bell Witch, but every visitor to the Bell home heard her all too well. One person described the voice as "a nerve-wracking pitch when displeased, while at other times it sang and spoke in low musical tones."

But Kate was capable of more than just hate and could demonstrate a benevolent spirit at times, as when she rescued the young boy trapped in the cave. Kate seemed to adore the mother, Lucy Williams Bell, and greatly respected John Bell, Jr., for his courage in standing up to something as fearsome as the disembodied spirit she was.

It was daughter Betsy Bell that Kate seemed to fixate on the most. The spirit would constantly follow Betsy around. When the young girl went to visit the homes of friends, Kate would go with her, sometimes terrifying whatever friends were playing host to Betsy. The spirit especially hated one of Betsy's suitors, Joshua Gardner, and warned Betsy repeatedly not to marry him for reasons Kate never divulged. Whenever Betsy and Joshua would meet, Kate would torment and embarrass them. Gardner was subjected to so much violent taunting that he eventually split from Betsy and moved out of the area. Betsy later married Richard Powell, her schoolteacher, and some theorized that Powell had created all the "effects" of the ghost to scare his rival Gardner away.

ANDREW JACKSON CONFRONTS THE BELL WITCH

News of the Bell Witch spread and soon crowds were traveling to the family's property from all over to hear the spirit's shrill voice or witness a manifestation of its vile temper. In his Christian charity, John Bell, Sr., never turned any visitors away and even fed some of them at his own expense. The crowds would wait by candlelight for the witch to show herself, and over time the interlopers tore up the Bell property with their wagons and horses, draining the family's finances and affording the Bells little privacy.

Andrew Jackson, who at the time was a general in the Tennessee militia, had heard about the Bell Witch from the courageous John, Jr., who served under Jackson during the Battle of New Orleans in 1815. When word of the haunting reached Nashville, Jackson felt it was time to gather some friends and journey to

Adams to investigate.

Jackson had earned a reputation for toughness and strength in many conflicts with Native Americans and was determined to either expose the Bell Witch as a hoax or drive the spirit away. Jackson's party came on horseback, bringing along a wagon loaded with a tent and provisions and looking forward to a good time investigating the witch. When one of the men openly questioned Kate's existence, the wagon mysteriously stopped of its own accord and became stuck in spite of how the road was smooth and level. The driver cracked his whip and shouted to the team of horses; the horses pulled with all their strength, but could not move the wagon an inch.

The general ordered all the men to dismount, put their shoulders to the wheels and give the wagon a push, but to no avail. The wheels were removed one-by-one and examined and found to be all right, revolving easily on the axles. At this point, Jackson could only raise his arms and exclaim, "By the eternal, boys, it is the witch!"

Then came the sound of a sharp, metallic voice from the bushes, saying, "All right, general, let the wagon move on. I will see you again tonight." The bewildered group looked in every direction to discover where the voice had come from but could not explain the mystery. The horses then started – unexpectedly and of their own volition – and the wagon rolled on as though there had never been a problem.

Some versions of the Jackson encounter story say that Jackson did in fact meet the witch. As Betsy screamed all night from the pinching and slapping she suffered from Kate, Jackson's covers were ripped off faster than he could pull them back on again; he and his entire party of men were also slapped, pinched and had their hair pulled by the witch until morning, apparently in retaliation to one of the men's demand that Kate show herself. Jackson and his men decided to hightail it out of the area as the sun rose on a new day. "I'd rather fight the British in New Orleans than have to fight the Bell Witch," Jackson was alleged to have said in the aftermath.

THE TRIUMPH OF THE WITCH

By 1820, John Bell, Sr., was weak and exhausted after years of physical abuse from the Bell Witch. As he walked one October day with his son Richard to the family's pigsty, one of the old man's shoes was yanked off his foot. Richard tied his father's shoe back on, only to see the other one pulled off in the same way. The air was suddenly filled with horrifying sounds, and the elder Bell felt totally overcome and began to pray for deliverance. He was led back inside the main house and took to his bed for several weeks, growing steadily weaker and more ill. On the morning of December 19, he failed to wake up and couldn't be roused. John Jr. frantically searched the medicine cabinet but could find only a strange vial filled with a brownish liquid.

When the local doctor arrived, Kate began to laugh and taunt the family and claimed she had switched the medicine for a vial of poison. The doctor tested the liquid on a cat, killing it almost instantly.

John Bell, Sr. died the next day, but even in death he found no rest from Kate. At his funeral, attended by hundreds of friends and curiosity seekers, Kate laughed and mocked the family, singing loudly and joyously in her triumph. She stayed on the Bell property for another year, then told the family she was leaving but would return in seven years. She kept her word, returning in 1828, but stayed only a couple of weeks.

The remaining members of the Bell family either died or moved away. The old buildings have long since been torn down, the family plot is overrun with weeds, but, to this day, strange lights and ghostly apparitions have been seen in the area. Some believe that the elder John Bell's restless ghost still wanders the land he once owned and farmed.

Meanwhile, the spirit that tormented Bell into his grave is said to still live in the small cave on his former property, lying in wait to terrify anyone who comes her way.

The place where the Bell Witch tormented the living still stands today as a popular Tennessee attraction.

All signs point the way to a place where pure evil once dwelt.

Betsy Bell was the center of attention.

General Andrew Jackson — soon to become President Jackson — had his own run-in with the Bell Witch poltergeist.

The Bell Witch phenomenon has created numerous spinoffs, including a biker meet.

Bell Witch doppelganger circa 1871.

John Bell.

After leaving the house, the witch could be heard roaming the nearby woods.

Above: Bell Witch as a shape-shifting demon hound.

Below: The grave of Betsy Bell.

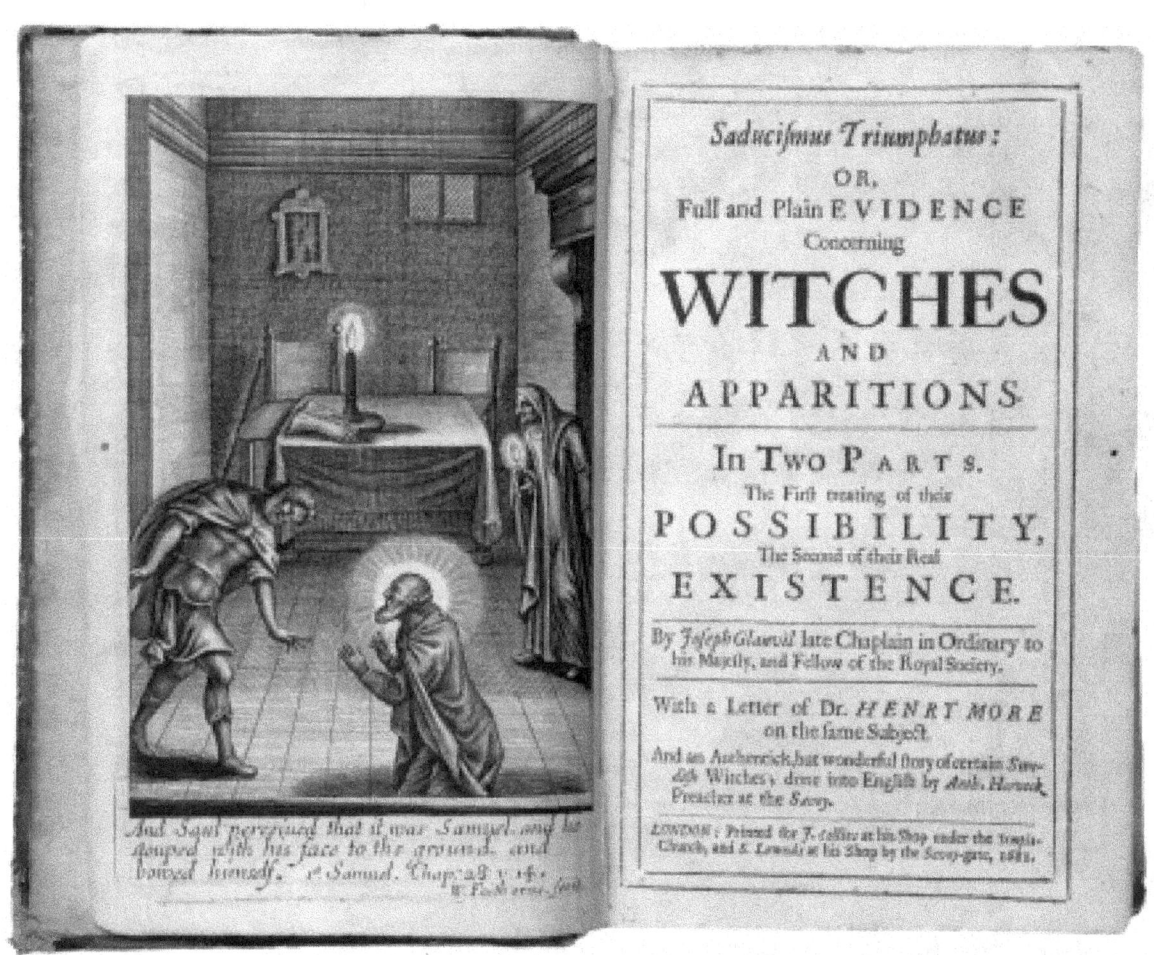

Above: A "Witch" book
Below: A YouTube banner courtesy "Laughing Historically."

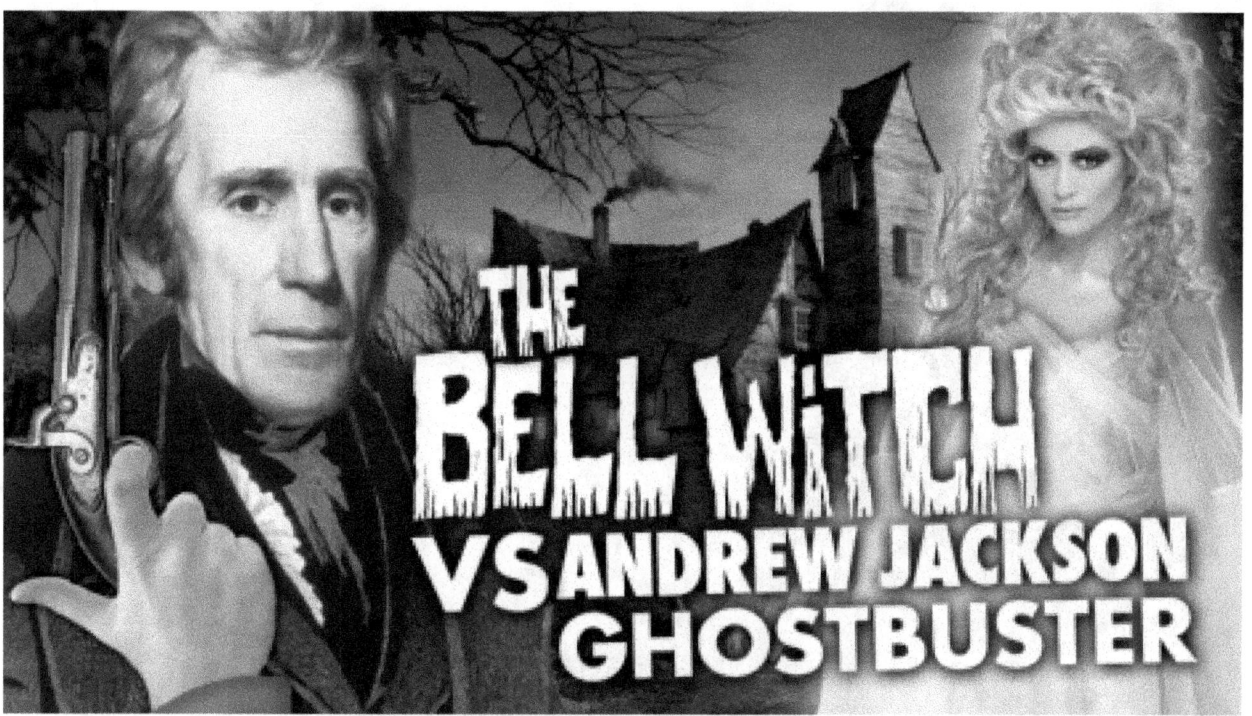

PAUL ENO'S TALES OF VAMPIRES

AND THE PARANORMAL IN EARLY AMERICA

By Timothy Green Beckley with Paul Eno

Paul Eno and I go way back. Well, not anywhere near as far back as his research into the paranormal in America has taken him.

Recently, I hopped on a northbound train out of Penn Station and headed up to Providence, Rhode Island, where the bearded icon of the psychic world was waiting for me in his cozy van outside the railway station.

It was the first time we had met mono et mono, though I had been on his weekly talk show "Behind the Paranormal" several times. Paul has hosted this program, along with this son Benjamin, for over five years. The father and son team broadcast out of the modest radio station WOON Radio 1240, located in Woonsocket, R.I.

I feel very much at home on the airwaves there because Paul allows a guest to set his or her own boundaries as to the direction the conversation will ultimately flow; my favorite topic on the show might be the relationship between UFOs and synchronicity. But another reason for that sense of comfort is because my association with the station itself actually goes back many years, when I first sat behind the microphone as a guest of Joe Ferriere.

Joe hosted a midday talk show on WOON Radio for nearly half a century, until he passed away several years ago. Though Joe seldom mentioned the topic of UFOs on his program, he was what is known as a "silent UFO contactee," a "UFO Repeater" who had taken dozens of photos of what he maintained were alien spacecraft observed hovering in our skies. Interested readers may want to pick up the book "UFO Repeaters: Seeing Is Believing! The Camera Doesn't Lie!," in which

Joe's photo collection is displayed along with his fascinating extraterrestrial encounters. Some of that material was furnished us by the subject of this chapter, Paul Eno.

Without hesitation, I would have to agree with what others have said about Paul when they proclaimed him "the most intelligent voice in paranormal research today," as "God's ghost hunter," and "one of the most visionary philosophers of our time," and "the ghost hunter with a brain." Several radio and television producers have called him "simply incredible" and "inspiring." I applaud them utterly for having the foresight and insight to make this unvarnished declaration.

Paul was among the first paranormal investigators of the early 1970s, beginning when he was studying for the priesthood. Today he is an award-winning New England journalist and holds a university degree in philosophy. Paul's many years of experience in the field of the strange and supernatural help him draw capacity crowds wherever he lectures, and he is the author of seven books.

VAMPIRES OF RHODE ISLAND

Among Paul's many areas of expertise is the folklore of his home state of Rhode Island. In a chapter from his 1998 book, "Faces at the Window," he recounts some fascinating case histories of real-life vampire encounters that took place in his neck of New England prior to 1900.

"Each of our six New England states has had vampire cases," Paul writes. "Several of the most striking incidents occurred in eastern Connecticut and Rhode Island in the period between roughly 1770 and 1900. Belief in vampires, in one form or another, has filtered down from the remote past. Vampires are mentioned in the lore of ancient Sumeria, Babylon, Greece, Rome and Israel and are found in mythologies as diverse as those of Brazil, China and the Rocky Mountains of North America.

"Of course, the world's vampire capital has always been central and eastern Europe," he continues. "The vampires that supposedly haunted New England, as well as the steps people took against them, corresponded almost exactly with the general folk belief of central Europe. In the known Rhode Island and Connecticut cases, the 'vampires' were believed to inhabit bodies of the dead and to prey only on members of their own families."

Paul notes that how these beliefs crossed the Atlantic and became implanted in the minds of these 18th- and 19th-century New England farmers, hardheaded children of the Puritans, remains a mystery. No eastern Europeans are known to have settled in Rhode Island or eastern Connecticut before 1850, so immigrant influence was not a likely factor.

Dr. Michael E. Bell, Rhode Island's official folklorist, has documented at least nine vampire cases in that state alone and suggests that these beliefs were always present and are a part of our Indo-European heritage. Paul quotes Bell as saying, "Mundane stories don't get passed on (from one generation to another.) It's the amazing stories that do."

PERMISSION TO DIG UP THE DEAD

One particularly remarkable case that Paul writes about took place in Cumberland, Rhode Island, on the border with Massachusetts, in 1796. The legal records of the incident can still be found in the vault at Cumberland Town Hall.

"On February 8 of that year," Paul writes, "one Stephen Staples petitioned the Town Council for permission to dig up the body of Abigail Staples, his 23-year-old daughter, because she was rising from the grave each night to drain the lives of her eight brothers and sisters."

Paul then quotes the relevant passage from the Town Council records, which explains that Stephen Staples wanted to dig up Abigail in order to "try an experiment" on Abigail's sister Lavina Chace, wife of Stephen Chace. Permission was granted. Lavina and several of Staples' other children were wasting away, almost certainly with the highly infectious disease we know today as pulmonary tuberculosis, called "consumption" in that era.

"The 'experiment' Staples performed was typical of the 'remedy' in New England's vampire cases," Paul writes. "It was believed that the cycle of consumption and death could be stopped if the body of the suspected vampire was exhumed, the bones broken to prevent its moving about, and the heart burned. To help ailing family members, the smoke from the fire might be inhaled or the ashes from the heart actually ingested in some way."

"SNUFFY STUKE'S" PROPHETIC DREAM

An 1888 Providence publication known as "Book Notes" (Vol. 5, No. 7) serves as Paul's source for another vampire account. The incident took place in West Greenwich in the mid-1770s and involved a family called the Stukeleys, headed by a handsome, well-to-do young farmer whom the locals nicknamed "Snuffy Stuke" because of the butternut-brown jacket he liked to wear.

He and his wife had been blessed with 14 children, several of whom had already reached their upper teens. One night, Snuffy had a disturbing dream in which he was the owner of a large orchard, half of whose trees suddenly died. The dream's meaning quickly became all too apparent when his oldest daughter, Sarah, developed what seemed to be consumption and rapidly wasted away. She died and was buried in the family graveyard on the Stukeley property.

Snuffy's strange dream became a recurring one, and soon his next-oldest daughter was taken with the same disease as her sister and began to wither away.

"But this time," Paul writes, "there was a big difference: The terrified girl complained of nightly visits from her dead sister, whom she said 'sat upon some portion of the body, causing great pain and misery.' Then she herself died. And so it went. One after another, the children sickened and died until six were gone and another, the first son, was taken ill. At the same time, Mrs. Stukeley starting complaining of nightly visits from Sarah."

The grief-stricken, terrified family held a council with "the most learned people," presumably local officials, physicians and clergy. After some discussion, it was agreed that a vampire was at work.

"Neighbors were called in to help," Paul writes, "and with picks and spades they opened the graves of the six dead children. When the bodies were viewed, five proved to be in an advanced state of decomposition. But one, the body of Sarah, the first to die, reportedly was in a remarkable state indeed. Sarah's eyes were open and fixed, her hair and nails had grown, and her heart and arteries were filled with fresh blood. It was clear to all that the cause of their troubles lay before them.

"Wasting no time," Paul goes on, "they cut the heart from Sarah's body and from the bodies of the five others and burned the organs on a rock in front of the Stukeley home. The bodies were then reburied. It was a remedy right out of the dark mountains of Transylvania. At last, peace descended on the troubled house, but not before a seventh victim had died. This was the sick son, a promising young farmer who had recently married and lived on an adjoining farm. He already had been too far gone. Thus was the dream of Snuffy Stukeley fulfilled, with the 'orchard' of his children depleted by half."

THE QUINTESSENTIAL CASE OF NEW ENGLAND VAMPIRISM

Drawn partially from the same source as the Snuffy dream story, the writings of one Sidney S. Rider of the publication "Book Notes," Paul writes about what he considers to be the quintessential case of New England vampirism. This story took place in Wakefield, Rhode Island, and concerned the Browns of Exeter, whom Rider called "a family of respectable surroundings."

"The Browns of Exeter were not country bumpkins," Paul writes. "They were well-off, respected farming people related to some of the most distinguished figures of Rhode Island's colonial history, including the founder of Brown University."

While the story of the Browns' encounter with vampirism was only just beginning when Rider wrote of it briefly, Paul says the complete account he offers here was more recently handed down by Lewis Peck of Exeter, whose grandmother, a Brown, recalled the incredible incident.

Mrs. Mary E. Brown died, apparently of consumption, on December 8, 1883, leaving her husband, George, with one son and several daughters. Six months later, the oldest daughter, 20-year-old Mary, died of the same disease. Then, around 1888, the son, Edwin, suddenly fell ill with consumption and relocated to Colorado in the hope of recovering. Declining rapidly, Edwin returned to Rhode Island, only to find that his 19-year-old sister, Mercy, had also contracted the disease and was in even worse shape than he.

As Edwin still battled for his life, Mercy died in January 1892. Twelve members of the Brown family conferred on what could be done for Edwin, who, given his former strength and health, should not be wasting away. They concluded unanimously that a vampire must be draining the life out of him – a vampire that likely resided in the grave of one of the three deceased family members. The Browns undoubtedly were aware of the local traditions about such things.

"So, on a cold March day in 1892," Paul recounts, "a grim assembly arrived at the Chestnut Hill Cemetery in Exeter, behind the Baptist church of that name. The remains of Mrs. Brown and Mary, buried for years, proved to be only skeletons. But in Mercy's grave was a startling find. Not only did the body look in the pink of health, with blood in the heart and arteries, but it had turned over part way in the coffin.

"The vampire-hunters cut the girl's heart from her body and burned it on a rock that still can be seen not far from the grave. Then all three bodies were reburied, and the ashes of the heart gathered up, for Edwin's doctor, a full believer in the vampire theory, had prescribed for him the ashes of his sister's heart, dissolved in medicine. This grotesque remedy evidently did Edwin no good; he died shortly thereafter."

This was the last known case of "vampirism" in New England, Paul writes, but it is by no means forgotten locally. Mercy's grave can be seen behind the still-active Chestnut Hill Baptist Church, as can those of Mrs. Brown and Mary.

Lewis Peck, the Brown descendant who passed the story along, talks about Mercy Brown only if prodded. When asked who brings the small flowers that are occasionally placed on Mercy's grave, Peck says he doesn't know. But the belief that Mercy really was a vampire has persisted, especially among certain old-timers in the region. Peck hedges as to his own position on the matter, saying only that "there are still a lot of people around here who believe in some pretty strange things." Peck does acknowledge that, when he was a child, "my mother and my grandmother told us never, ever to touch Mercy's gravestone."

Peck says one incident is forever embedded in his memory. It took place in the early 1960s, when he was in his thirties.

"I was in back of the church hall with a friend of mine," he recalls. "It was about 11 P.M., and suddenly we saw this great big ball of light right over Mercy's grave. I was scared to death! I've never seen anything like it before or since."

In a compelling twist to the Brown affair, a newspaper clipping about the case reportedly was found among Bram Stoker's Dracula notes after the author died in 1912.

THE SPECTER LEAGUERS

As the book you are now reading was being written, the ever-prolific Paul Eno was hard at work on a new book of his own, coauthored with his son, Ben, and called "Cosmic Journey: Behind the Paranormal." Paul shared an as-yet-unpublished chapter with me entitled "The Paranormal in Human History" that includes the following fascinating story of the Specter Leaguers.

"One apparently paranormal incident might have prompted the Salem witch hysteria in Massachusetts," Paul writes, "and the social and religious reforms that eventually followed it. This is the little-known but well-documented 'invasion' of Cape Ann, Massachusetts, in 1692, by what came to be called 'The Specter Leaguers,' seemingly an army of ghosts, demons, aliens or Frenchmen, depending on your point of view."

The controversial Puritan chronicler of early New England, the Reverend Cotton Mather, tells the story in his classic work "Magnalia Christi Americana," which translates as "The Marvels of Christ in America."

No, this is not Paul Eno digging down into some subterranean base in the Antarctic. Rather, it's the "Behind The Paranormal" host trying to dig out of his Woonsocket, RI, driveway circa winter of 2015.

The Rev. Eliakim Phelps played a vital role in the unsettling case of the Stratford poltergeist.

Tormenting and hanging witches became the order of the day.

Cumberland vampire being exhumed.

The estate stood tall and proud and seemingly "normal" when looked at from the outside — but once inside, all hell is said to have broken loose!

Several hundred years ago, the Stratford poltergeist wandered the halls and rooms of this grand estate.

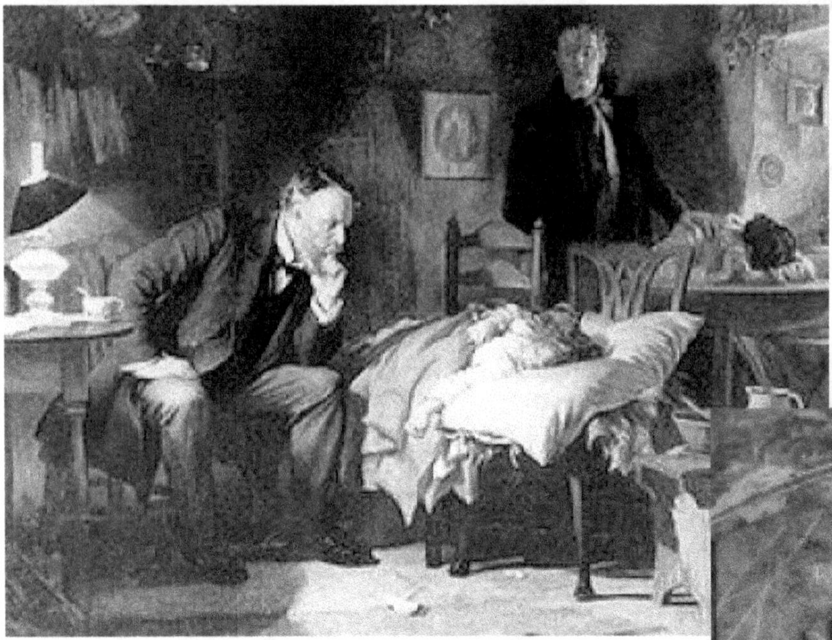

Relatively unknown, vampires were running amuck throughout early America, draining the lifeblood of many an unsuspecting colonialist.

Mercy Brown tombstone.

Son Benjamin and father Paul Eno have been hosting "Behind The Paranormal" for over five decades on WOON Radio. Their show can be found Monday Drive-Time Radio, 6-7 pm Eastern, 3-4 pm Pacific, 11 pm 12 am British www.BehindTheParanormal.com programs are also archived.

"The witch hysteria began that same year on the Massachusetts North Shore, in and around Salem and Danvers," Paul writes. "We suspect that this spectral incident at Cape Ann, only about 20 miles up the coast from those towns, had much to do with stirring people up about the paranormal. Mather writes that he got the story from Reverend John Emerson (1625-1700) of Gloucester, Massachusetts. Emerson reported how 'a number of rollicking apparitions, dressed like gentlemen, in white waistcoats and breeches, kept that and the neighboring towns in a state of feverish excitement and alarm' for at least two weeks."

It began in the home of one Ebenezer Babson. He and his family "almost every night heard noises as if some persons were walking or running hither and thither about the house." Coming home late one night, Babson saw two strange men emerge from his own front door. Upon seeing him, the two men ran into a cornfield. When Babson entered his house and asked his family who the men were, they insisted no one had been there.

"Confused and frustrated," Paul continues, "Babson grabbed his gun and went looking for the intruders. A short distance from the house, he flushed them from behind a log. As they high-tailed it into a swamp, Babson reported that one man said to the other, 'The man of the house is now come, else we might have taken the house.' Then Babson lost sight of them."

In another incident, three intruders were chased away while snooping outside the local fort and ran toward a swamp. When one man fired at them, all three fell to the ground. The shooter approached what he expected to be three dead men, but the figures suddenly rose up and ran away "without hurt or wound of any kind." At one point, residents heard some of the intruders speaking in "outlandish jargon" and "could not understand a word."

The intruders, called "unaccountable troublers" in the vernacular of the time, demonstrated that they were impervious to lead or steel and could show themselves "first in one place, then in another." More of these specters appeared, both by night and day, dressed in white and carrying "bright guns," though they acted more like hooligans than soldiers. As the sightings increased, the local residents feared an attack by the Indians, the French, or worse. Others believed it was an invasion by demons and that the Devil was loose at Cape Ann. Whoever the phantoms were, they grew more emboldened every day.

"They threw stones, beat upon barns with clubs, and otherwise acted more in the spirit of diabolical revelry than as actuated by any deadlier purpose," Paul quotes Mather. "They moved about the swamps without leaving any tracks like ordinary beings. It was evident that such beings as these were must be fought with other weapons besides matchlocks and broadswords; consequently, a strange fear fell upon the Cape."

With the realization that "the Cape was in great peril from this diabolical invasion, the aid of the surrounding towns was invoked in this truly alarming crisis." Sixty men were sent from nearby Ipswich to battle "the Powers of Darkness," but the strange phantoms were now so bold that they "treated their pursuers with open contempt."

The incidents reportedly ended as suddenly as they began. Once it was settled that these "insults" proceeded from specters and not from beings vulnerable to weapons of mortal make, "the unequal contest was abandoned. When this was done, the demon's occupation being gone, they too disappeared."

"As far as we know," Paul writes, "the Specter Leaguers never troubled Cape Ann again."

THE STRATFORD POLTERGEIST

Paul also offered up an account of a 19th century poltergeist haunting taken from the files of well-known researcher of the strange and author Troy Taylor. The events took place in Stratford, Connecticut, in 1850, and the case remains a mystery even more than a century and a half later.

The story begins when the Reverend Eliakim Phelps purchased a sprawling mansion on Elm Street in Stratford, planning to retire in his new home. He had been widowed in his late 50s and his children were all grown and had long since left home. Phelps was unique among Presbyterian clergymen in that he was known to have an interest in mysticism, mesmerism and the growing Spiritualist movement in America. He devoted most of his time to reading and exploring these interests.

At age 59, Phelps married again, this time to a much younger woman who already had three children: Anna, 16, Henry, 11, and another girl, who was six. Phelps and his new wife had a son together; he was three years old when the strange happenings on Elm Street began.

In spite of outward appearances, the family was not entirely happy. Mrs. Phelps disliked the town of Stratford and her neighbors as well. She was constantly tired and upset, while Anna was said to suffer from a "nervous disposition." Their stress will be relevant to the story to come.

"It began on Sunday, March 10, 1850," Troy writes. "The entire Phelps family returned from church services that morning to find the doors of their house standing wide open. Dr. Phelps was shocked by this. As the maid was away, he had been sure to secure the entire house, locking not only the exterior doors and windows, but the interior ones as well. The only keys were in his pocket. But now they discovered that all of the doors had been flung open, both inside and out."

Inside, Dr. Phelps discovered total chaos. The place had been thoroughly ransacked, with furniture knocked over, dishes smashed, and books and papers scattered everywhere. He saw that his gold watch, the family silver and his loose cash were in plain sight but had been left alone, which ruled out robbery as a motive.

Upstairs in the bedrooms was a sight even more unnerving. Someone had spread a sheet over one bed and placed one of Mrs. Phelps' nightgowns on top of it. Stockings had been placed at the bottom of the nightgown to suggest feet and the arms had been folded as though crossed in preparation for a funeral. Was this some intended message from the vandals?

The family tried to straighten the house up before Mrs. Phelps and the children left for afternoon services. Dr. Phelps remained behind, hoping to catch the interlopers if they returned. He hid in his study, armed with a pistol, and waited in silence. After a few hours, he left his hiding place and went to the lower floor.

When he opened the door to the dining room, he suddenly saw what he thought at first was a crowd of women. They had entered without making a sound and now stood silent, standing and kneeling in positions of religious devotion. Several of them held Bibles, while others bowed their heads. A few moments later, Phelps could see that the women were really lifelike effigies that had been fashioned from the family's clothing in a way similar to the figure in the bedroom upstairs. The dresses had been filled with rags, muffs and other materials around the house.

But how had the dummies been created and positioned in the short time that Mrs. Phelps and the children had been at church and while Phelps himself had been so vigilantly standing guard? How could it have been done, and, more importantly, what did it mean?

Over the months to come, nearly 20 more similar effigies appeared in the home, without warning and with no clue as to how they were so quickly and silently constructed. On the day after the initial vandalism, the activity became even more frantic, with objects moving around the house. An umbrella jumped in the air and traveled nearly 25 feet. Forks, spoons, knives, pens and assorted small objects launched from places where no one had been standing. This continued all day long but fell silent by nighttime. But the next morning, the activity started all over again. A few days later, objects began to drop from nowhere, beginning with a potato landing on the breakfast table.

A MADNESS ALL THE WORLD COULD SEE

Observers, friends and the curious also witnessed the objects flying about of their own volition. Whenever someone claimed it was a kind of trickery, Dr. Phelps would invite the skeptics to see for themselves. He was hospitable to newspaper reporters, permitting them to come to the house and stay as long as they liked, which often resulted in the outsiders seeing the disturbances firsthand and coming to believe in the family's bizarre predicament.

The outbreak went on, becoming both a physical and psychological attack on the entire family. The nighttime hours were filled with rapping, knockings, voices, screams and bizarre sounds. Daughter Anna and young Henry soon became a more direct target.

A reporter from "The New York Sun" wrote that he saw Anna's arm jerk and twitch. Anna said that she had just been pinched. The reporter rolled back Anna's sleeve and stated that her arm bore several savage-looking red marks. At other times, Anna was slapped by unseen hands. Those present would only see the girl shake or jerk her head but reported hearing the sound of a slap. Red marks and welts would often appear on her skin.

Meanwhile, Henry was just as tortured. He was beaten, struck and sometimes rendered unconscious and abducted. One newspaper reporter claimed to have seen Henry carried off his bed by an unseen force and dumped on the floor. The young boy was thrown into a cistern of water and had his clothing torn apart in front of visiting clergymen.

Locals said the haunting was caused by the ghost of a woman named Goody Bassett, who was hanged near the house for witchcraft in 1651. Many believed that the house had been invaded by intelligent spirits bound and determined to wreak havoc with the family. Another theory is that the phenomena were the result of unconscious or involuntary psycho-kinesis, perhaps fueled by the bitterly unhappy Mrs. Phelps or the "nervous" adolescent Anna, although that would not explain the mysterious effigies of women that appeared in locked rooms.

Desperate for information, Dr. Phelps decided to conduct a séance on his own and easily made contact with an entity that claimed to be a spirit in hell enduring torment for the sins he had committed in life. The spirit asked for a piece of pumpkin pie and a glass of gin and said he had been causing all the trouble "for fun."

After months of madness, the family pulled up stakes and moved back to Philadelphia. The spirits did not accompany them there, where the family spent the winter and spring, returning to Stratford in the early summer of 1851. The house remained calm and still and the supernatural forces seemed to have resolved themselves.

To find out more about Paul Eno and his work, go to:
www.newenglandghosts.com

The website for his radio show is at www.behindtheparanormal.com

SUGGESTED READING

Paul's books include:

"Faces at the Window," New River Press 1998, Second edition 2001

"Footsteps in the Attic," New River Press 2002, Third edition 2012

"Turning Home: God, Ghosts and Human Destiny," New River Press 2006

"Rhode Island: A Genial History" (By Paul F. Eno and Glenn Laxton), New River Press 2005

Troy Taylor's books include:

"Into the Shadows: American Unsolved Mysteries and Tales of the Unexplained," Whitechapel 2002

"Cabinet of Curiosities," Whitechapel 2005

"The Haunted President" (from Troy's "Haunted Illinois" Series), Whitechapel 2005

"Rolling Heads" are created when victims of particularly violent murders rise from the dead to seek revenge. They devour their victims, leaving them void of flesh.

An actual "ghost dancer," circa 1880, ready to bring down the spirits.

NATIVE AMERICAN GHOSTS AND MONSTERS

By Sean Casteel

It should come as no surprise that the colonizers of the Americas did not import ghosts and monsters to this country. Among the Native Americans, legends and folkloric tales of the strange and frightening were an integral part of what was considered at the time to be a backwards, primitive culture. We are only now beginning to learn that things the white man of old called "superstition" and "ignorance" were in fact born of a "white hot" connection to a very real world of spirits and fiends run amuck.

THE MOURNFUL CRIES OF THE SWAMP WOMAN

In the folklore of the Wabanaki, "Swamp Woman" is a ghost that lives in the swamps and makes mournful cries. Anyone who tries to follow the sound of her crying will be lost in the swamp and killed. Some stories depict Swamp Woman as an evil creature, intentionally luring children to their deaths out of spite or so that she could eat them. Other stories paint her as a tragic figure, saying she is the ghost of a childless woman who calls children to her out of sheer loneliness, only to have them die when her ghostly hands touch them. She was often employed as a bogeyman by parents to scare children away from straying into the swamp.

THE SCALPED MAN

"The Scalped Man" is a character from Arikara and Pawnee ghost stories, a warrior who returned to life after being killed and scalped in battle. He now roams the world as a fearsome spirit with the top of his head missing. In most stories, Scalped Man frightens and threatens people; in other stories, he is a pitiful creature who haunts his old village and helps people when they are not looking.

Daniel Leed's House, Leeds Point, Atlantic County, NJ
"Birthplace of the Jersey Devil"

The Leeds house way back in the pine barrens is where the Jersey Devil is said to have been born.

Native Americans draw upon the energy to open the portals between this world and the next.

According to the oral tradition of the Arapahos, a talking skeleton saved the life of one of its best braves.

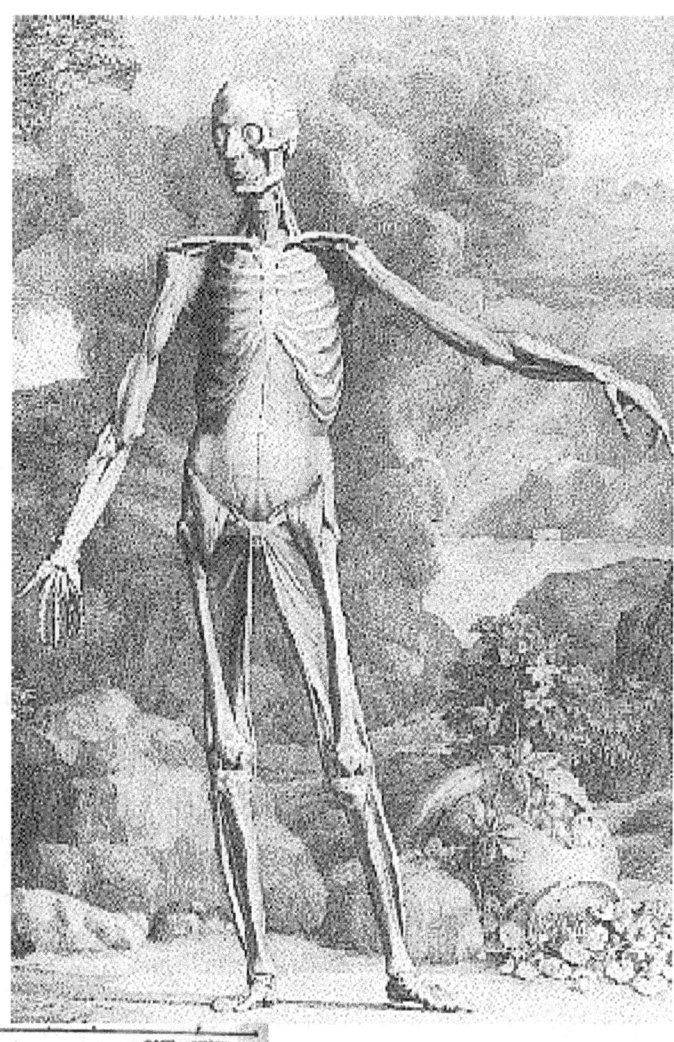

Tales of the Jersey Devil's appearance have been chronicled by the press throughout the years.

Even films have been made about the legend of the Swamp Woman.

According to the Wabanaki, "Swamp Woman" is a ghost that lives in the swamps and makes mournful cries.

THE WALKING, TALKING SKELETON

From the Arapahos comes the story of the lame warrior and the skeleton. In the days before horses (which were actually introduced in America by European colonists), a group of young men were hunting wild game in the western mountains. One warrior felt a sudden sharp pain in his ankle as the party was crossing the rocky bed of a shallow stream. The ankle swelled and grew increasingly painful, so they pitched camp for the night. The next morning the ankle was so badly swollen that it was impossible for the young man to continue the journey with the others.

His fellow travelers built a makeshift teepee shelter for him and left him plenty of firewood. He was instructed to return to the village when his ankle was well and not to try to catch up with them. After several days, the ankle was still too painful to walk on. A heavy snowstorm fell, and the young warrior was nearly out of food. As luck would have it, a herd of buffalo were rooting in the snow for grass close enough for him to kill one with his bow and arrow. He crawled out to the carcass, skinned it, and began to roast its ribs.

Night had fallen as he reached for his first piece of meat. He next heard approaching footsteps crunching in the snow. Unable to flee whoever was there, he reached for his bow and arrow and waited. The tent flap opened and there stood a skeleton wrapped in a tan-colored robe. The robe was pinned tight at the neck so that only the skull was visible above the skeleton feet below. Frightened, the warrior turned his eyes away.

The skeleton spoke in a hoarse voice, saying, "You must not be frightened of me. I have taken pity on you. Now you must take pity on me. Give me a piece of those roast ribs to eat, for I am very hungry."

The warrior was still greatly unnerved by the appearance of the unexpected visitor, but he offered a large piece of meat to the stranger's bony hand. To the young man's amazement, the skeleton chewed the food with its bared teeth and swallowed it.

"It was I who gave you the pain in your ankle," the skeleton said. "It was I who caused your ankle to swell so you could not continue on the hunt. If you had gone on with your companions, you would have been killed."

The skeleton informed the warrior that the rest of the hunting party had encountered an enemy war party who had slain the young warrior's fellow tribesmen. The skeleton had saved the young man's life. The creature next rubbed the warrior's ankle with its bony hand, and the pain and swelling were instantly healed. Having restored the warrior's ability to walk, the skeleton warned the young man that enemy warriors were still all around him.

"But if you follow me," the creature said, "I can lead you safely back to your village."

When the warrior reached his home, the skeletal ghost vanished.

THE MONSTROUS CANNIBAL ROLLING HEADS

The monstrous Rolling Heads of Native American lore are almost too horrifying for the movies, though it would be just the sort of thing current CGI technology could do a good job with. There are several different variations of this particular legend but most of them start with the story of an isolated Indian family.

Every day, before going out to hunt, it was the custom of the father to cover his wife in red paint as a form of sacred medicine intended to protect her from harm. She would then leave their two children alone in the lodge while she went to the nearby lake to fetch some water. At the lake, she would disrobe, as if to bathe. She then commanded a snake to appear, which rose out of the lake, obligingly enough. The snake said she should come and lie with him since her husband had gone hunting. The woman obeyed the snake and did so every morning.

Upon his return one day, the husband asked his wife what had made the paint come off her. She answered that she had taken a bath. The husband decided to follow her secretly the next morning instead of doing his usual hunting. From his hiding place at the lake, the husband saw his wife summon forth the snake, strip naked and begin having intercourse with the reptile. In a jealous rage, the husband killed the snake, cutting it into several pieces with his knife. Then he caught his wife and killed her; he cut her up and took her meat home. He cooked his wife, and the children unknowingly ate their mother.

The husband left the children at the lodge, saying he was going to retrieve some meat he'd left behind. The children began to wonder what had happened to their mother.

Soon after, their mother's head came rolling up to them and said, "I am very sorry that my children have eaten me up." The children fled the Rolling Head, but it was in hot pursuit. When they were too tired to run any further, the elder child drew a line on the ground and dug such a deep hole that the pursuing head could not cross over to them. The children were eventually adopted by a kindly family and their father was torn apart by lions in punishment for what he'd done.

The forgoing tale of domestic strife and murder is only one version among many tales of the Rolling Heads phenomenon. According to legends of the Midwestern and Plains tribes, Rolling Heads are man-eating monsters that appear as an undead, disembodied head with long, tangled hair. The head rolls along the ground chasing humans to kill and devour.

Rolling Heads are created when victims of particularly violent murders rise from the dead to seek revenge. In most stories, this takes the form of an angry man who murders his unfaithful wife, although in some versions the victim is killed for witchcraft or violating some taboo. The story is sometimes made more gruesome by the addition of forced cannibalism, such as feeding the flesh of the mother to the unsuspecting children or feeding the wife part of her own meat as she lays dying.

Eventually, the series of evil acts leads the Rolling Head to rise from the victim's grave and take revenge on the killer. It then proceeds to terrorize its own children and/or the neighboring people until someone manages to destroy it. Some stories say that Rolling Heads can only be killed by drowning, while others say this is accomplished with magical powers or by causing the heads to fall off cliffs or into pits.

THE JERSEY DEVIL'S NATIVE AMERICAN ORIGIN

Said to inhabit the Pine Barrens of southern New Jersey, the Jersey Devil is frequently described as a flying biped with hooves, a snake's tail, bat wings and a head that resembles a horse. The overall effect of the hodgepodge of parts is that it looks like a dragon, which is a term many of the early witnesses used. The Jersey Devil is said to glow and can project fire or poison water with its breath, both classic dragon characteristics. It also emits bone-chilling screams.

The Lenape tribes call the Pine Barrens area "Popuessing," meaning "place of the dragon." The creature's origin in Native American myth echoes that of similar creatures – such as Bigfoot and the Chupacabra – whose legends have crossed over from the Indians and been "rediscovered" by later white settlers.

The dragon-like creature is also called the "Leeds Dragon" because of a woman named Deborah Leeds, the mistress of a British soldier who was suspected of being a witch. The story goes that Leeds had given birth to twelve normal children, but, when she became pregnant for the thirteenth time, she cursed the unborn child. The curse resulted in her bringing forth a creature with hooves, a goat's head, bat wings and a forked tail. The "baby," who was allegedly fathered by the Devil himself, killed the midwife before flying up the chimney and escaping toward the pines.

There still exist genealogical records of a Deborah Leeds who bore twelve children between 1704 and 1726. Her father-in-law, Daniel Leeds, had arrived in America from England in 1677 and settled in Burlington, New Jersey. He published an almanac that made use of astrology, causing his Quaker neighbors, who considered astrology an unholy belief system, to condemn Daniel as "Satan's harbinger." His son Titan would later redesign the almanac's masthead and add a family crest of three dragon-like creatures with clawed feet and bat-like wings, the very image of the Jersey Devil.

In the mid-1700s, when anti-British sentiment was building, the Leeds family had supported the royal governor of New Jersey, Lord Cornbury, and incurred the wrath of their more revolutionary-minded neighbors. The family was accused of somehow being mired in the occult and the Leeds/Jersey Devil became a symbol of political ridicule and scorn.

Nowadays, the NHL team the New Jersey Devils use the creature as their namesake, and New Jersey is the only state in the union to have an official state demon.

DEMONIC POSSESSION AND WITCHCRAFT IN EARLY AMERICA

By Sean Casteel

The first American settlers came from Europe in search of religious freedom and held deeply engrained views about the nature of witchcraft and the continual presence of a palpably real Satan who warred against the upright and moral with an unrelenting determination. These beliefs were part of the newcomers' overall cultural memories after the European Inquisition and its tortuous persecution of so many mostly innocent women.

In the late 17th century, during the time of the Puritans, witchcraft and possessions ran rampant among the populace, or at least were thought to. Demonic possession is spoken of as far back as the Christian New Testament; people afflicted with diseases were thought to be possessed by demons. While for some in the ancient world the root word "daimon" could refer to either a good spirit or a bad one, the term progressively took on the evil cachet of being solely associated with Satan.

When the unexplainable happened, it was attributed to acts of God or the Devil, but over time such events were blamed increasingly on magic, the occult – and on the humans capable of putting their dark desires into action through supernatural means. Such was the mindset that fueled the Salem witch trials of 1692-93.

A HOUSEHOLD SERVANT BECOMES A SLAVE TO SATAN

But 20 years before the infamous Salem witch trials began, a young woman named Elizabeth Knapp suffered what was believed to be a bona fide case of demonic possession. The daughter of a farmer, Elizabeth was 16 years old and worked as a servant in the house of Samuel Willard, a prominent preacher in the Puritan village of Groton, Massachusetts, located 32 miles northwest of Boston.

Willard was known for his sermons about damnation and obedience to God, warning his listeners that "although God is ready to receive them, the Devil is ready to devour them." When Elizabeth, a member of his own household, began to show signs of a demonic possession, Willard took a careful, even scientific approach to the situation. He called in a medical doctor on several occasions in the hope of curing her symptoms. When the doctors found no medical cause for her "fits," Willard declared that Elizabeth was possessed. Throughout the entire process, Willard kept notes about the case in his journal, starting on October 30, 1671, the night Elizabeth first showed signs, until January 12, 1672.

At first, Willard wrote, Elizabeth complained of pains throughout her body and would clutch at her leg, breast and neck and yell out, particularly about strangulation. She would go through emotional fits, sometimes laughing hysterically, weeping or screaming. Hallucinations then followed. She claimed to see two persons walking around her and a man floating over her bed. She would convulse on the ground and at one point tried to throw herself into the fire. On the first Sabbath Day after the symptoms began, the young girl became violent, leaping and contorting her body to the point where it took three or four people to hold her down. When throwing these fits, Elizabeth would shout out the words "money, money, sin and misery, misery."

According to Willard's journal, on the night of November 2, 1671, Elizabeth confessed to having met the devil, a characteristic of most possession cases. She stated that for three years the devil had promised her money, youth, ease from labor and the ability to see the world. The devil had shown her a book of blood covenants which were signed by other women as well. The devil had tried to get her to kill herself and others, including Willard and his family, but she could not do as the devil asked. After a fit that lasted for two days, Elizabeth became catatonic. When she emerged from that condition on December 8, she said that she had been assaulted by the devil, then made a pact with him and allowed the fiend into her bed.

THE USUAL TERRIFYING SYMPTOMS

Throughout the next month, Elizabeth went in and out of her violent fits, spoke in a strange, deep voice and made animal sounds. The devil spoke through her and called Willard "a rogue minister." Elizabeth told Willard that the devil controlled her body and was more powerful than she was. The devil took hold of her speech and she had no control over what she was saying.

Elizabeth began a fit of hysterical weeping and Willard held her to comfort her. Afterwards, she was speechless for several days. Willard ends his documentation of the case on January 15, 1672, saying he would leave the situation to those more "learned, aged, and judicious" than he was.

However, Willard did make some final remarks regarding why he felt Elizabeth's possession to have been genuine. For one thing, it would have been physically impossible to fake the extremely violent thrashing and writhing of Elizabeth's fits, especially the incredible strength she had displayed at those times. Something diabolical had to be present there. While some observers had doubted that the devil had really spoken through Elizabeth, Willard said on several occasions she spoke with her mouth closed, her throat swollen up like a balloon, and he heard voices emanating from her that were not her own.

On the other hand, he did not believe she had made a genuine pact with the devil because her various accounts of what was said between her and the possessing spirit contradicted each other so much. Willard went on to give powerful sermons in the village of Salem during the trials there in 1692, but, after he stopped making entries in his journal, whatever became of Elizabeth remains unknown.

A SHORT HISTORY OF THE SALEM WITCH TRIALS

The Salem witch trials were a series of hearings and prosecutions of people accused of witchcraft in colonial Massachusetts between February 1692 and May 1693. The trials resulted in the executions of twenty people, most of them women. Despite being generally known as the Salem witch trials, the preliminary hearings were conducted in several towns in the Province of Massachusetts Bay, to include Salem Village (now Danvers), Salem Town, Ipswich and Andover.

The episode is regarded as one of the nation's most notorious cases of mass hysteria and has served as a cautionary tale about the dangers of religious extremism, false accusations and lapses in due process of law. It was not unique but simply an American example of the much broader phenomenon of witch trials in the time period.

The concept of a continual demonic presence was a carryover from Europe, where it had been common for peasants to use a form of witchcraft or charms to ensure good fortune for farming and other mundane household concerns. Over time, such "white magic" came to be regarded as evil and associated with demons and evil spirits; the persecutions for witchcraft kept pace with this change in the understanding of the "reality" of the spirit world.

The well-known hellfire minister Cotton Mather was a firm believer in the existence of witchcraft. In his book "Memorable Providences Relating to Witchcrafts and Possessions," Mather writes of the family of Boston mason John Goodwin, whose eldest child had been tempted by the devil to steal linen from a washerwoman named Goody Glover.

Glover was a disagreeable woman whose own husband denounced her as a witch; she was accused of having cast spells on the Goodwin children. Four of the children began to have strange fits, what was called "the disease of astonishment," which quickly became associated with witchcraft. Loud, random outcries, loss of control of their bodies, flapping their arms like birds and violent attempts to harm themselves and others were among the symptoms. The children's symptoms would help to fuel the craze of 1692.

THE ACCUSATIONS THAT STARTED IT ALL

In Salem Village, in February 1692, two young girls began to have fits described as "beyond the power of epileptic fits or natural disease to effect." The girls screamed, threw things around the room, uttered strange sounds, crawled under the furniture and contorted themselves into peculiar positions, according to witnesses. The girls also complained of being pinched and pricked with pins. A doctor could find no medical cause for the ailments. Meanwhile, other young women in the village began to exhibit similar behaviors.

The first three people accused of allegedly afflicting the victims were Sarah Good, a homeless beggar, Sarah Osborne, who rarely attended church services, and Tituba, who was a black or Indian slave and most likely targeted for being ethnically different from most of the other villagers. Each of these women were outcasts of a kind, but, when more upstanding, prominent women were subsequently accused of witchcraft as well, the townspeople concluded that anyone could be a witch and church membership was no protection from accusation.

Among the accused was Bridget Bishop, who had a reputation for gossiping and promiscuity, but declared herself innocent of any familiarity with the devil.

Elizabeth How was a kind soul who tended to her blind husband. Nevertheless, she was accused by her neighbors of causing both their cows and young daughter to die after they quarreled with How, which they interpreted as supernatural acts of revenge. How was also accused of sending her spectral form to attack a young girl and attempt to drag her into a Salem pond. Even though other witnesses vouched for her good character, she was convicted and executed.

An elderly woman in poor health and a respected member of the church community, Rebecca Nurse was among the second wave of suspects accused by the children. As she protested her innocence, her youthful accusers cried out in fake pain and performed contortions to suggest that they were being tormented by her. Prosecutors took Nurse's impassive reaction to the demonstration to be a sign of her guilt. She was bound over for trial and executed

And the list of the executed continued. Eventually the colonial government acknowledged that the trials were a mistake and compensated the families of those convicted. But that vindication came too late for the 19 defendants who were executed. A 20th victim, Giles Corey, was pressed to death when he refused to plead, and as many as 13 others died in prison.

THE SALEM WITCH TRAIL OF 1878

Nearly 200 years after the infamous Salem witch trials, another man was brought up on charges resembling witchcraft in the same vicinity.

In a civil trial held in May of 1878, in Salem, Massachusetts, a woman named Lucretia Brown, an adherent of the Christian Science religion, accused fellow Christian Scientist Daniel Spofford of attempting to harm her through his "mesmeric" mental powers. The last witchcraft trial held in the United States, it garnered significant attention for its bizarre claims and because it took place at the scene of the 17th century trials.

The case had its roots in the infighting among Christian Scientists in the formative years of the religion. The new faith was led by Mary Baker Eddy, the author of the book, "Science and Health with Key to the Scriptures," which the defendant Spofford had helped Baker to publish. Spofford had even introduced the former Mary Baker Glover to her future husband, Asa Gilbert Eddy.

No good deeds go unpunished, however. When Spofford and Mrs. Eddy disagreed over the terms for publishing a second edition of Eddy's book, he was cast out of the religion on the grounds of "immorality." In her writings, Eddy had developed the concept of "malicious animal magnetism," or MAM, a form of hypnosis or controlled mental energy that could harm another person. Eddy believed such "mind crimes" could be stopped by having people in close proximity to her "intercept" these mental emanations.

At the time of her lawsuit, Lucretia Brown was a 50-year-old spinster who lived in Ipswich, Massachusetts, about 12 miles northeast of Salem. She had been an invalid since childhood because of a spinal injury, but she believed Christian Science had healed her. She suffered relapses in 1877 and 1878 and accused

Spofford of having interfered with her health through "mesmerism." Her suit declared that his mind influenced and controlled the minds and bodies of his victims and that he had used those abilities wrongfully and maliciously against her, causing her great suffering.

The presiding judge dismissed the case, noting that the claims made by Brown were vague and that it was not clear how one could prevent such mental control even if Spofford were imprisoned.

It was never established whether Mrs. Eddy was behind Brown's lawsuit or not, but the case garnered widespread attention in the news media, much of which was strongly critical of Eddy.

One had no way of knowing what sort of demon or ghost would be lurking behind the next door.

Contacting the departed was a common practice in early America.

Sometimes ghostly dwellers could outnumber the living.

Witches and poltergeists could easily levitate objects and scare the hell out of those in a haunted house.

If the need arose, it might be useful to throw a witch into a burning fire to rid a dwelling of its curse.

The clergy were at the forefront of questioning and then hanging a suspected witch — leaving it to God to sort out the concubines of Satan from the innocent.

    The Headless Horseman is a fictional character from the short story "The Legend of Sleepy Hollow" by American author Washington Irving. The story, from Irving's collection of short stories entitled *The Sketch Book of Geoffrey Crayon, Gent.*, has worked itself into known American folklore/legend through literature and film.

    The legend of the Headless Horseman begins in Sleepy Hollow, New York, during the American Revolutionary War. Traditional folklore holds that the Horseman was a Hessian artilleryman who was killed during the Battle of White Plains in 1776. He was decapitated by an American cannonball, and the shattered remains of his head were left on the battlefield while his comrades hastily carried his body away. Eventually they buried him in the graveyard of the Old Dutch Church of Sleepy Hollow, from which each Halloween night he rises as a malevolent ghost, furiously seeking his lost head.

WELCOME TO SLEEPY HOLLOW, WHERE STRANGE THINGS ARE ALWAYS HAPPENING

By Timothy Green Beckley and Circe

Ghost stories – especially those of a historic nature – have always fascinated me. I remember organizing a "Haunted Tour of Manhattan" for Channel 5 news a long, long time ago. I was running the New York School of Occult Arts and Sciences, which was probably one of the first – if not the very first – metaphysical institutions in the United States. Many a great parapsychologist cut their (vampire) teeth on 14th Street, on the second floor, where we held events most nights of the week. There was Alan Vaughn, Shawn Robbins, Witch Hazel (yep, that was her real name; she even had it changed on her driver's license; I know. I made her show it to me!), Carol White, Max Toth, Stanley Krippner, Ted Owens, Rod Chase, and Walli Elmlark, the white witch of New York. If you're on the Internet, Google Walli Elmlark and David Bowie and you will find an article I wrote on their strange, supernatural relationship.

When autumn comes around and you're looking for a good reason to leave town, you can head upstate toward New England in search of the perfect pumpkin. If you have children, you will want to take them on a seasonal outing along the Hudson River. It's beautiful. Still mild, and there is such a difference in the air compared to Manhattan. Hey, and you can even do a bit of sky-watching. The sky near Pine Bush, New York, has been full of UFOs on and off for centuries, the locals maintain. To find the best places to observe the heavens in search of Mr. ET, bring along a copy of our book "UFO Repeaters – Seeing Is Believing – The Camera Doesn't Lie." You will want to turn to the chapter about Ellen Crystall, and be sure to look at the many remarkable photographs she took near the Jewish Cemetery in Pine Bush, a small town that now has an annual alien parade and has been the center of much media attention in regard to UFOs.

Recently, we deployed our company ghoul and likeable horror movie host, Mr. Creepo (aka "Mr. UFO" - Tim Beckley, that's me!), along with sexy vamp hunter and Creepo henchwoman Circe (or is that wench-woman?) to check out rumors of a revival of paranormal activity in the dreamy village of Sleepy Hollow, New York, and neighboring Tarrytown.

Though our budget was small, the researchers managed to drink and eat – mainly drink – themselves into a tizzy as if possessed by gluttonous spirits. Very much, we fear, like the early farmers whose wives accused them of "tarrying" too long on market day at the local tavern. Thus the name Tarrytown was born. In any respect we present their – pardon the expression – "sobering" – report.

The cool autumn air sets in just before twilight, and a breeze starts to drift in from the Hudson River, just down the road a bit from where legend has it Ichabod Crane was chased by the Headless Horseman.

Hey, I have great sympathy for Ichabod Crane. I can just imagine how frightened he must have been to be chased into the wind by the Headless Horseman. I know this fleeing for dear life is not to be taken literally, since it is fiction, but accounts of numerous headless horsemen abound in the pages of history. In fact, my grandfather on my dad's side of the family supposedly was once confronted by this faceless terror. My dad's folks were brought up in Kentucky and were very religious Baptists who didn't even like to joke around about such serious matters as ghostly hauntings. Yet one hell-bound demon caught up with my grandpop behind the barn one fall evening. Now, there is no way of proving this, as I told George Noory on Coast To Coast AM when I was his guest a year or so ago. But supposedly my grandfather's headless "friend" became headless through no fault of his own when he was hit by a Yankee's cannonball directly between his shoulders.

Granddaddy would never talk about what he saw. He kept his silence to the grave for fear of the wrath of the Almighty. He spoke about it once and only once, so it is more or less hearsay. But taking into consideration all the other things that have happened to my family paranormal-wise, I give the incident a high probability rating for having actually transpired pretty much like he said.

Returning to my sojourn with Circe, we observed that the bridge and adjacent brook where Crane soiled his pants in an attempt to run for his life still stands, although the locale is now part of the main drag that goes through town, a road used by truckers, buses and SUVs coming up from Manhattan, a scant 40-minute drive away.

Many commuters unwilling to drive in the midst of quite ghostly (I mean ghastly) traffic take to the rails, hopping onboard one of the numerous commuter trains that make the trip from the Big Apple all day and well into the evening hours.

Folding back the pages of the "New York Post" (we are much too blue collar to read the "Times") and gazing out the window, one would hardly guess that the area is particularly rich in paranormal lore. But as you pass White Plains and the office buildings start to diminish in height and number, you can start to be thankful that Circe is your traveling companion, as ghouls know well to leave her be. We figure it has to be the garlic in her bag, but she insists it is the lovely charms she makes and wears to ward off negativity and things that go bump in the night.

But, indeed, the truth sometimes can be very strange. For it is along this very route to Sleepy Hollow, back in 1982, that thousands craned their necks out of car windows to watch as a silent, giant, black triangle filled the sky, much like the cloak of the Headless Horseman is said to have done as the phantom glided through the thickets and glades of this same community in the early 19th century.

One of our first destinations was the Sleepy Hollow cemetery to visit some of the community's founding members. Circe (made infamous for her role of "Muffy" in my low-budget vampire flick, "The Curse of Ed Wood") was perched on a tombstone while I frolicked with the angels near the grave of Washington Irving.

Switching into a serious mode, I remarked how I could recall numerous conversations with fellow researcher Philip Imbrogno, whose book, "Night Siege: The Hudson Valley UFO Sightings," fairly well documented the numerous close encounters in the area. I told Circe how Phil, a teacher by profession (strange, wasn't Ichabod Crane also a teacher?), had started out as a conservative investigator of unexplainable aerial phenomena only to end up photographing ghost lights and confronting time distortions (to find out more, order my book "Our Alien Planet: This Eerie Earth" from the Conspiracy Journal bookstore). All within a few square rural miles of where we were now standing.

During the course of our investigation in the area, we drove over into Connecticut to hunt down giant Jack 'O' Lanterns known to be harassing residents near an outdoor farmers market. This was pretty much the same trek truck drivers had been on that fright-filled night in 1982 when they overflew 18-wheelers with a "thing" the size of a 747 that tailed them at less than a thousand feet in the air. Around the same time, the mysterious Men-In-Black showed up to persuade witnesses to back off from telling of their encounters with the unknown. Many similar tales exist from the time of Washington Irving, who also spoke of nightmarish figures cloaked in black who stalked those who dared discuss their own paranormal misadventures.

Those who have followed such matters will be able to confirm that oftentimes places that have a reputation for being "haunted" have a long history of other diverse paranormal phenomena as well.

Indeed, it was Circe that reminded me that Washington Irving had also speculated on this very "coincidence" in his "Legend of Sleepy Hollow" story. To prove her point, she cracked opened the copy of Irving's book we had just purchased at the Kyjuit gift shop on the Rockefeller Foundation estate, scene of the annual Halloween activities that tourists flock to in this region along the Hudson every autumn.

To quote Irving: "A drowsy, dreamy influence seems to hang over the land and to pervade the very atmosphere. Some say that the place was bewitched by a high German doctor during the early days of the settlement; others, that an old Indian chief, the prophet or wizard of his tribe, held his powwows there before the country was discovered by Master Hendrick Hudson. Certain it is, the place still continues under the sway of some witching power that holds a spell over the minds of the good people, causing them to walk in a continual reverie. They are given to all kinds of marvelous beliefs, are subject to trances and visions, and frequently see strange sights and hear music and voices in the air. The whole neighborhood abounds with local tales, haunted spots, and twilight superstitions; stars shoot and meteors glare oftener across the valley than in any other part of the country..."

One almost has to scratch one's head in disbelief that this paragraph was written two hundred – give or take – years ago. It seems like something a contemporary ghost hunter, like our pal, Joshua P. Warren, might write in one of his scripts for the Discovery Channel.

As we hunkered down for the evening, after hours of paranormal musings, we couldn't help but reflect on how the area seemingly abounds in the macabre. In fact, all around us were signs and symbols that a spooky October was in the works for the area just up the river from our vampiric crypts.

Author Phil Imgrogno "guards" one of several dozen mysterious stone structures that dot the New England landscape in an area besieged by the supernatural throughout the history of America.

Many are buried here, including Washington Irving.

If you think this is a fictional tale, you are wrong. The bridge stands to this day where the school teacher escaped from the Headless Horseman.

At night, when the shadows are just right, the Headless Horseman may appear.

THE HAUNTED 19TH CENTURY LIVES ON

By Sean Casteel

While the Bell Witch haunting continues to enthrall those interested in paranormal Americana, it stands alongside numerous other ghost stories from a time when the country was still relatively young.

One such rival to the Bell Witch legend is the haunting of a farmer and his family in the Edgefield District of South Carolina in 1829. It was one of the most publicized hauntings of the pre-Civil War era and the spirit involved is commonly referred to as the "Edgefield Ghost."

ANOTHER HARDWORKING FARMER

As in the Bell Witch haunting of a few years previous, the Edgefield ghost chose a hardworking farmer and his family to bedevil and bewilder. By all accounts, Isaac Nuel Burnett was a stable man, not prone to fantasy or exaggeration. He had built his farm by strenuous effort and took respectable care of his large family, which by 1829 included his wife Hetta and seven children. Among Burnett's children was a ten-year-old daughter named Martha, who seemed to be singled out for special attention from the ghost.

It all started with the sound of someone mimicking noises around the Burnett farm. The local newspaper, "The Edgefield Carolinian," reported in its July 11, 1829 edition that: "The voice was first heard in October last, imitating various noises, such as that of the spinning wheel, ducks, hens, etc. It was first heard by Mr. Burnett about twenty yards from the house, which led him to suppose it was some of the neighbor's children hiding in the weeds and trying to frighten his children. It was afterwards heard in the loft of the house and Mr. B., supposing it to be a bird, sent a boy up to drive it out, but nothing could be seen. It thus continued to perplex the minds of the family for some time until, at length, one of the children said he believed the thing could talk and commenced asking questions, which it answered by whistling, much like a parrot."

The conversations between the "voice" and the family continued; the mysterious intruder gradually began to speak in actual words. As the news of the supernatural conversing spread among the neighbors, a local man named John Sheppard, considered to be "a pious and worthy citizen," visited the Burnett home. Sheppard was a state legislator, a veteran of the War of 1812, and, in 1850, would become the father of a future governor of South Carolina. In terms of the credentials of respectability, Sheppard seemed to have sufficient.

In an attempt to ascertain the extent of its knowledge, the newspaper article continued, Sheppard asked the voice questions about local residents and their circumstances which the voice answered correctly. The voice also knew Sheppard's name and the names of his children and could name most of the people present in the room.

When Sheppard asked why the voice had come to the Burnetts' home, the eerie reply came, "Because I have no other place to go." When asked if it intended to do the Burnett family any harm, it replied in the negative, saying it loved the family. As to whether it also loved Jesus Christ, the voice gave no answer and refused to answer any further questions as well. It told the family it was going away and did in fact disappear from the Burnett home but made visits to several neighbors who had previously conversed with it. After two weeks, the voice returned to Isaac Burnett's farm.

WHISTLING IN THE DARK

The Burnett family grew increasingly concerned about the nature of the ghost and called on a local minister, Reverend Hodges, to drive the spirit away. But the spirit would not speak when Hodges was present, even after the minister made several visits to try to cleanse the family's home. When Hodges and Sheppard together visited the home of a neighbor of the Burnetts, however, the spirit was present there and did speak. It said it knew the Reverend and did not like him. Hodges countered by saying he intended to drive the voice away, and it replied, "Do so, if you dare."

The conversation between the Reverend and the ghost continued for an hour, but there is little record of what was actually said. At one point, Hodges challenged the ghost to whistle a song, but it answered that it did not know any songs. Hodges then whistled a hymn, to which the ghost responded by saying, "This will not do" and then "whistled 'Yankee Doodle Dandy' very distinctly."

At this point, Mr. Burnett decided his children should no longer communicate with the voice and forbade them to do so. As a result, according to "The Edgefield Carolinian," the ghost "is now seldom heard."

RECOILING FROM THE NAME OF JESUS

For a time, the Edgefield ghost had focused a great deal of attention on ten-year-old Martha Burnett, but the child was not flattered by its "affection." She did not enjoy conversing with it, as did some of her family and neighbors, but was instead simply terrified of it. A pious friend of Martha's recommended that she quote a certain Biblical passage to the offending spirit, First Timothy, 1:15, which reads, "The saying is sure and worthy of full acceptance, that Christ Jesus came into the world to save sinners. And I am the foremost of sinners."

As in the case of James Sheppard recounted earlier, the ghost seems to have recoiled immediately from the mention of Jesus. This became even more evident when Isaac Burnett placed a Bible in the loft area of the house, from which the voice often seemed to originate.

The Edgefield ghost faded from public memory over the years. Martha Burnett died in 1860 at the age of forty-one. Her father outlived her by six years. Many descendants of the family still live in Greenwood and Edgefield Counties in South Carolina. The haunting site today is unmarked and on private property.

The Cumberland house associated with vampires would cause even the most steady to quake.

The quaint New England town of Edgefield saw the appearance of the Edgefield ghost.

To this day, Aaron Burr's spirit roams a popular spot in New York City's Greenwich Village, perhaps still suffering the shame of his duel with Alexander Hamilton more than two centuries previous.

AARON "BURR" SENDS SHIVERS DOWN THE SPINE

What was once the site of Aaron Burr's carriage house is now occupied by an "unmarked" restaurant in New York's West Village in Manhattan called "One if by Land, Two if by Sea." In the present era, there are frequent sightings at the swanky eatery of Theodosia, the daughter of Aaron Burr, the onetime vice president who is most famous now for having killed fellow statesman Alexander Hamilton in a duel.

In December 1812, Theodosia was returning to New York from South Carolina on the schooner "Patriot." When the ship disappeared at sea, Theodosia's spirit is thought to have journeyed to the location where the restaurant now stands to be closer to her father. She is said to cause poltergeist activity at "One if by Land, Two if by Sea" that includes champagne glasses tumbling from tables and paintings inexplicably falling off walls, among other spectral events. The staff at the restaurant have reported seeing spirits coming down the stairs at night, and the dining room manager adds that his workers are not permitted to drink on the job.

There is more ghostly activity related to Aaron Burr. He and Alexander Hamilton represented a man accused of murdering his fiancée in So Ho and got him off the hook at the trial. According to the legend, after the verdict came down, the victim's cousin put a curse on both lawyers. This may explain Burr's lingering presence in New York City, where he occasionally joins his daughter at her "One if by Land, Two if by Sea" stomping grounds. Or maybe his ghost is simply bitter over dying in disgrace for killing Hamilton in the notorious duel that happened just a few years after the trial.

Another of Burr's scandals is centered on what is said to be Manhattan's oldest building, the Morris-Jumel Mansion, which served as George Washington's headquarters during the Revolutionary War. It was later home to a wealthy married couple named Eliza and Stephen Jumel. Burr had an affair with Eliza and, soon after, her husband Stephen was found dead. He had, suspiciously enough, fallen out of a window and landed on a pitchfork. Eliza and Burr married right away; Burr was 77 at the time and was rumored to be after Eliza's money. Burr and Eliza divorced three years later and Burr died the day it was finalized.

After the divorce, Eliza's mental health deteriorated drastically and her behavior became erratic. Following her death in 1865, she was often spotted roaming the mansion in a white dress. Some still claim to see Burr's ghost at the house as well.

EDGAR ALLAN POE, RAPPING FOREVERMORE

Edgar Allan Poe died on October 7, 1849, at Washington Medical College in Baltimore, Maryland. Two days earlier, a man had encountered Poe "in great distress" and wandering the streets of Baltimore in need of immediate help. Poe was found wearing someone else's clothes and repeatedly called out the name "Reynolds," but he died before he could explain what he was talking about or what had made him so ill. Newspapers at the time claimed that Poe died of "congestion of the brain" or "cerebral inflammation," common euphemisms at the time for alcoholism, but the cause of death is uncertain because Poe's medical records are long lost.

Poe's spirit may be "long lost" as well. Some people believe the author and poet still lurks around his former home at 203 North Amity Street in Baltimore. According to "The Baltimore Post-Examiner," several people in the 1970s felt taps on the shoulder but turned around to see no one behind them. One person was spooked when a window sash appeared to fly across the room and land at his feet. Reports of "creepy feelings" and an "eerie presence" are not uncommon around Poe's house.

His ghost is also said to wander over to a Baltimore pub called "The Horse You Rode In On," where bartenders attribute swinging chandeliers to Poe and believe he's responsible for a cash register that repeatedly pops open by itself. The pub is thought to be one of Poe's favorite drinking spots; the employees there now call the ghost "Edgar" and speak to him regularly, acknowledging his presence and perhaps comforting him.

A YOUNG WOMAN'S "CRISIS APPARITION"

Psychical researcher Frank Podmore.

Frank Podmore was an English author and psychical researcher who wrote a series of books on paranormal subjects beginning in the late 1800s. He was generally well-reviewed by the scientific community because he gave rationalistic explanations for the psychical phenomena he studied – in other words, a debunker.

But even as a debunker, Podmore collected many interesting stories. In his 1909 book, "Telepathic Hallucinations: The New View of Ghosts," he reprinted the letter of a young woman named "Miss Gollin" of Brooklyn, New York. The letter was dated March 2, 1905, and related events that had happened to Gollin in 1886.

"I was employed in the office of a certain newspaper in this city," Gollin writes. "On Saturday, the 25th of January, 1896, at about 12:30 P.M., while attending to my work, all at once I felt conscious of a presence near me. In fact, it was the same feeling one has when someone is intently looking at you and you feel an inclination to turn to see who it is. This feeling was so strong that I turned almost involuntarily, and there, at the back of my chair, I saw the full figure of a young man with whom I was well acquainted; in fact, engaged to marry. I wish to state here that this young man had never been in this office. The figure was very distinct. In fact, it was all so plain that I felt the young woman sitting next to me must see it also, and though very much overcome and not understanding it at the time, I turned to her and asked, 'Did you see anyone just now standing back of my chair?' She replied, 'No,' and, of course, wondered why I asked."

Gollin says she had been at church with the young man to whom she was betrothed the previous Sunday to the incident and he was apparently in good health, though he had earlier been ailing somewhat due, it was thought, to working too hard at his college studies. The couple agreed to meet again in the middle of the coming week, but Gollin instead received a letter from her young man's sister saying he had a cold and might not come to see her until the end of the week.

In reply, Gollin had written that perhaps, given the wet weather, they should agree to meet on the following Sunday to allow her young man time to fully recover. She heard nothing further and fully expected to see the young man on Sunday. When she reached home after work on the Saturday she saw his image at the office, she found a telegram urging her to come see her fiancé at once. She hurried to his home and was told he had died at 12:30 P.M. of typhoid fever. Gollin said she had seen the figure "fully dressed in a black suit of clothes," which may suggest funereal garments for the departed.

Gollin's friend from the office also sent a letter to Podmore in which she corroborated the story told by Gollin. She recalled being asked to see if there was someone behind Gollin's chair and said she is sure that no one in the flesh had approached her. Gollin later told her that she had received a telegram stating that her fiancé had died at exactly the same time the apparition had appeared to her at work.

In a "crisis apparition," when the image of an absent person suddenly appears to a friend or family member, it is usually not a vague, wispy apparition. It seems to be the very person, as when Gollin states the figure was "very distinct" and "plain," meaning it appeared to be physically real. In some crisis apparition reports, the phantom appears at the time of the person's death, sometimes from thousands of miles away.

In spite of how the story is presented by Podmore as part of a larger effort to explain ghosts away as mere hallucinations, the crisis apparition phenomenon has been reported since ancient times along with other ghostly manifestations that may one day prove to have "outlived" the debunkers who seek to silence their otherworldly voices.

Every room has its spooky tale at the Ghost City Inn.

All are welcome in Jerome. The population has varied over the decades. Often there may be more spirits than the living.

A lonely main street in Jerome with only our co-author Tim Beckley to be seen. Looks like the party is over - 100 years ago! Actually, there is still plenty to do in town. (Photo by Charla Gene)

THE TOWN OVERRUN BY GHOSTS

JEROME, ARIZONA

THE WICKEDEST CITY IN THE WEST

By Timothy Green Beckley

Jerome winds along one of Arizona's scorching and dusty trails. As we drove the length of Highway 89A, which stretches between Sedona and Phoenix, I couldn't help but feel compassion for the Spanish Conquistadors led by Antonio de Espejo, who passed through the Verde Valley in the mid-16th century dressed to honor the King in heavy metal helmets and confining, polished armor. If it was anything like what today's modern traveler experiences, it had to be like trekking through the chambers of hell. It's the land where the temperature rises to 102 degrees by the time you awake, and the air becomes so burning hot by midday that you want to crawl under a rock – if you could find one!

Historians tell us things were a bit more tempered back in the days of the Conquistadors, so we don't think Espejo and his men were hallucinating or had heat stroke when they told the local Yavapai Indians that they had come to lay claim to the vast fortune that was theirs through God's grace. They had heard as far away as Spain about the existence of El Cibola, better known as the Seven Cities of Gold. Some conjecture that El Cibola was the stronghold of a band of the Knights Templar who had fled from Europe with a vast treasure of religious artifacts and set up shop in the territory around 1150. It is said that seven bishops assigned to Cibola (thus the distinction of seven cities) amassed a bloody fortune which they buried in the earth for safekeeping. Though worthy of only minor consideration, this tale of vast wealth buried in the ground does add a mystique to our sojourn and makes us wonder if Espejo didn't know a little something more than academia might credit to him.

Over a period of the next couple of hundred years various artifacts of considerable value were found and polished. There was enough copper and gold lying about to make even the biggest fool's heart flutter. And, in addition, those traversing the region had conferred with the local Indians who showed them an opening in the mountain that was filled with treasures. This landmark became known as Cleopatra Hill, and eventually word spread far and wide of a possible huge mother lode. By 1876 the town had been established and multitudes were coming to stake their claim. In 1889 the United Verde Copper Company opened up several mines around Jerome, and those not wishing to look to prospect for prosperity on their own had as much work as they wanted – though toiling under the prevailing conditions at the mines could easily be dangerous to life and limb. An estimated ONE BILLION DOLLARS worth of valuable minerals – gold, copper and silver – were extracted from the earth over the decades, but many a determined young man died in the process of making a few elite individuals exceedingly wealthy.

Accompanied by fellow ghost hunter, paranormal enthusiast, shutterbug and an insatiable Arizona explorer, Charla Gene was the perfect travel companion to hit the ghostly byways with. Inquisitive and adventuresome, she was primed to see if the stories of spirits rumored to abound in Jerome were over-exaggerated or on the level. Once boasting a vibrant – and often violent – population of 15,000, the living residing there today number only around 444. And, in a twisted irony of sorts, the dead seem to require the living to endure as much as the living need those that have departed in order to survive in an economically troubled world. For, in addition to its tough reputation as being the Wickedest Town in the West, it has seen death and destruction that is almost unparalleled in American history. Anyone existing under these conditions must certainly feel that they were being taken advantage of on the most primitive level.

As we put our gas-guzzling Ford Explorer into second gear to climb the rather steep scenic back mountain roads that lead into Jerome, we did not have to remind ourselves why we were heading to a place where time ostensibly has elapsed. We thought of ourselves as tried and true "ghost hunters" on a mission to reveal to the world the plight of those residing directly across from us on the opposite side of the veil. You may wonder what might make it easier to establish contact with spirits in Jerome – more so than most other places – and our answer would be that it must have something to do with what many say is the "indefinable energy" in the earth that is found at various particular locations.

In a sense, we were representing the downtrodden, which included prostitutes, underpaid miners working under hazardous conditions, Mexican immigrants, gunslingers, out-of-luck gamblers and hopeless alcoholics who could not afford a decent legal defense. In short, any and all troubled spirits, many of whom laid down their lives to settle what became a significant part of America's Wild West.

We had made special arrangements with the hosts of "Higher Vibrations" to stream a live ghost hunt from Jerome's Ghost City Inn, which was to serve as base camp while staying in town. Previously a creaky boarding house and illegal distillery, the multiple-story landmark has a history of legitimate haunts that we were anxious, if possible, to verify firsthand. The program's offbeat hosts, Alex "Friend of Putin" Scully and King Ron, have been broadcasting locally in Las Vegas, Nevada, on KLAV-AM, 1230, every Tuesday at 9 PM. This was to be their first Saturday night broadcast, which they had heavily promoted for weeks, hoping to have a larger than normal audience. Streaming worldwide over the Internet, their show is dedicated to educating people on the subjects of UFOs and other paranormal phenomena. Thus, as it turned out, we were – as Jack Blues proclaims in "The Blues Brothers" musical comedy – "On A Mission From God" to be the "messengers of choice" on the evening of June 18, 2011.

Tour guide and ghost hunter Shotgun Sadie has no trouble meeting up with visitors from the next world. (Photo by Charla Gene).

The town was nearly destroyed by mining fires several times.

During the influx of miners, saloons and bordellos were among the most popular establishments. Here is Norma Butterball's famous house of "ill repute."

The Spanish Conquistadors came in search of vast wealth - and may have found it and hidden it somewhere near Jerome.

A VISIT BY THE GHOST OF GRANDMA GARCIA

The structure that is now the Ghost City Inn was initially established in 1885 as a place for the mine's middle management to reside. The town was expanding to and fro with construction going on day after day in an attempt to provide adequate space for everyone to live, even if it was under strained and crowded conditions.

After three devastating fires, a landslide and various other upheavals in Jerome, the entire structure of the city and the land it stood on shifted significantly, as did the town's population, which expanded and shrunk like an accordion at various intervals in its history. In fact, a number of the town's structures actually slide down the mountainside to a lower altitude, including the town's jail, which ended up down the ridge 225 feet below its original position. But the earliest incarnation of what was later to become the Ghost City Inn changed in 1920 when the building was purchased by the Garcia Family, who turned it into a boarding house for the miners themselves. The current owners, Jackie and Allen Muma, have run what has become a very charming Bed and Breakfast for about a decade. They maintain that a number of visitors have confronted them with the fact that the place is haunted just like the rest of the town. Though she described herself as a nonbeliever in the supernatural before becoming the Inn's most recent proprietor, Jackie has come to concede that the B&B hosts some really interesting unregistered guests. Not by coincidence, one of them just happens to be the previous owner!

They called her Grandma Garcia, and she took care of the miners the best she could despite the overcrowded conditions.

"The miners worked in shifts," Jackie explained. There were several shifts a day, so they had to rotate when they could sleep. We are in touch with Grandma Garcia's daughter, who is still alive and living in California in her late 80s. She says her grandmother used to go into the rooms upstairs and kicked the cots real hard to wake up whoever was sleeping so that another person could take their place and get some rest."

Apparently, Grandma Garcia was short and had a humpback.

"The doors were smaller and lower down," Jackie continued, "so that a normal person might hit their head if they didn't duck when walking from one room to another. She also had a stove and some other furniture that was closer to the ground."

A spooky apparition in the Hotel Jerome.

Originally most of the dwellings were built on the side of the hills outside town only to slide down and be destroyed.

Take heed as danger lurks nearby.

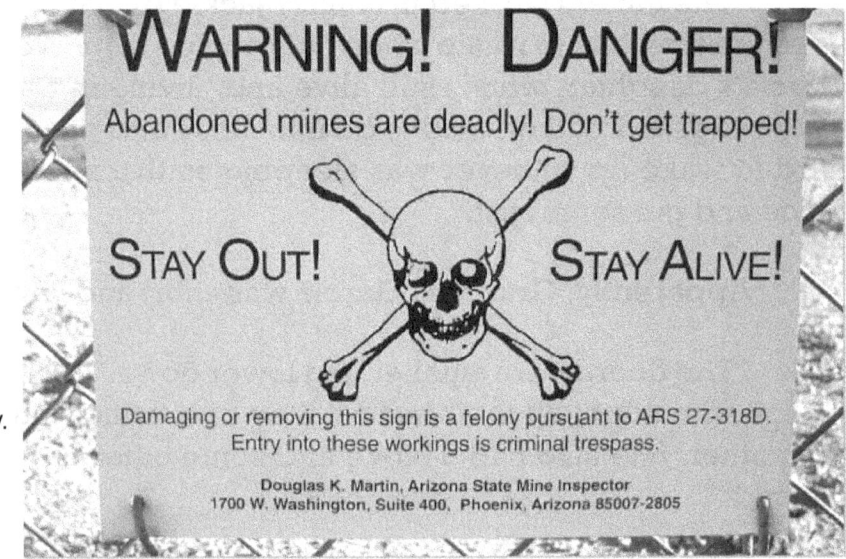

Among the many vices enjoyed in Jerome was the consumption of alcohol during prohibition.

"There was an illegal distillery in the house which Grandma claimed she knew nothing about," Jackie said. "In one of the rooms on the first floor there was a big area rug, and when you pulled it back there was a hatch door, and when you descended the ladder there was all this booze. One day there was an explosion that blew out the windows on the second floor. It charred the chimney and damaged the iron stove. Grandma always liked to say she didn't know what was going on in her own place."

After that day, Mrs. Garcia had a great fear of fire and being burned alive.

"She was so afraid that she wouldn't let anyone light a match or have an open flame anywhere around her," Jackie went on. "And even her ghost seems to be adversely affected by anything to do with fire. Mainly in the back bedroom, where she lived for over 50 years, sometimes when guests stay overnight in the room they will relate how their packs of cigarettes or lights will be missing or will have moved. Sometimes they even smell coffee in the middle of the night. Well, Grandma loved her coffee, because she always had a pot brewing since she was up day and night cooking to feed the men as they came home at various times from their shifts in the mines."

CONFRONTING SPIRITS ON MAIN STREET

Outside, in the much cooler evening air, Shotgun Sadie was conversing with a group of tourists who had gathered for the Haunted Tours of Jerome, for whom Sadie is a knowledgeable tour guide. They were in the process of walking around town and taking in the chilling sites when we came across them congregating on the corner of Main and First Streets. Each of the tour's guests had been given a rather impressive ghost detector that theoretically flashes rapidly when a spirit is present. The detectors were going crazy!

Shotgun Sadie explained that we were standing in a particularly active "hot spot," thus the noticeable disturbance.

"A hotspot?"

"Oh yes!" she replied. "You see, when the town was booming, its residents were out on the streets drinking at all hours of the day and night. There were maybe three or four shifts at the mines which let out at various hours. Midnight might have been as busy as noon in the alleyways around town where people went to sleep it off. The bars and gambling halls never closed. Fights were pretty common, as were knifings and shootouts. People were dying pretty appalling deaths."

Shotgun says she has stood on this spot on Main and First and actually heard disembodied voices. "A number of times I have heard someone say very loud, 'Liar! Liar!'" The voice gives her chills.

A bit of investigation provoked another possibility.

A check of the town's records tells a horrific tale of fires that almost destroyed this wild and wooly town on more than just a few occasions. The Jerome Volunteer Fire Department list these as major historical blazes:

In the late 1890s, the town was devastated by one conflagration after another:

·April 24, 1894 - Two blocks in the commercial district burned down.

·December 24, 1897 - Christmas fire destroyed the business district and many homes.

·September 17, 1898 - Once again, the business district and many homes went up in flames.

·May 8, 1899 - 24 saloons, 15 Chinese restaurants and many homes were burned.

·1902 - Four homes on the hogback.

·1907 - Eight homes in the foreign quarter.

·1911 - Four homes and the T.F. Miller warehouse.

·1915 - The famous Montana Hotel burned.

·1917 - An entire block burned, including rooming houses and homes, displacing 90 families.

·1918 - 60 homes burned in the gulch.

·1926 - Jerome Hotel and 26 homes burned.

The publisher of Jerome's now-defunct newspaper once stated that it almost got to the point where he felt like having the front page type already set which would read JEROME BURNS AGAIN!

I mentioned to Sadie that I was getting a rather strong psychic impression that the voice she heard might actually have been shouting "Fire! Fire!" instead of "Liar." She concurred that this was indeed a good possibility and a matter of what could be a misinterpretation. Were the spirits speaking forthrightly, trying to get a message across to us that they did not want to be incinerated in one of the infernos that swept over Jerome?

LADIES OF THE NIGHT

Though prostitution was never formally legal in Jerome, it was tolerated by city lawmakers and essentially flourished for as long as anyone can remember. There are even "Official Bordello Inspector Badges" on display in some of the tourist shops. Among the first to arrive to seek out her fortune in Jerome was Nora "Butter" Brown, an enterprising Madam who saw more than gold in them there mines. She and some of the other Madams eventually became "respectable" later on in life and were to become some of the wealthiest residents of the state.

The strangulation murder of Sammy Dean has never been solved and some say the ghost of the glamorous prostitute still walks the back streets of Jerome.

Ron Roope, owner of Haunted Tours of Jerome, reminded us that Jerome even had its own Red Light District known as Husband's Alley. "The women of the night often underwent cruel hardships at the hands of their clients. There were beatings, stabbings and strangulation. There was also the specter of alcoholism and opium addiction, to say nothing of disease."

Ron admits that the vast number of murders associated with prostitution in Jerome cannot even be guessed at. They can only be included among the over

9,000 accident victims who wound up in Jerome's hospital over the years, the majority of them ending up in the morgue. If we didn't know better, it would seem that Jack the Ripper might have moved here from England had it not been for the fact that these deaths occurred over more than half a century.

"Sammie Dean is probably the most famous case of a lady of the night who was murdered under horrendous circumstances," notes Ron the guide. "It was in 1931, at the peak of the most recent hunt to strike it rich here. Only thirty, Sammie was one of the most popular gals in town. She worked out of Diamond Lily's bordello and was known to have many influential gentleman friends.

Ron, who is also active in the Jerome Historical Society, adds that "The police said there was no evidence to go on. But folks in the neighborhood said the last caller to see her had been the Mayor's son. Apparently, he had taken her to dinner at the English Kitchen and proposed marriage, but she had turned him down. The next morning she was found brutally strangled to death. No charges were ever made or substantiated, but he did leave Jerome soon after Sammie's death."

The spirits of other not-so-famous sporting gals still can be seen and heard wandering the streets down by the town's community center, which has been tagged "Spook Hall."

It was in this area that some of the less fancy street girls plied their trade, working out of dilapidated shacks. One of these gals was savagely stabbed to death on the way home and refuses to take her death lying down. To add credence to the body of evidence that the ghosts of the girls of the night lay in wait around Spook Hall is the fact that there is alleged to be a heavy aroma of perfume that lingers in the air there.

THE MYSTERIOUS LEDGER

Back in the Ghost City Inn, we were still attempting to lock horns with an unadulterated spirit. Was there a phantom of any sort in the Miners Suite that would like to communicate with either Charla or myself? We had been told that every room in the Inn had its own presence that was – pardon the expression – dying to get through to the living. Could ours be any different? During the broadcast, the hosts of "Higher Vibrations" wanted to know if I could feel the presence of anything unusual in the Miners Suite where we had hunkered down. I was seated in an antique chair, telephone in hand, answering any and all questions that King Ron and his paranormal partner Alex Scully tossed my way. And while I have to confess I wasn't getting the vibe – perhaps it was too early in the evening – across the room from me Charla was holding a ghost detector supplied to us by paranormal investigator and "Speaking of Strange" talk show host Joshua P. Warren. The instrument was flashing on and off as she held it in the doorway. Later, we learned from the manager on duty that this is the exact spot where an apparition has been seen or felt from time to time in the Miners Suite.

So were we alone or not? I am no expert on the sensitivity of ghost detectors and prefer my own psychic intuition. Apparently, others who had stayed in the Miners Suite had been determined to do precisely the same thing.

A ledger near the bed seemed to flip open, though it was probably a gust from the air-conditioning unit that was operating on a thermostat system that made the AC go on and off. Nevertheless a closer look at the journal's pages might be in order, I thought.

As it turns out, there were numerous references to phenomena reportedly seen, felt, sensed and smelled in our cozy quarters. The following are random postings made by previous guests over a period of about five or six years.

MICHELLE AND SCOTT

PEORIA, AZ

TWO YEARS AGO WE CAME TO Jerome for my birthday with my two sisters. We stayed in Room 33 at the Grand. (The former hospital where the 9000 came to expire.) My sister was awakened by moans and sounds of carts.

LINDA M.

Something pulled the covers off on the left side of the bed. I saw a dark shadow and I began to scream.

MARRY ANN

BURBANK, CA

We had a ghost with us last night. As I sat quietly in bed I noticed the bathroom door move and it scared me to death.

RANDY AND KATHY

SURPRIZE, AZ

My wife was tired and went to bed before I did. I went to bed at 11 PM. About a half hour later, I was awakened by noises in the ceiling and in the wall near our headboard. It sounded like a large party and people talking. I could hear someone running across the floor. I saw a figure standing in our bedroom at the foot of the bed. I quickly got up out of bed and turned on the light and the figure just vanished. I checked the bathroom, ground floor and even the front door to make certain it was locked. Later, I felt a hand on my chest. It wasn't my wife's hand as she was turned away from me on the bed.

OUR VISITOR

FEB, 2009

I was sleeping in the master bedroom, which was cold one minute and then would really get warm the next. So when I was warm I would uncover my feet and fall asleep. I was woken up by a pin prick to my hip and something trying to pull at my feet. I got this overwhelming energy coming from the bathroom. It was so strong. I kept trying to lose the feeling but I knew someone was watching me.

So what are the chances a "stranger" was lurking around that we could not see?

A VANISHING COWBOY

The Inn's proprietor, Jackie, says that, before devoting her fulltime to working in and promoting the Bed and Breakfast, she was still a fulltime Registered Nurse in Jerome's Emergency Room, often working the night shift. Jackie outlined one incident fully: "My husband, Allen, who is now the Chief of Police in Jerome, would fill in for me and told me that often the departing guests would share some strange stories about what happened to them during the night.

"We thought perhaps they had too many drinks before going to bed. But one afternoon, while running the vacuum upstairs, there was a man standing in the doorway of what was a shared bath back at that time. I turned off the vacuum and told him that we didn't have a public restroom. I knew he wasn't a guest so I assumed someone had left the main door unlocked and he had wandered in from the street. He was wearing a heavy canvas or leather coat that reminded me of a trench coat which was visibly dusty. He had long gray hair that hung to his shoulders; unkempt, naturally curly.

"When I spoke to him, he turned his back to me and went further into the bathroom and around the corner toward the commode. I followed directly and when I made the turn he was nowhere in sight. Mind you, there was nowhere for him to have gone as there was one door leading in and out. I looked everywhere, but no trace of him. I called my husband at the police station. Initially, he thought maybe the 'stranger' had rushed past me when I confronted him, but I told him that was simply not the case. Then he said maybe it had been a reflection, but that didn't add up as there was no such picture anywhere that would have made the impression of a cowboy. Plus, it wasn't a quick encounter, it was a few seconds. Anyway, it got my attention. Later in the week I called my Mom (from Michigan) and told her what I had experienced. Her response was, 'Oh honey, I wouldn't share that story with anyone, if I were you.' I think she thought I had fallen off the deep end.

"In another incident, I was in the dining room cleaning up after breakfast, after all the guests had checked out. It had never happened before, but I heard music coming from upstairs; it was really loud and was old time music. I walked up and followed the sound; it led me into the Verde View Room. It was coming from the alarm clock radio, so I unplugged it and went back downstairs. It came on a second time, even louder than the first. I went up again, into the same room, flipped the unit over and opened the battery compartment to find there were no batteries. Immediately, I turned the volume all the way down and again called my husband. His response was that electronic devices can sometimes store power and come on from time to time without batteries or electricity. Yeah, right."

Thoroughly puzzled, Jackie began to think that maybe her guests weren't so daffy after all. Now she was seeing and hearing things herself.

This ghostly encounter with a cowboy doesn't seem to end here, as the Ghost City Inn owner explains.

"Sometime later a guest was staying in the Verde View room and he was hoping to have an encounter. When I came in the morning to make breakfast, he met me at the door and told me that he had been awakened in the night by a cowboy who said his name was Jake Stark and made him yell out loud that Cecil Thompson had 'done it,' killed him, and he wanted everyone to know it. He also wouldn't let [the guest] go back to sleep until he wrote it down so he wouldn't blow it off in the morning thinking it had been a dream."

The guest desperately wanted to know who Cecil Thompson was, but Jackie told him she had never heard the name. She thought it would end there. But it did not!

"He later went uptown to mail a package and he was talking to one of the locals, Ingrid, who has since moved back to Sweden, telling her about his experience. She said to him, 'I was just reading a book called "They Came to Jerome," and here, on page 150-something, is the name Cecil Thompson and a paragraph about how he and his family were thrown out of town for being hell raisers.'"

Many people over the years have seen the disappearing cowboy.

Jackie says, "He will sit on the bed in the night, awakening the unsuspecting guest, and, if he is told to leave, he simply stands up and walks through the solid wall. A medium once told me that he was a cattle herder and would come to Jerome monthly to spend his wages when apparently he was murdered by Cecil Thompson."

Eventually, we fell asleep, exhausted from the evening's ghostly activities. However, the next morning, as we dragged our equipment down the stairs, we were overcome by a feeling of resistance, as if the spirits at the Ghost City Inn and in the entire city of Jerome were not harmful as much as they were anxious to get their tragic tales across to the world — to allow the living to know that the departed do not forget what has occurred to them in life after putting off this mortal coil. Despite their standing in life, they deserve the same treatment and respect as anyone else, regardless of that individual's fancier clothes or their relative wealth. Indeed, the "old" mining town of Jerome came to a final halt in 1951, when the mines dried up and almost everyone began drifting away. But Jerome and its residents — the living and the dead — are not about to give up as they venture into a new era of cooperation between spirits and those still residing in the physical realm.

Gaining speed as we wound our way back down to the highway, we couldn't help but feel as if we had left another world – a world where the living and the dead share many of the same concerns. The spirits had entrusted us with a story to tell and — though there is much more that could be said — we are more than happy to present an important part of their legacy to you until another opportunity comes along!

\# \# \#

REFERENCES

www.ToursOfJerome.com

www.Sawaufo.com/higher-vibrations-special-ghost-hunt-with-tim-beckley-live-from-the-ghost-city-inn/

www.GhostCityInn.Com

www.Jeromefd.org/

www.JeromeHistoricalSociety.com

THE BELL WITCH PROJECT

Chapter 1

Introduction

Before entering upon an investigation or going into details of the acts and demonstrations of the Bell Witch, it is proper that the reader should know something of the Bell family and citizens of the community who witnessed the manifestations, expended their energies in trying to discover the origin and force of the phenomena, and who in connection with the Bell family, give credence to the truth of these statements. The story will not be altogether new to thousands who have heard graphic accounts from the lips of the old people who witnessed the excitement and have, perhaps, also read short newspaper sketches. No full or authentic account, however, has ever been published. Newspapers were few and far between at the time these events transpired, and there were no enterprising reporters or novelists abroad in the land. Several writers in later years undertook to compile the story, but could not obtain the authentic details. Williams Bell, it seems, was the only one who kept a diary of what transpired, which he put in shape in 1846, twenty-six years after the culmination of the tragic events in the death of John Bell, Sr. It appears also that he was inspired to write the sketch by the intensity of the living sensation that sent a tremor through every nerve of his body, as it kept fresh in the memory of every one, the astounding manifestations that continued to be rehearsed at every fireside and in every social gathering, taking on new phases and versions far from the truth.

Some enterprising person, wise in his own conceit, undertook to solve the mystery, and failing to arrive at any satisfactory conclusion, gave currency to a suspicion that the young daughter, Betsy Bell, actuated by her brothers, John and Drewry, was the author of the demonstration, and that the purpose was to make money by the exhibitions. This version found lodgment in many minds not acquainted with the facts, and the discussion became very distasteful and irritating to the family, and Williams Bell determined to write the incidents and truth of the whole story and let the public pass upon the injustice of such a judgment. After it was written, the brothers consulted over the matter, and finally for good reasons then existing, agreed not to publish the statement during the life of any member of John Bell, Sr.'s immediate family.

Williams Bell died a few years after, this, and gave the manuscript to his eldest son, James Allen Bell, who has carefully preserved it. The writer was raised within a few miles of the Bell place, and has been familiar with the witch story from his youth up, and becoming intimately acquainted with Joel and Allen Bell during his residence in Springfield, about 1867 applied to Joel Bell for the privilege of writing the history then, while himself, sister Betsy, Frank Miles, Lawson Fort, Patrick McGowen, Johnson, and others acquainted with the facts, were still living. Joel Bell assented to the proposition, but Allen Bell declined to furnish his father's manuscript, and the matter was dropped until recently. Since the death of all of the family who were victims of the frightful disturbance, Allen Bell has consented to the use of his father's statement in connection with other testimony. The further explanation of the Publication of the history of these stirring events, after the lapse of many years, will be found in the following correspondence:

ADAIRVILLE, KY.

July 1st, 1891

M. V. Ingram, Esq., Clarksville, Tenn.:

DEAR SIR - Some years ago, while you were engaged in publishing a newspaper at Springfield, Tenn., Uncle Joel Bell applied to me for the manuscript of my father, Williams Bell, stating that the application was made at your request for the purpose of incorporating the same in a full and complete history of the so-called Bell Witch, which proposition I declined to accede to at that time, for several reasons that need not now be mentioned. However, one objection was, that after writing his own memories, and the recollections of other members of the family, father consulted with Uncle John Bell in regard to the matter, and they determined that in view of all the surrounding circumstances, it was best that it should not be published during the life of any of Grandfather John Bell's immediate family, and he gave me all of his notes just before his death with this injunction. So many painfully abhorrent misrepresentations had gone out concerning the mystery that he desired the writing should be preserved, that the truth might be known in after years, should the erroneous views which had found lodgment concerning the origin of the distress continue to live through tradition handed down to an enlightened generation under a version so disparaging.

This history was written by father during the Fall and Winter of 1846, and is the only sketch ever written in detail by any one cognizant of the facts and demonstrations. Now, nearly seventy-five years having elapsed, the old members of the family who suffered the torments having all passed away, and the witch story still continues to be discussed as widely as the family name is known, under misconception of the facts, I have concluded that in justice to the memory of an honored ancestry, and to the public also whose minds have been abused in regard to the matter, it would be well to give the whole story to the World. You having made the application years ago, and believing you are capable, and will if you undertake it, being already acquainted with many of the circumstances, compile a faithful history of the events, I am willing to let you have this manuscript and notes, on the condition that you will agree to include all other corroborative testimony still to be had, and write a deserved sketch of Grandfather John Bell and family, and those associated with him in any way during the period of the unexplained visitation which afflicted him and gave rise to the excitement.

Respectfully,

J. A. BELL

CLARKSVILLE, TENN.

July 5th, 1891

Hon. J. Allen Bell, Adairville, Ky.:

DEAR SIR - In reply to your favor of the 1st inst., I remember distinctly the discussion between Mr. Joel E. Bell and myself in 1867, in regard to the publication of the history of the Bell Witch, and also his after report of the interview with you, which caused the matter to be dropped. Joel Bell was a gentleman whom I esteemed very highly for his moral worth and generous friendship. His earnestness impressed me with the views so decidedly expressed in favor of the publication then, believing the facts would correct the erroneous impressions which had been created. I will accept your proposition and undertake to compile such testimony as may still exist; as you suggest, and will endeavor to make a faithful record of the facts.

I have always regarded the so-called Bell Witch as a phenomenon for which

THE BELL WITCH PROJECT

the Bell family, who suffered the infliction and misfortune, could in no wise be responsible, but were entitled to all of that sympathy so generously bestowed by the good people of that community who knew John Bell only to honor him. But in undertaking the work, it shall not be my purpose to account for the series of dramatic events that so confused and mystified people at that time, but compile the data and let readers form their own conclusion. I believe the publication will do good, not only in correcting a false impression, but will recount historical events and facts concerning the most remarkable visitations, in the early part of the present century, that ever afflicted any community, giving the present generation some idea of the grounds for the superstition that possessed the early settlers of this country.

Very truly, your friend,

M. V. INGRAM

THE BELL WITCH PROJECT

Chapter 2

The Early Settlers - Society and Religion - Kate the Witch - The Bell Family - The School Master and Betsy's First Lover

More than two hundred years ago, the Star of Empire took its course westward, following the footprints of the advance guard who had blazed the way with blood, driving the red man, whose savagery rendered life unsafe and civilization impossible, from this great country, then, as now, teeming with possibilities. Couriers carried back the glad tidings of peace and safety, and a glowing account of the rich lands, fine forests, great water courses - rivers, creeks, brooks, and bubbling springs. In short, the land of milk and honey had been discovered in Tennessee, then the far west, and the flow of emigration from North Carolina, Virginia, and other old States, became steady and constant, rapidly settling up the country. They were of the best blood of the land; men of brawn and brain. They came with the axe, the hoe, the plow and sickle. They brought with them their customs and notions of civilization and Christianity, having the Bible and the American Constitution for their guide. Wild speculations and schemes of laying out great, cities and building railroads, had not entered the dreams of men then. Good lands and farming was the object, and only young men of muscle, nerve, honesty of purpose, and a courageous disposition to work, possessed of self-reliance and frugal habits, were among the immigrants.

Along with this tide of immigration came John Bell and his amiable wife Lucy and family of promising children, also a number of likely Negroes, then slaves. They landed with their train of wagons and splendid teams in the west end of Robertson county, Tennessee, near where Adams Station is now located, on the Southeastern line of the Louisville & Nashville Railroad, in the year 1804, and met with a hearty reception by old friends who had preceded them. There was general rejoicing in the community over the accession to the quiet happy neighbor hood. Mr. Bell purchased a home partially improved, with good houses, barns, and a fine young orchard, surrounding himself with about one thousand acres of the best land on Red River; and settled down for life, clearing more land and opening a large and fertile farm. His commanding appearance, steadfast qualities, and force of character, at once gave him rank and influence in the community. Mrs. Lucy Bell was an exemplary mother among matrons, ruling her children with the glowing passion of a tender loving mother's heart; even the stern husband yielded to every glance of her gentle piercing eyes and loving smiles. Everybody was in love with Mrs. Bell, and wondered at the power of her influence, and the charming discipline exercised in her home. It was indeed a happy and very prosperous family, as every one recognized.

The principal families composing this delightful neighborhood at that time were Rev. James and Rev. Thomas Gunn, the pioneers of Methodism; William Johnson and James Johnson, the founder of Johnson's Camp Ground, and his two sons, John and Calvin Johnson; John Bell, Jerry Batts, the Porters, Frederick Batts, the Long family, James Byrns, the Gardners, Bartletts and Dardens, the Gooch family, Pitman, Ruffin, Mathews, Morris, Frank Miles and brothers, "Ninety-Six" Needham, Justice and Chester; and just across Red River, between that and Elk Fork Creek, was the large Fort settlement, the Sugg family, McGowen, Bourne, Royster, Waters, Thomas Gorham, Herring, and many other good people. Rev. Sugg Fort was a pioneer Baptist minister and a man of great influence. These people raised large families, and formed the aristocratic society of the country, and no man whose character for morality and integrity was not above reproach was admitted to the circle.

The circle, however, widened, extending up and down the river, and into Kentucky, embracing a large area of territory. Open hospitality characterized the community, and neighbors assisted each other and cooperated in every good move for the advancement of education and Christianity. They established schools, built churches and worshipped together. Churches took the name of the river, creek or spring of the location, and it was nothing uncommon for people to go ten or fifteen miles to church and visiting. The Baptist took the lead in building houses of worship, Red River Church being the first established in that community, which was in 1791. It still maintains the name and organization under the control of a new generation, but has changed the location, moving a short distance to Adams Station, building a new and more commodious house. Drake's Pond Church on the State line, one mile east of Guthrie, Ky., was the next congregation of worshippers organized. This church was held by the Predestinarian Baptist when the split took place in the denomination later. Rev. Sugg Fort was pastor of both churches, and the two congregations visited and worshipped with each other a great deal, the churches being only seven miles apart. The Methodists, in the meanwhile, established several churches in the circle, presided over by Rev. James and Rev. Thomas Gunn, who itinerated a wide scope of country, evangelizing with great success, and it was not uncommon for them to travel fifty miles to marry a couple or preach a funeral. The people of the Bell neighborhood were about equally divided in their church affiliations between the Baptist and Methodist, but toleration, Christian fellowship, and a spirit of emulation prevailed. They worshipped together, and the ties of friendship grew and strengthened; families intermarried, and these fond relations still exist in the present generation.

Like all new countries, the settlement became infested with robbers and horse thieves, and it was almost impossible for any one to keep a good horse. It seemed that the legal authorities were powerless to detect and break up the vandalism and the situation necessitated some active measures on the part of the citizens. Nicholas Darnley, who lived on the Tennessee side of Drake's Pond, several of 'the Forts and Gunns, taking the matter in hand, quietly organized a large vigilance committee to ferret out such crimes, and were not long in detecting the criminals. The ring leaders of the band proved to be men connected with respectable families; one lived in the bend of Red River below Port Royal, and the other a highly connected citizen of Kentucky. The regulators took the two thieves into the dense forest and swamps between Drake's Pond and Sadlersville (as now known), strung them up to limbs of trees and whipped them from head to foot with keen switches. The men were then set free, and warned that if caught again after three days they would be hung. The thieves emigrated at once, crossing the Mississippi River, and finally settled in Louisiana, reformed, leading more honorable lives, and soon became extensive cotton planters and died respected, leaving handsome fortunes.

Both raised large families, ignorant of this stain, and therefore their names are prudently withheld from this sketch, but the circumstance, which was not very uncommon in olden times, illustrates the fact, that the hickory used by our fathers was more potent in correcting bad morals than the penitentiaries of today, and was not less humane. Convicts who darken the door of a modern prison, suffer the same character of punishment, laid on with greater brutality, and other cruelties, and rarely is one ever reclaimed. Whatever may be said of the barbarity of the old whipping post law, it was certain punishment for the convicted, and a greater terror to law breakers, than the penitentiaries of the present day, and was more effective in every way, giving bad men a chance to reform. No criminal cared to show his face in the community after going to the whipping post. They invariably moved and led better lives.

The principal trading points for this locality at that time were Port Royal, Tenn., and Keysburg, Ky., the oldest towns in this country and just as large then as now; also Adairville, Ky., 8pringfield, Clarksville, and Nashville, Tenn. Merchants bought their goods in Philadelphia and New Orleans, hauling them out by wagons until steamboats were brought into use. People, how ever, bought but very few goods. They raised cotton and flax, sheep for wool, and made their clothing at home, using the hand gin, cards, spinning wheel, and old-fashioned loom, and had a cobbler to make up the hides, tanned in a neighboring tannery on shares, into shoes. Doctors were scarce in the country, and the few located at the trading points, did the medical practice of the entire country, riding from five to fifteen miles to see patients.

Some twelve years have passed since John Bell commenced a happy and prosperous career in his new home on the south bank of Red River in Robertson County. A very interesting family of children have grown up, and fortune has smiled on him at every turn. He has become one of the wealthiest and most influential men in the community, respected for his integrity of character, Christian devotion and generous hospitality. His house had become the home of every passing stranger, and neighbors delighted in frequent calls and visits. Many were the pleasant social gatherings at the Bell Place, in which Prof. Richard Powell, the handsome bachelor school teacher, found pleasurable mingling. He was a man of culture and force of character, distinguished in his profession, which was a high calling at that day and time. Every one liked Dick Powell for his fine social qualities and genial manners. He kept a large school in the settlement, and was the educator of several of Mr. Bell's children, especially his young daughter Betsy, whom he gave four years of tuition, and relished every opportunity for praising her virtues to her mother, telling Mrs. Bell what a bright, sweet girl she was, and no one was disposed to controvert his judgment on this point. Betsy was now ripening into lovely girlhood, and the lads who had grown up with her under Richard Powell's tutorship, were as firmly impressed with her charms as was the teacher.

However, the boys were yet a little shy of any demonstrations giving expression to their convictions, as Betsy was considered too young to receive the attention of beaux, and bashful youngsters made excuses for calling at Mr. Bell's to visit his boys. There was one very gallant youth, however, who made no effort to disguise his admiration for the blue-eyed beauty, and his attentions to Betsy were not discouraged. Joshua Gardner was a very handsome young man, graceful in appearance and cultured in manners, and very entertaining socially. He was of a good family, and had won the distinction of being the sprightliest youth in School. Every one conceded that Josh was a fine fellow, who would make his way in the world, and his attentions to Betsy were not displeasing to the old folks nor her brothers.

THE BELL WITCH PROJECT

About this time a mysterious visitor, claiming to hale from the old North State, put in appearance, taking up headquarters at John Bell's, and persisted, in spite of opposition, in remaining indefinitely to fulfill certain missions. This was "Kate" the witch, which the reader is doubtless growing very impatient to know something about. The first evidence of the mystery, or the appearance of things out of ordinary course of events, occurred in 1817. Mr. Bell, while walking through his corn field, was confronted by a strange animal, unlike any he had ever seen, sitting in a corn row, gazing steadfastly at him as he approached nearer. He concluded that it was probably a dog, and having his gun in hand, shot at it, when the animal ran off. Some days after, in the late afternoon, Drew Bell observed a very large fowl, which he supposed to be a wild turkey, as it perched upon the fence, and ran in the house for a gun to kill it. As he approached within shooting distance, the bird flapped its wings and sailed off, and then he was mystified in discovering that it was not a turkey, but some unknown bird of extraordinary size. Betsy walked out one evening soon after this with the children among the big forest trees near the house, and saw something which she described as a pretty little girl dressed in green, swinging to a limb of a tall oak. Then came Dean, the servant, reporting that a large black dog came in the road in front of him at a certain place, every night that he visited his wife Kate, who belonged to Alex. Gunn, and trotted along before him to the cabin door and then disappeared.

These strange apparitions, however, passed for the time unnoticed, exciting no apprehensions whatever. Very soon there came a strange knocking at the door and on the walls of the house, which could not be detected. Later on the disturbance commenced within the house; first in the room occupied by the boys and appeared like rats gnawing the bed posts, then like dogs fighting, and also a noise like trace chains dragging over the floor. As soon as a candle was lighted to investigate the disturbance, the noise would cease, and screams would be heard from Betsy's room; something was after her, and the girl was frightened nearly out of her life.

Mr. Bell now felt a strange affliction coming on him, which he could not account for. It was stiffness of the tongue, which came suddenly, and for a time, when these spells were on, he could not eat. He described it as feeling like a small stick of wood crosswise in his mouth, pressing out both cheeks, and when he attempted to eat it would push the victuals out of his mouth.

John Bell endured such things for a long time, perhaps a year or more, hoping that the disturbance would cease, charging his family to keep the matter a profound secret and they were loyal in their obedience. As frightful as were the demonstrations, not a single neighbor or friend outside of the family had any knowledge of the facts until the affliction became insufferable when Mr. Bell, in strict confidence, laid the matter before James Johnson and wife, narrating the circumstances, insisting that they should spend a night at his house, hoping that Mr. Johnson could throw some light on the mystery. The wish was very cordially acceded to and at the hour of retirement Mr. Johnson led in family worship, as was his custom, reading a chapter, singing a hymn, and then offering prayer. He prayed very earnestly and fervently for a revelation of the cause, or that the Lord would remove the disturbance. As soon as all were in bed and the lights extinguished, the frightful racket commenced, and presently entered Mr. and Mrs. Johnson's room with increased demonstrations, stripping the cover from their bed. Mr. Johnson was astounded and sat upright in bed in wild amazement; but he was a man of strong faith and cool courage, and recovering from the confusion he collected his wits and commenced talking to the spectre, adjuring it to reveal itself and tell for what purpose it was there. The effect of the entreaty convinced Mr. Johnson that the demonstrations came from an intelligent source of some character, but beyond this he had no conception whatever. He however insisted that Mr. Bell should let the matter be known, and call in other friends to assist in the further investigation. This was agreed to, and there was no end to the number of visitors and investigations. Kate, however, developed more rapidly, and soon in answer to the many entreaties, commenced talking, and among the first vocal demonstrations, repeated Mr. Johnson's song and prayer offered on the night of his first visit, referred to, word for word, personating the old gentleman, assimilating his character so perfectly that no one could distinguish it from his voice and prayer.

Kate had now become a fixture, attaining eminence as chief among citizens, at home in the excellent family of John Bell, Sr., and distinguished as the Bell Witch. He, she, or it - whatever may have been the sex, has never been divined made great pretentious for religion taking Mr. Johnson for a model of Christianity, calling him "Old Sugar Mouth," frequently observing "Lord Jesus, how sweet old Sugar Mouth prays; how I do love to hear him." Kate delighted in scriptural controversies, could quote any text or passage in the Bible, and was able to maintain a discussion With the ablest theologians, excelling in fervency of prayer and devotional songs - no human Voice was sweet. Kate made frequent visits to North Carolina, John Bell's old neighborhood, never absent longer than a day or an hour, but always reporting correctly the news or events of the day in that vicinity. With all of these excellent traits of character, Kate behaved badly toward visitors and all members of the family except Mrs. Lucy Bell, to whom the witch was devoted, declaring that "Old Luce" was a good Woman, but manifesting very great aversion for "Old Jack" - John Bell, Sr. He was most detestable and loathsome in the eyes of Kate, for which no cause was ever assigned. But the witch often declared its purpose of killing him before leaving the place.

THE BELL WITCH PROJECT

Kate was also averse to the growing attachment between Joshua Gardner and Betsy Bell, and remonstrated, punishing Betsy severely in divers ways for receiving his devoted attentions. Esther, Betsy's older and only sister, married Bennett Porter, just before the witch had fully developed, and Betsy was now the pride and pet of the household. Like all other girls, however, she made bosom companions of two of her female associates. These were Theny Thorn and Rebecca Porter. They were Betsy's seniors by one or two years, but were both vivacious, charming girls, and had many admirers. Becky Porter was a sister of Bennett Porter, and Theny Thorn was the adopted daughter of James Johnson and second wife, also a niece of Mrs. Johnson, who had no children, and they were greatly devoted to her. In fact she was petted and almost spoilt, and knew them only as father and mother. The three girls were classmates in school, close neighbors, the families all on the most intimate terms, and they grew up together like sisters, almost inseparably attached to each other, going together in society, and were the chief attraction for all the young men in the country. Especially was young James Long devoted to charming Becky Porter, and Alex. Gooch felt a strong pulsation in his heart for lovely Theny Thorn.

Kate the Witch never slept, was never idle or confined to any place, but was here and there and everywhere, like the mist of night or the morning sunbeams, was everything and nothing, invisible yet present, spreading all over the neighborhood, prying into everybody's business and domestic affairs; caught onto every ludicrous thing that happened, and all of the sordid, avaricious meanness that transpired; divining the inmost secrets of the human heart, and withal, was a great blabber mouth; getting neighbors by the ears, taunting people with their sins and shortcomings, and laughing at their folly in trying to discover the identity of the mystery. Kate, however, held fast to Christianity, and was a regular fire-eating Methodist while associating with "Old Sugar Mouth" and his son, Calvin Johnson; was a regular attendant at Mr. Johnson's prayer meetings; calling the amens, thumping on the chairs, and uttering the exclamation "Lord Jesus."

People now concluded that a good spirit had been sent to the community to work wonders and prepare the good at heart for the second advent. Kate's influence was something like that exercised over a "whiskey-soaked town" by Rev. Sam Jones at the present day, only more forceful. The sensation spread hundreds of miles and people were wild with the excitement, and traveled long distances on horseback and in vehicles to witness the demonstrations, and Mr. Bell's home was continually overflowing with visitors and investigators. John Bell's hospitality, however, was equal to the great strain. He fed all visitors free of charge. Citizens of the community soon learned to respect Kate's presence and councils, as they feared and abominated the witch's scorpion tongue. Everybody got good;

the wicked left off swearing, lying and whiskey drinking, just as people do now for Rev. Sam Jones. The avaricious were careful not to covet or lay hands on that which belonged to their neighbors, lest Kate might tell on them. No man allowed his right hand to do anything that the left might be ashamed of. No citizen thought of locking his smoke house or crib door, or of staying up through the night to guard his hen roost or watermelon patch. Negroes were too sleepy to leave their cabins after night, and white people went out only in companies after dark to attend prayer meetings. The wickedest man in the country could break new ground all day with a fiery team and kicking colts, singing psalms, and never think of cursing, though he might be laid out in a trance a dozen times by a punch from the frisky plow handles. No incident out of the regular routine of every day transactions occurred that the witch did not know all about the affair, and would tell the circumstance to some one in less than an hour.

What a great factor in politics this warlock would be at the present time? The whole country would vote Kate an honorary life membership of both houses of Congress, and the right to preside in all departments at Washington, with the privilege of compelling witnesses, books, papers, and giving reports to the newspapers. The witch might also spread out over the entire land during election times to warn the people who was fit for office. If so, only those commended by the mage would ever attain to office, for no amount of money could bribe the witch to conceal the schemes and purposes of designing men. Whatever else may be said of the Bell Witch, Kate evinced an exalted opinion and profound respect for an honest man, and never hesitated, when occasion seemed to require, to remark the distinction of character in men, as in the case of the two brothers, John and Calvin Johnson. John was pronounced a sly trickster, frank and genial in his outward appearance and association, but secretly planning in his own mind some crafty scheme to detect the mysterious oracle. Calvin, however, was an honest man with a pure heart, free from guile, and he was permitted to feel the gentle pressure of the seer's velvety hand, which, when laid on others, produced a smarting sensation, like the chastising palm of an irate mother when laid on a disobedient boy. However, this semblance of deep piety did not hold out. It answered a good purpose in the prayer meetings, serving to promote Christian Fellowship and unify different denominations in devotional exercises, in alternate meetings at Brother Johnson's (Methodist), and Brother Bell's (Baptist) but Kate at last undertook too much for the most renowned wizard. Satan, it is said, was once a respected angel, and becoming too presumptuous, fell from his high state, and so from the same kind of rashness Kate "tumbled." This came of attending the preaching of Rev. James Gunn and Rev. Sugg Fort, thirteen miles apart; on the same day and same hour, trying to reconcile the Arminianism of the one and Calvinism of the other, mixing Methodist fire with Baptist water. This was too much even for so

THE BELL WITCH PROJECT

great an oracle as the Bell Witch.

The preachers were all right, and their sermons and doctrines both got taken one at the time, and a regenerated person could, hardly miss heaven on either line, but it would perplex an angel, much less a presumptuous zealot, to run on both schedules at the same time. This is what Kate undertook to do, and succeeded to the extent of taking in both sermons; but the mixture was too strong for the witch's faith, and the whole stock of piety was soon worked out at a discount. After this Kate backslid and fell from grace, took up with unregenerated spirits, held high carnivals at John Gardner's still house, coming in very drunk, cursing and fuming, filling the house with bad breath, spitting on the Negroes, overturning the chairs, stripping the cover from the beds, pinching and slapping the children, and teasing Betsy in every conceivable way and to such an alarming extent that her parents feared for her to remain alone in her room a single night, and when it was not convenient for Theny Thorn or Rebecca Porter, or both to stay with her, they sent her from home to spend the night. This is something of the general character of Kate, the unknown citizen, which is authentically recorded in detail by Williams Bell and others further on.

THE BELL WITCH PROJECT

THE BELL WITCH PROJECT

Chapter 3

Biographical Sketch of the Bell Family and Reminiscences

John Bell, Sr., was born in 1750 in Halifax County, North Carolina. He was a son of William Bell, a thrifty farmer and prominent citizen. John was given a good country, school education, and was brought up on the farm, where he acquired industrious and steady habits in youth, and grew to manhood noted for his indomitable energy and perseverance, combining all of those good qualities which fits a man for usefulness and success in life, coupled with good practical sense and a keen quick perception. In the meantime he learned the cooper's business, which was a valuable trade at that day, and with all he was a handsome, prepossessing gentlemen.

In 1782 John Bell wedded Miss Lucy Williams, daughter of John Williams of Edgecombe County, North Carolina, a man of considerable wealth and prominence in the community. Lucy was a very handsome, winsome lady, possessing those higher qualities of mind and heart and grace of manners which go to make up that lovely female character she developed all through life, as the reader has already been informed. John Williams approved the match, and gave his daughter a young Negro woman, Chloe, and her child, named Dean, and with the means John had saved up, they bought a farm in Edgecombe County, beginning a prosperous career. They both embraced the Baptist faith and became earnest Christian workers, living up to their religion through life.

Twenty-two years of prosperity having now attended the happy union, John Bell and wife found a large family growing up around them – six children had been born to them, and Chloe had eight, that had become valuable as slaves - a family of seventeen. There was absolute necessity for more elbow room; more land to give their boys a chance in life. Then it was that Mr. Bell determined to emigrate to Robertson county, Tenn., settling, as he did, on Red River, some forty miles north of Nashville, which history the reader is already familiar with.

THE BELL WITCH PROJECT

At the time the remarkable events in this history begun, they had nine children, seven sons and two daughters: Jesse, John, Jr., Drewry, Benjamin, Esther, Zadok, Elizabeth, Richard Williams and Joel Egbert. Benjamin died young; Zadok was educated for the bar, and became a brilliant lawyer. He settled in Alabama, and died in the flush of young manhood, having a promising future before him. The other seven lived to mature age, honored and useful citizens.

John Bell made it a rule to owe no man. He paid as he went, and accumulated rapidly from his farm by economy in management. He was always forehanded, having money ahead, and was accommodating to his neighbors, who were not so fortunate. He was as firm in his convictions as he was dignified in character and generous in hospitality, consequently he was a tower of strength in the community. His sons and daughters, and the present generation of grandchildren, have been no less honored, and no family name has made a stronger impress on that county.

The first marriage in the family was that of Esther, who wedded Alex. Bennett Porter, July 24th, 1817, Rev. Thomas Gunn officiating at the altar. Esther was a very prepossessing young lady, gifted with many graces and charms which made her attractive. Bennett Porter was also popular, and the wedding was quite a noted event. Jesse Bell, the eldest son, married Miss Martha Gunn, daughter of Rev. Thomas Gunn. This marriage took place several months later. Both couples settled in the neighborhood, making a fair start in life, sharing the confidence and good will of the community. A year or two after the death of John Bell, Sr., the two families emigrated to Panola County, Miss., where they settled for life and raised large and interesting families, and have many descendants there at present. John Bell, Jr., the second son, was said to be the very image of his father, and developed the old gentleman's character to a great degree, and was distinguished for his firmness and stern integrity. He was a successful, farmer and a progressive citizen, and enjoyed the fullest confidence of the community. He served as magistrate during a term of years. John Bell, Jr., married Elizabeth Gunn, daughter of Rev. Thomas Gunn, and raised an interesting family. He died in 1861. John, Jr., Drew, and Alex. Gunn engaged in flat boating in 1815. They built generally two or three boats during the summer season, in Red River, at Thomas Gorham's, now known as the Sugg mill place.

The boats were constructed of rough hewn and sawed timber, and were cabled to the bank, awaiting the Winter or Spring rise in the water, when they were loaded with all kinds of produce, tobacco, flour, corn, oats, bacon, whiskey, dried fruits, butter, turkeys, chickens, eggs, etc., and were cut loose on the first current of sufficient tide to float the crafts out, each boat having two men at the

THE BELL WITCH PROJECT

oars and the captain at the stern with one oar, to steer the boat in the proper current to avoid snags and breakers, as the craft drifted on with the flow to the great Father of Waters, and down to New Orleans, the southern mart. This was the only way people had at that time for shipping their produce to market, except by wagons. It was very slow, but generally sure, and always got there with the tide that left Red River. Each one of the partners would take charge of a boat as captain or master, and first loaded, first off. After arriving at New Orleans, and selling the cargo, the boats were worthless except for fuel or secondhand lumber, and they were sold for what the timber would bring, and the boatmen made their way home as best they could, generally walking, and arriving in time to build more boats for the next season. A bill of lading for the last one of these trips, still in existence, was made out to Alex. Gunn, April 1818, for fifty hogsheads of tobacco weighing 64,166 pounds gross, probably not over 52,000 pounds net, every hogshead numbered, for which he brought in returns a draft on a Nashville bank for $1,000, two hundred pairs of boots, $800, and $211 in sugar and coffee. This was probably after paying freight charges, about three cents per pound, for the tobacco.

About this time two steamboats, the General Green and the General Robertson, entered the Cumberland River, driving most of the flatboats men out of the business, having a monopoly of the shipping trade up to 1822, making Clarksville the principal shipping point, which was then a town of only forty families - 215 white population, and a number of Negroes.

The want of some satisfactory explanation, or the failure of all investigations to throw light on the witch mystery, gave rise to a speculative idea that John and Drew Bell had learned ventriloquism and some subtle art while on these trips to New Orleans, and taught the same to their young sister Betsy, for the purpose of attracting people and making money. This conjecture was widely circulated, and checked many people in their purpose of visiting the scene of the excitement. Notwithstanding this explanation was accepted by many, it was the silliest of all solutions attempted. If the parties were able to perform such wonders, they only had to make the fact known to have reaped a fortune. But to the contrary, they tried to keep it a secret, and when known it brought both suffering and loss to the family. Moreover, John Bell, Jr., was absent, visiting relatives in North Carolina, six months or more during the height of the excitement, and he could not possibly have had anything to do with it. Drew was also absent at times, and still no difference was observed in the manifestations when they were both absent or present.

The witch entertained visitors in the reception room just the same when Betsy was present or retired to her own chamber. There was also knocking on the doors and outer walls, and rattling on the housetop heard, when every member of the family were known to be within. And as soon as the family and visitors retired for sleep, every room full, doors and windows securely closed, the cover was stripped from every bed and pillows and sheets jerked from under strong men. If the Bell brothers and sister, had been capable of making such demonstrations, could they have continued the exhibitions so long undiscovered by the shrewd detectives who were constantly on the alert? Or would they have heartlessly inflicted so much distress upon their father and family? No one in that community, familiar with the facts and demonstrations, knowing the affections of the children for their parents, and devotion to each other, ever believed it. They knew it was impossible.

Betsy was not only frightened, but was severely punished in so many ways that she cheerfully submitted to any and every investigation proposed, even to the ridiculous treatment of cranks, conjurers, and witch doctors, in the hope of relief from some source. Drewry Bell never married. He lived quite a secluded bachelor's life, accumulating considerable property. He died at his home in that vicinity January 1st, 1865. It is said by neighbors that he lived under forebodings and dreadful, apprehension that the witch would visit some calamity on him. He charged every strange noise and occurrence to the haunt, reciting mysterious occurrences to his friends, believing that the spirit was ever present about his premises, and through fear he kept some man employed on the place to keep him company.

Richard Williams Bell settled on his portion of the land inherited from his father's estate, buying other interests, and devoted himself to agriculture. He was endowed with a strong intellect, and was the most cultured of the family, noted for his splendid business qualifications and frugality, and especially was he distinguished for his integrity of character, his deep piety and devotion to his religious principles, his tender nature, and promptness in lending a helping hand where help was needed, he was one of nature's noblemen - a good man and valuable citizen. He had not an enemy in the broad land. His neighbors trusted him implicitly, and relied upon him as a true friend and safe counselor in all things, and his name is cherished to this day by all who knew him.

Williams Bell was a boy at the time of the witch affliction, which the Bell's have always alluded to as "our family trouble," but he was old enough, and probably just the right age, to receive a deep and lasting impression of what occurred, what he saw, felt and heard, things that were well calculated to impress a boy's mind. He waited upon his father during the last year of his life, and when able to go out, accompanied him wherever he went about the farm or in the neighborhood, witnessed his contortions and excruciating sufferings, and heard the derisive songs and fearful anathemas pronounced against him by the witch - terrifying invectives that were calculated to appall the stoutest heart and leave an impress seared as by fire.

The imprint was never erased, and every recurring thought of the dire events came like a convulsing nightmare. After mature years he consulted with his brothers and sister Betsy, comparing their recollections with the notes of his own memory, from which he wrote the thrilling details of "Our Family Trouble," and no reader who ever knew the writer will question the truth of a single word of it, no matter what may be their faith or opinion concerning the mystery, or their views about witch craft of olden times. Williams Bell died October 24th, 1857, at the age of forty-six years, just in the prime of life and his greatest usefulness. He left a good estate for his widow and children.

He was three times married, his first wife being Sallie Gunn, daughter of Rev. Thomas Gunn; second marriage with Susan Gunn, daughter of Rev. James Gunn, and third wife, Eliza Orndorff. James Allen Bell was the eldest son by his first wife. He received careful training at the hands of his father, and developed steady business habits and strong convictions, attaining to prominence quite early in life, taking a leading place in politics and public affairs, and about 1870 was nominated by the County Democratic Convention and elected by the people to represent the county in the State Legislature. At the close of the term he sold his farm and other interests in Robertson County and moved to Adairville, Ky., engaging in the tobacco business, where he still resides, and is highly esteemed by the people of both Logan and Robertson counties. He married Miss Eugenia Chambers, a lady of many personal charms and accomplishments. They have raised three children, a son and two daughters, of whom they have just cause to feel proud. Williams Bell's youngest son, Ninyon Oliver, by his last marriage, is a substantial farmer and owns a fine home adjoining the old Bell place in fact his farm includes the old residence site and surroundings.

Joel E. Bell was the youngest child of John and Lucy Bell. The writer enjoyed a personal acquaintance with him for twenty-five years, and learned to appreciate his warm and generous friendship. He was a man of noble impulse, clear practicable head and settled convictions, favored by an indomitable spirit full of fiery enthusiasm, and always left a strong and pleasing impress on those with whom he came in contact. He took a leading part in all matters looking to the advancement of the public welfare, and his zeal for the accomplishment of whatever he undertook knew no bounds. He was a strong Baptist, a religious enthusiast, always overflowing with the love of God, and his last days were spent in zealous work for the Master's cause. He attended the associational meetings, delivered happy little speeches pregnant with practical ideas, infusing spirit in the members, giving freely of his own means for the advancement of religious enterprises. There are but few Baptist ministers and prominent laymen in Tennessee and Southern Kentucky Who do not remember old Brother Bell with tender emotions. He died in 1890 at the age of seventy-seven years, ripe for the enjoyment of that sweet repose which remains for the righteous. Joel Bell sold his farm in the west end of the county, the place now occupied by Lee Smith, about 1855, and moved to a large brick dwelling at the cross roads four miles north of Springfield - the Adairville road - where he died. He was twice married, and was fortunate in both matches.

THE BELL WITCH PROJECT

Chapter 4

Betsy Bell and Her Trials

Elizabeth, the youngest daughter of John and Lucy Bell, was born in 1805, and was only twelve years of age when "our family troubles" commenced - a lighthearted, romping lass whose roguish beauty and mischievous glance made the hearts of the boys go pit pat, while she yet enjoyed most the gay notes of the woodland songsters, or a stroll with her associates in search of wild flowers, berries, etc., along the riverside where the murmuring waves lent an enchantment to the pursuit. Betsy, however, developed rapidly, and at the age of fifteen had ripened into lovely young womanhood, and was noted for her extraordinary beauty and winsome ways. She was a blonde, symmetrical in form, presenting a charming figure of uncommon grace, with a fine suit of soft silky hair, which hung in beautiful waves, in contrast with her fair complexion, and with all, there was enchantment in the mischievous twinkle of her large deeply set blue eyes.

She was also characterized for her keen wit and sparkling humor; nor had her domestic education, that which added most to a young girl's popularity in olden times, been neglected, to all of which must be added industrious habits, gentleness and womanly dignity. It is no wonder that she was the pet of the family and the favorite in society, nor is it surprising that young Joshua Gardner should have lost both his head and heart in admiration for the fair beauty in whom the observing bachelor school master discovered so many charms. Gardner had now become very earnest in his devotions, and was never more happy than when in her society. And it was said that the sentiment was reciprocated, he being the first young man to impress her with his attentions. In fact their fondness for each others society became the subject of general remark among the young people.

They were regarded as lovers, and Joshua was the recipient of many congratulations on his good fortune in winning the affections of the fairest beauty in the land. The affiance was marked by a passionate tenderness and adoration which neither could well conceal, and it was given still more notoriety by the witch, whose keen observations and cutting remarks frequently drove them from the presence of other company, for a walk in the lawn or seats under the favorite pear tree. However, it was the manner in which Kate appeared that caused serious forebodings. It was a soft melancholy voice, sighing in the distance and gradually approaching nearer with gentle pleadings in loud whispers, "Please Betsy Bell, don't have Joshua Gardner. Please Betsy Bell, don't marry Joshua Gardner." Over and over was this entreaty earnestly repeated by the mysterious voice in the most beseeching and supplicating tones, so doleful and disconsolate that it caused a shudder to creep over every one who heard it. It was so intensely persuasive, gentle and sweet, so extremely mystifying, that it not only bewildered the lovers, but brought perplexity and confusion into every social circle where the matter was discussed as the most absorbing theme. Why should Betsy Bell not wed Joshua Gardner? He was handsome and gracious, well educated, intelligent and entertaining, high spirited, industrious and energetic, and noted for his strict moral character and pleasing deportment; he was highly connected and possessed sufficient means for a good start in life. His integrity was above reproach, and he stood before the community as a model young man.

Then why this dismal foreboding of the witch? Why should Betsy Bell spurn his manly devotions? No one could surmise or conjecture a single reason, and all hearts warmed in deep sympathy for their betrothment. Betsy had suffered extreme torture, the anguish of terror by contact with the frightful ghost, and was deeply impressed with the witch's earnest solicitude as a premonition of some dire consequence. Joshua, however, was stouter of heart. The burning passion which thrilled his soul was like a consuming flame, and grew stronger as the persecutions increased. He had his own opinions and conjectures about the mystery, and though he could not solve it, he was willing to brook all danger of the witch's power to visit distress or greater evil than had already been inflicted, and he was ready to endure all for the sake of her whom he loved so tenderly, madly. He was assured that Betsy loved him as passionately in return. Hers was a stronger, a more rational devotion, looking also to the future, weighing deliberately the consequences that might result from a mistake, and thought it best to prolong the engagement and await further developments, hoping that the mystery might be solved or the witch would disappear, leaving them in the full enjoyment of each other's love and all of their sweet anticipations of uninterrupted happiness.

This was the agreement, and there was no abatement in their devotions; the attachment grew stronger and the ties more tender and passionate. Betsy was not without friends, sympathy and consolation all through this long and trying ordeal. Her parents were deeply sensible of her sufferings and the cloud of sorrow that overshadowed her, threatening to crush the spirit and hope of her young life, and did all that was in their power to alleviate her distress. Her mother, Mrs. Lucy Bell, whose influence was the controlling power, and swayed like magic in molding and shaping the character of her children, was watchful of her every want and care. The brothers were not negligent in providing diversions for her relaxation. Theny Thorn and Becky Porter never deserted her in moments when courage was needed to withstand the dreadful scenes that were enacted. They witnessed the fearful convulsions of hysteria which so frequently came on suddenly, with the announcement of Kate's presence, suppressing her breath until life was almost extinct.

They had heard her frantic screams from violent pain, complaining that the "old thing" was sticking pins in her body. They had heard the sound of the blow, and saw the tinge left by the invisible hand that slapped her cheeks. They had seen her tucking comb snatched by magic from her head and slammed on the floor, her beautiful hair disheveled and all tangled in an instant, and heard Kate's hilarious laughter enjoying the freak. They had witnessed her shoes coming unlaced and slipping from her feet at the witch's suggestion, and observed many other terrifying and tormenting acts, accompanied with vile threats, while watching with Betsy night after night, gossiping with the witch that she might have some rest. But few girls could be persuaded to withstand such frightful scenes under apprehensions of greater calamity, but timid as they were their sympathy and devotion made them strong; courageous to endure and suffer with their friend in any misfortune that might come. Their presence and sympathy encouraged Betsy to bear her persecutions, and hold out bravely in the hope that the mystery would soon be dispelled. James Long and Alex. Gooch were frequently around contributing to some diversion, and Joshua Gardner continued his rapturous attentions, foregoing every desire of his own heart for her pleasure and comfort. Prof. Richard Powell had ended his career as a pedagogue and was not so much about the Bell home. He had entered the political arena and become a leading politician and foremost in all public affairs. He was several time selected to the State Legislature, where he distinguished himself as a lawmaker of ability and gained wide popularity.

THE BELL WITCH PROJECT

THE BELL WITCH PROJECT

Chapter 5

The Homestead — Graveyard — Witch Stories and Surroundings

The old Bell farm is about one mile from Adams Station, a village that sprang into existence in 1859-60, during the building of the Edgefield and Kentucky Railroad, which is now the Southeastern branch of the Louisville and Nashville system. It lies on the south side of Red River, bordering some distance on that pretty stream, stretching back nearly one mile over a beautiful fertile valley. The greater portion of the farm was cleared by John Bell during the first twenty years of the present century. Here Dean, the faithful Negro who proudly mastered the big wagon and team in the train from the old North State, that landed the family safely, deserves honorable mention. He was noted for being the best axe man and rail splitter that ever entered the forest of this country. He was small in statue, but powerfully muscled, and no two men were ever found who could match him in felling timber, he taking one side of a tree, against two men on the opposite, and invariably cutting the deepest kerf; and so with the mall and wedge, he could beat any two of the best rail splitters in the country.

Dean was as proud of this distinction as ever John Sullivan was of his pugilistic championship, and he was indeed a valuable man in the forest at that time, as he was faithful and useful every way, and Mr. Bell thought a great deal of him and treated him kindly, as he did all of his Negroes, but money could not buy Dean. Red River is a bold strong stream, with some interesting scenery, and bubbling springs bursting out along its banks. During the early settlement the stream abounded with game and fish, furnishing much sport for the natives, and young people frequently gathered at favorite places for picnics and fishing frolics. The noted spring mentioned by Williams Bell in this sketch, designated by the witch as the hiding place of a large sum of money, breaks out on the southeast corner of the place, near the river, from which flows the bubbling waters of Lethe.

The residence was a double log house, one and a half stories high, a wide passage or hallway between, and an ell-room with passage, the building weatherboarded on the outside, furnishing six large comfortable rooms and two halls, and was one of the best residences in the country at that time. It was located on a slight elevation in the plane, nearly a half-mile back from the river, a large orchard in the rear, and the lawn well set in pear trees. The farm has been divided and the old buildings were long since torn away and the logs used for building cabins, still standing on the Joel Bell place, now owned by Lee Smith. No one cared to occupy the premises after the death of Mrs. Lucy Bell, when it was vacated, and for some time used for storing grain. The only sign now remaining is a few scattered stones from the foundation, and three of the old pear trees that surrounded the house, planted about the time or before John Bell bought the place, some ninety years ago. One of these trees measures nearly seven feet around the trunk; it, however, shows signs of rapid decay. The public highway, known as the Brown's Ford and Spring field road, ran through the place within one hundred yards of the house, and it was no uncommon thing during the witch excitement to find a horse hitched to every fence corner of the long lane, by people calling to hear the witch talk and investigate the sensation.

Many stories were told regarding spectres and apparitions of various kinds seen, and uncommon sounds heard along this lane - strange lights and jack-o-lanterns flitting across the field. There is nothing, how ever, authentic in reference to these things except the incident told by Dr. Gooch, who saw the old house enveloped in flames, and the musical feast at the spring, related by Gunn and Bartlett. There were many superstitious people in the country who believed the witch was a reality, something supernatural, beyond human power or comprehension, which had been clearly demonstrated. This is the way many reasoned about the mystery.

Kate arrogantly claimed to be all things, possessing the power to assume any shape, form or character, that of human, beast, varmint, fowl or fish, and circumstances went to confirm the assertion. Therefore people with vivid imaginations were capable of seeing many strange sights and things that could not be readily accounted for, which were credited to the witch. Kate was a great scapegoat. The goblin's favorite form, however, was that of a rabbit, and this much is verified beyond question, the hare ghost took malicious pleasure in hopping out into the road, showing itself to every one who ever passed through that lane. This same rabbit is there plentifully to this day, and can't be exterminated. Very few men know a witch rabbit; only experts can distinguish one from the ordinary molly cottontail. The experts in that section, however, are numerous, and no one to this good day will eat a rabbit that has a black spot on the bottom of its left hind foot. When the spot is found, the foot is carefully cut off and placed in the hip pocket, and the body buried on the north side of an old log.

Some of these people believed the spook escaped from an Indian grave on the Bell place, by the reckless disinterment of the red man's bones, but Kate's own statement, which was afterwards contradicted, is the only shadow of evidence found to sustain this opinion.

The Bell graveyard is located on a gravelly knoll about three hundred yards north of the side of the old dwelling, where repose the dust of John Bell, Sr., his wife Lucy, and sons Benjamin, Zadok, and Richard Williams, the last named who tells the story of "Our Family Trouble." A beautiful grove of cedar and walnut trees surround the sacred spot, keeping silent watch over the graves of loved ones whose bodies rest there. Wild grape vines, supported by large trunks, spread their far-reaching tendrils over every branch and twig of the trees, forming a delightful alcove. Native strawberries grow all about, and wild flowers of many varieties blossom in their season, filling nature's bower with grateful fragrance, and decorating the graves in living beauty. It is here that the wild wood songsters gather to chant their sweetest lays, and the timid hare finds retreat and hiding from the prowling huntsman. Sweet solemnity hovers over the scene like the morning halo mantling the orb of light in gorgeous beauty.

There are numbers of unregenerate men who can perhaps muster sufficient courage to pass a city of towering shafts and monuments, but can: not be induced to approach near so sacred a spot as this after the sun has hidden his face behind the shadow of night. It presents nothing fanciful, or inviting to their view, but rather a scene of the ideal home of weird spirits. But to people who trust Providence, admire tile beauties of nature, and fear not devils, this bowery alcove of woodland trees, evergreens, vines and flowers, sheltering sacred dust, appears one of the most lovely and majestic spots on earth.

Let those who feel the need of it, have magnificent stately monuments and lofty shafts mounted with a dove, or a pinnacle finger pointing heaven ward, but give me such a paradise of living green as this, planted and nurtured by the hand of the All Wise Creator, where angels may delight to meet and commune, breathing sweet incense distilled by the zephyrs from nature's own flowers, keeping vigilance until the last trump shall sound, and why should I care for a granite shaft reaching to the skies, or grumble at a poor scrawny spook for wanting to hide beneath its cover, to catch a pure breath while hazing around to avoid Satan?

On the opposite side of the river from the Bell place, is the William La Prade farm, now owned by M. L. Killebrew, and just below Killebrew's, all between the river and Elk Fork Creek, is the Fort settlement, a large and influential family, distinguished among the pioneers, and whose descendants still maintain the honored name. On the east was located the Gunns and Johnsons, all having good farms. James Johnson and two sons, John and Calvin, were Bell's nearest neighbors, and next the Gunn families. James Johnson was a grand old man. He was the founder of Johnson's Camp Ground on his place, which was kept up by his sons, the Gunns and other good people, long years after his death, as late as 1854. Great crowds of people from a circle of twenty or thirty miles, gathered there annually, spending weeks in a season of religious enjoyment. Many descendants of these excellent families - Gunns and Johnsons - make up the present citizenship maintaining as a precious heritage the good names left to them. Also the Goochs, Longs, Porters, Jerry Batts, Miles, Byrns, Bartlett, Ruffin, and other good names among the early settlers, are still well represented.

One mile above Bell's the Clark brothers had a mill to which the early settlers carried their grain and grist. Later, Fort's mill was built below, and several other mills erected on Elk Fork. Morris & Merritt bought out the Clarks and converted the old mill into a cotton ginning, thread spinning and wool carding factory. It was said that the witch took up at this factory after seven years absence and return. The manager told the story to customers, that frequently after shutting down the mill, the operators would hardly reach home before the machinery would be heard apparently in full movement, and returning hastily, opening the door, he would find everything perfectly still as he had left it. There is, however, no evidence to be had now verifying the statement.

THE BELL WITCH PROJECT

Chapter 6

Mrs. Kate Batts and the Witch

It is proper that the reader should, before perusing "Our Family Trouble" and other accounts of the witch, be introduced to Mrs. Kate Batts, who was a noted lady in that community, remarkable for her eccentricities, who survived long after John Bell and is well remembered by many citizens still living. There were two Batts families, who were in no way related. Jerry Batts was a very prominent man, and his descendants make up part of the present good citizenship of that community.

Frederick Batts and wife Kate had three children, Jack, Calvin and Mary. They had no relatives and lived very much unto themselves. Their children died in advance of the turn of life and the family has become extinct. The boys were all, spindling and gawky, and very droll, and did not take in society. Mary, however, was a beautiful bright girl and very popular. Frederick Batts was an invalid, a helpless cripple, the greater part of his life, and his wife Kate assumed control of the farm, the family and all business affairs, and was successful in accumulating by her management, keeping the one idea of money-making before her. They were well to do people, owned a very good farm, a number of Negroes, and were forehanded, having always some money to lend. Nothing of a disreputable nature attached to the family character. They were respectable people, except for Mrs. Batts' eccentricity, which made many hold the family at as great a distance as possible.

She was a large fleshy woman, weighing over two hundred pounds, and was headstrong and very exacting in her dealings with men. She was exceedingly jealous of her rights, not always knowing what they were, conceiving the idea that everybody was trying to beat her out of something. Her tongue was fearful. She did not hesitate to tackle any man who came under the ban of her displeasure, with a scourge of epithets. This, however, was tolerated as a weakness, and excited the sympathy of the better class, who humored her whims, but no one cared to encounter her organ of articulation when she was in a bad humor, and especially the ladies, who were generally afraid of her, and could not endure her methods and dominating spirit. The superstitious believed that she was a witch, and this conjecture was strengthened by her habit of begging a brass pin from every woman she met, which trifle was supposed to give her power over the donor, and some ladies were careful to put their pins far away when "Old Kate" came in sight. Notwithstanding Mrs. Batts was around every few days, traveling her circuit once a week, trading and gossiping, the superstitious were careful to keep their apprehensions concealed from her. They were all smiles and joy, and spared no opportunity to make "Aunt Kate" happy in everything but one and were exceedingly regretful that there was not a pin on the place.

Mrs. Batts kept her Negro women employed mostly at spinning, weaving cotton, flax and wool, making jeans, linsey, linen, etc., and knitting stockings after night until late bed time, and always had something to sell, and would buy all the surplus wool rolls and other raw material wanted in her business, and this furnished her an excuse for visiting regularly over the neighborhood. Mrs. Batts was very aristocratic in her own conceit, believing that her property entitled her to move in the highest circle of society, and she put on extraordinary airs and used high sounding bombastic words, assimilating, as she thought, aristocracy, which subjected her to much ridicule and made her the laughingstock of the community. Moreover, she was anxious to give her timid boy, Calvin, a matrimonial boost, and never hesitated to invade the society of young people, who were amused by her quaint remarks. The girls, however, dreaded her presence in mixed company, lest she should unwittingly say something to cause a blush. However she never neglected to put in a word for her noble boy, who resembled a bean pole. "Girls, keep your eyes on Calvin; he's all warp and no filling, but he'll weave a yard wide" - referring to her own large proportions.

Mrs. Batts kept an old gray horse expressly for the saddle. Old Gray was saddled every morning as regular as the sun shone, though Aunt Kate was never known to ride. She invariably walked, carrying a copperas riding skirt on her left arm, two little Negro boys walking by her side, and Phillis, her waiting maid, in front leading the old gray horse. This caravan was known as "Kate Batts' troop." No difference where she went, if entering the finest parlor in the country, Aunt Kate would habitually spread the copperas skirt over the seat offered her, and set on it. With all of these peculiarities and eccentricities, "Sister Kate" was an enthusiastic Christian, always expatiating on the Scripture and the goodness of God, and would have her share of rejoicing in every meeting, and it never required an excess of spiritual animation to warm her up to business. She was a member of

THE BELL WITCH PROJECT

Red River Church and a regular attendant, always late, but in time to get happy before the meeting closed.

On one occasion, Rev. Thomas Felts was conducting a revival meeting, which had been in progress several days, and a deep religious feeling had been awakened, the house being crowded every day with anxious people. Just as Parson Felts had concluded a rousing sermon awakening sinners to repentance, and called the mourners to the front, and the whole audience engaged in singing rapturous praise and transporting melody, the Batts' troop arrived. Phillis observed "Old Missus" had already caught the spirit and was filling up on glory, hurriedly hitched Old Gray and made a rush for the house. The meeting had reached its highest tension, the house was packed, and the congregation on foot singing with the spirit.

The interest centered around Joe Edwards, who was down on his all fours at the mourner's bench, supplicating and praying manfully. Joe Edwards was a good citizen, but a desperately wicked and undone sinner, and everybody was anxious to have him converted. Especially were his religious friends in deep sympathy, sharing the burden of sorrow he was trying to throw off, as he seemed to be almost at the point of trusting, and the brethren had gathered around, instructing and urging him on. Just at this critical moment Sister Batts rushed in, and elbowing her way into the circle, she deliberately spread her copperas riding skirt all over Joe Edwards and sat down on him. The poor man did not know what had happened; he felt that he was in the throes of the last desperate struggle with Satan and that the devil was on top. He shouted and yelled the louder, "Oh I am sinking, sinking. Oh take my burden Jesus and make the devil turn me loose or I will go down, down, and be lost forever in torment. Oh save me, save me, blessed Lord."

A good brother invited Sister Batts to another seat, but she politely declined with a flourish of big words, as was her custom when putting on dignified airs. "No I thank you; this is so consoling to my disposition that I feel amply corrugated." "But," insisted the good deacon, "you are crowding the mourner." "Oh that don't disburse my perspicuity; I'm a very plain woman and do love to homigate near the altar whar th'r Lord am making confugation among th'r sinners." "But, Sister Batts, the man is suffocating," still interposed the deacon. Yes, bless Jesus, let him suffocate; he's getting closer to th'r Lord," exclaimed Sister Batts.

The situation had now become serious. The whole house had caught on, and was bursting with tittering laughter. Sister Batts felt the foundation beneath her giving away, and was caught by two brethren just as she threw up her hands, in time to prevent a still more ludicrous scene. Joe Edwards rose up shouting joyously for his deliverance, as if some unknown spirit had snatched him from the vasty deep. Sister Batts clasped her hands and shouted, "Bless th'r Lord, bless my soul, Jesus am so good to devolve His poor critters from the consternation of Satan's mighty dexterity." The affair had reached such a comical and extremely ludicrous stage, that the audience could no longer restrain its resistibility to a simper, and many left the house hurriedly for an outdoor open air free laugh. This ended the service, breaking up the meeting. The preacher could do nothing but dismiss the remainder of the congregation, who were suffering from a suppressed tittering sensation, holding their sides out of respect for the minister and religion.

Phillis was a strong believer in "Ole Missus." Describing the incident she said: "I neber seed Satan whipped outen er meetin so quick in all'er my bawn days. Sooner an Ole Missus sot down on dat man de devil tuck out under der flo an de man hollered glory, glory, lemme up, lemme up. Ole Miss paid no tention tu enybody. She sat dar, an menced gittin happy herself, an all de folks in de house menced shoutin'. De man he got so full of glory he ware gwinter git up anyhow an menced drawing hiz hine legs up sorter like er cow, an den drapped back, kase Ole Miss ware still dar, an she want'er gwineter git up tell ole Satan wuz mashed clean outen him. Hit made Mister Joe Edwards sweat like er hoss, but he am got mighty good ligion now, dat will last him tell der next meetin."

As soon as the loquacious visitor developed the propensity for articulation, people became importunate in their entreaties, begging the mysterious voice to disclose its character, nature, who or what it was, and what its mission, to which importunities various answers were given, but no explanation that seemed to satisfy the anxious curiosity. Finally Rev. James Gunn undertook in a conversation with the gnome to draw out the information. The goblin declared that it could not trifle with a preacher or tell Brother Gunn a lie, and if he must know the truth, it was nothing more nor less than old Kate Batts' witch, and was determined to haunt and torment old Jack Bell as long as he lived.

This announcement seemed to fit the case precisely and satisfy a certain element to a fraction. Less superstitious and more considerate persons did not expect the witch to divulge the truth, and of course did not believe a word concerning Mrs. Batts' agency in the matter; that was impossible. But the explanation pleased those, who wanted it so. It served for a brand new and most startling sensation in the mysterious developments, and all tongues were set to wagging. Men and women looked aghast, and said that was just what they had believed all the while. Various suspicious circumstances were recalled to confirm the witch's statement. The most inconvertible evidence was that a certain girl in the vicinity was given the task of churning, and after working the dasher diligently for two hours without reward, and no signs of butter coming, she declared that old Kate Batts had bewitched the milk and she was determined to burn her. Carrying out this decision, she stuck an iron poker in the fire, and after it had come to a white heat, she soused the iron into the milk, setting the churn away; then making some excuse for the visit, she called on Aunt Kate to ascertain the result of her experiment, and found Mrs. Baits sitting in the corner nursing a burnt hand, which had been badly blistered through a mistake in taking the poker by the hot end that morning.

Another circumstance, Mrs. Batts had been heard to speak harshly of John Bell in regard to a transaction she had with him years back when he first moved to the settlement, declaring that she would get even with him. Mrs. Batts was not in the habit of saying many good things about any one, unless she got the best end of a bargain in her dealings, but it is most probable that the old transaction referred to had been forgotten by both parties until brought out by the witch, and John Bell hardly believed Mrs. Batts capable or culpable in the mystery. However, many were satisfied with the explanation, and from this time on the witch was called "Kate," and to this name the incomprehensible voice was always pleased to answer. But there was music in the breeze when this new sensation reached the ears of Mrs. Batts. Her eyes flashed fire, and her tongue was let loose at both ends, rolling off epithets like streaks of lightning. She kept every path in the neighborhood hot for a month trying to find the "corrigendum who dared to splavicate her character with the spirifications of John Bell's witch. She would show him the perspicuity in the constipation of the law." Sister Batts, how ever, never found the author of her discomfiture. The corrigendum was a shapeless, invisible, irresponsible thing, and not subject to the law.

THE BELL WITCH PROJECT

THE BELL WITCH PROJECT

Chapter 7

Witchcraft of the Bible

Opinions of Rev. John Wesley, Dr. Clark, and other Distinguished Divines and Commentators

The writer has no theory to present regarding the Bell Witch phenomena, nor has he any opinion to advance concerning witchcraft, sorcery, spiritualism or psychology in any form, but prefers quoting from Scripture, and the reasoning of distinguished men, learned in theology, and experienced in psychical research. He frankly confesses his ignorance of such matters, and the total lack of both inclination and ability to enter into the investigation of the fathomless subject.

Having known the history of the Bell Witch from a boy's earliest recollections, and now having collected and compiled the testimony, he is convinced by the overwhelming evidence, that the circumstances detailed by Williams Bell, and supported by others, as unreasonable as they may appear, are literally true - such things did happen, but no further can we venture.

Knowing the character of the men and women who testify to these things, no one can disbelieve them, or believe that they would have willfully misrepresented the facts; nor can it reasonably be said that so many reputable witnesses had fallen into an abnormal state of mind, and were so easily deceived in all of their rigid investigations.

A man may be arraigned for trial on the charge of murder, the court and jury knowing nothing about the facts and circumstances, but they are bound by both physical and moral law to believe and find the man guilty on the testimony of reputable witnesses, detailing the facts and circumstances, and yet may form no opinion or idea as to the state of mind or cause that prompted the prisoner to commit the murder. So it is in this instance; the testimony is convincing of the truth of the wonderful phenomena, at John Bell's, but the motive or cause is beyond our comprehension, and to this extent the facts must be accepted. It would be a shameful display of one's ignorance to deny on general principles the existence of the thing or fact, in the face of such evidence, because he did not witness it, and cannot comprehend it. Might as well the jury, after hearing the evidence, discharge the prisoner on the grounds that they did not see the act committed, and could not believe the man guilty of a deed so atrocious.

The writer, however, wishes to present every phase of the Bell Witch phenomena, together with some quotations from the Bible on which many people in all ages have based their superstition; also the reasoning of some spiritually enlightened and successful ministers of Christ's doctrine, and opinions on ancient witchcraft as presented by the Bible, together with the ideas of modern spiritualism, for the benefit of those who are disposed to investigate. Christianity of the present day has generally abandoned the doctrine of "ministering spirits" as a faith leading up to a danger line where there can be no distinction between that and modern spiritualism. Dr. Bond, a distinguished Methodist divine and editor, who has most forcibly combated the faith on the grounds that, that which cannot be explained is not to be believed, and for the best reason that many deeply pious minds have become involved in confusion and error in trying to exercise this discriminating faith, and he argues that all premonitions, omens and spectral appearances are a common phenomena of disordered senses, and that the doctrine of the spirit world is unscriptural and dangerous in the extreme, and that theologians have no right to say that the spirits of the dead live about us, and commune with us, and minister to us.

Notwithstanding all such arguments and the efforts to put away superstition, to ridicule and laugh it out of existence, there is scarcely any one who is free from every form of superstition. Certainly the Christian world gets its superstition from the Bible, if it is not innate, and it is very hard to discard, and still accept all other things that the Book teaches as divine revelation. There are but few people, however, who are willing to admit their superstition, lest they be laughed at and characterized as weak-minded, crazy, etc. Even Dr. Clark, the great John Wesley, the founder of Methodism, and many other distinguished writers and commentators, have not escaped this criticism. Mr. Wesley, however, was bold in speaking his sentiments and rather boasted of his belief in witchcraft. He wrote and spoke about the Epworth ghost that haunted the family some thirty years.

Rev. L. Tyerman, in his Life and Times of Wesley, says Wesley has been censured and ridiculed for this credulity. Did Wesley deserve this? The reader must not forget the undeniable, though mysterious, supernatural noises in the

THE BELL WITCH PROJECT

Epworth rectory. He must also bear in mind that one of the most striking features in Wesley's religious character was his deep rooted, intense, powerful and impelling convictions of the dread realities of an unseen world. This great conviction took possession of the man, he loved it, cherished it, tried to instill it into all of his helpers, all of his people, and without it he would never have undertaken the Herculean labor, and endured the almost unparalleled opprobrium that he did. Besides his own justification of himself is more easily sneered at than answered. He (Wesley) writes:

"With my last breath, will I bear my testimony against giving up to infidels one great proof of the invisible world; I mean, that of witchcraft and apparitions, confirmed by the testimony of all ages. The English in general, and indeed, most of the men of learning in Europe, have given up all accounts of witches and apparitions as mere old wives' fables. I am sorry for it, and I willingly take this opportunity of entering my solemn protest against this violent compliment, which so many that believe the Bible pay to those who do not believe it. I owe them no such service.

I take knowledge these are at the bottom of the out cry which has been raised, and with such insolence spread throughout the nation in direct opposition not only to the Bible, but to the suffrage of the wisest and best of men in all ages and nations. They well know (whether Christians know or not) that the giving up of Witchcraft is in effect giving up the Bible; and they know, on the other hand, that if but one account of the intercourse of men with separate spirits be admitted their whole castle in the air: deism, atheism, materialism - falls to the ground. I know no reason, therefore, why we should suffer even this weapon to be wrested out of our hands. Indeed, there are numerous arguments besides this, which abundantly confute their vain imaginations. But we need not be hooted out of one; neither reason nor religion requires this. One of the capital objections to all of these accounts is, 'Did you ever see an apparition yourself?' No, nor did I ever see a murder; yet I believe there is such a thing. The testimony of unexceptionable witnesses fully convince me both of the one and the other."

Was Mr. Wesley right or not? John Wesley was perhaps the greatest evangelist the world has produced since the days of Paul, and now after more than one hundred years can we, judging from his wonderful work, deny that the spirit of God, and even ministering angels as he claimed, attended him in his mighty spread of the gospel? Was any living man ever endowed with such a wonderful capacity for traveling, preaching and writing, under so many hardships and privations? And does it not appear that he was inspired and guided by the same power that supported Paul? The infidel may find some way of denying this, but the Christian believer, hardly.

Then to deny Wesley's teachings respecting Bible authority for witchcraft; or charge his faith to a disordered mind, is to accuse God with raising up a great man to propagate a monstrous error, and furthermore is to discard the hundreds of passages all through the Bible from Genesis to Revelations, and agree with infidelity that all such Scripture is false, and that being false, there can be nothing reliable in God's Word. For illustration take the case of the witch of Endor, whom Saul approached in disguise after night, because he had ordered all witches and wizards put to death, and the witch of Endor was shy of violating the order. Now God had withdrawn from Saul and answered him no more, and he sought a familiar spirit, promising the woman that no harm should come to her for this thing. I. Samuel xxviii, 3: Now Samuel was dead and all Israel had lamented him, and buried him. Then said the woman, Whom shall I bring up unto thee? And he said, Bring me up Samuel. And when the woman saw Samuel, Saul asked what form is he of? And she said, An old man cometh up, and he is covered with a mantle. And Saul perceived that it was Samuel, and he stooped with his face to the ground, and bowed himself. And Samuel said to Saul, Why hast thou disquieted me, to bring me up?

Read the whole chapter - Saul's trouble and Samuel's prophecy of what was to occur tomorrow, etc. There can be no doubt that this was the identical Samuel who had anointed Saul King of Israel, if the Bible be true; moreover the witch did not know Saul until after Samuel appeared. This cannot be placed in the catalogue of God's miracles, because it was the woman's profession; and she is supposed to have brought up bad, as well as good spirits, and she was popularly known in the country as a witch possessing this power, and therefore Saul was directed to go to her. If this be a miracle, then God used witches and wizards to perform miracles, and Paul and others who cast out devils in the name of Christ, were wizards or seers. How will Christian people who deny Mr. Wesley's position reconcile this question? Furthermore, additional light on this subject will be found in I. Chronicles xiii. Saul died for asking counsel of one that had a familiar spirit, to inquire of it. Evidently God did not approve of the works of this woman, though He permitted such works. And why? Because it is in accord with the philosophy of creation of worlds, the reign of devils on earth, and designs of the Almighty in the scheme of redemption, answers the believers in a spiritual world. They hold from the teachings of such Scripture, that there is a spiritual world, just as this is a natural or material world. They hold that the inner man, or life, is a refined substance, which, when separated from the natural body by death, passes into the spiritual world as tangible to those in the spiritual world as the body is to the material world. Also that bad as well as good spirits enter this spiritual kingdom, and that there is a continual struggle between the good and bad in that world as in this.

They believe that the spiritual body is a very refined substance, like electricity, and that matter is no obstruction to it, that it may and does have communion with the spirit in the body, knows every thought and action of the human mind, our wants and necessities, and therefore departed spirits become ministering angels or spirits to friends in this world, and just in proportion as man lives in nearness to God, spiritually, rising high in the scale of mental, and heartfelt devotion, developing his spiritual nature - that refined substance called animal electricity or magnetism, which is the spirit - so much more is he capable of recognizing the presence of ministering spirits by communication or even by spiritual sight; and that it is through this medium that people see apparitions, receive premonitions and warnings of what is to occur. These believers hold that the visitation of angels so often recorded in both the Old and New Testaments, were simply ministering spirits, sometimes referred to as angels, and often, as "man" or "men" and spirits. As in the case of Paul, Acts xvi. 9: when "a man" appeared to Paul in the night, "There stood a man of Macedonia, and prayed him, saying: Come over into Macedonia and help us." Now the question, who was this "man?" Was he a spirit, a Macedonian? In Rev. xxii. the angel appearing to John, tells him that he was one of the prophets. The Psalmist says, "The angels of the Lord encamped around them, and delivereth them." And again, "He shall give his angels charge over thee to keep thee in all thy ways." The Apostle Paul says, speaking of angelic spirits "Are they not ministering spirits, sent forth to minister to them who shall be heirs of salvation?"

So it is believed from these and many other such expressions in the Bible, that the atmosphere possesses the property of telegraphing that is yet to be developed and better understood, by which the spiritual world is in constant communication with this, and that spirits travel like thought or the electric flash, throughout all space in an instant, and space is annihilated. It is, therefore, believed that the principles of the moral government of God are the same under every dispensation, that this could not be changed in the very nature of God's creation, and that the ministry of angels and exemplified under every dispensation, showing the uniformity of God's works and government.

The question is asked: Are angels not men, spirits that once dwelt in the body on earth? Who was "the man Gabriel" that spoke to Daniel of the four great monarchies? Who was the prophet that talked to John on the isle of Patmos? Who was the "young man" that stood in the sepulcher, clothed in a long white garment. Who were the "two men" that stood by them at the sepulcher in shining garments, telling the disciples that "He is not here but is risen," as recorded by Luke xxiv?

THE BELL WITCH PROJECT

Who were the "two men" that spoke to the men of Galilee when Jesus ascended from Mount Olivet? - Acts i., 9-11. This faith must be the most comforting thing on earth to the soul that can exercise it discriminately. But the danger is in going too far, losing sight of God, and relying on ministering spirits, for there may be evil as well as good spirits, and how can one know whether the manifestation is from Christ's Kingdom, or that of outer darkness? God showed His disapproval of Saul's act in calling up so good a spirit as Samuel through a witch medium, knowing that the Lord had withdrawn from him on account of his wickedness and disobedience; yet the witch was gifted with that power - perhaps just as the present day mediums have developed electrical force.

However, Mr. Wesley was not alone in pro claiming this belief in a spiritual kingdom and ministering spirits. Many learned theologians support this doctrine. Dr. Adam Clarke, the great scholar and commentator, in his Commentary, vol. xi., page 299, says: "I believe there is a supernatural and spiritual world in which human spirits, both good and bad, live in a state of consciousness. ... I believe that any of these spirits may according to the order of God, in the laws of their place of residence, hare intercourse with this world, and become visible to mortals." This doctrine is affirmed, from the reason that Samuel actually appeared to Saul; Moses and Elias talked with Jesus in the presence of Peter, James and John, and there are many other such instances recorded.

Dr. Richard Watson, of England, who was regarded as the most intellectual teacher the Methodist church ever had, referring to the case of Samuel, says: "The account not only shows that the Jews believed in the doctrine of apparitions, but that in fact such an appearance on this occasion did actually occur; which answers all the objections which were ever raised or can be raised, from the philosophy of the case, against the possibility of the appearance of departed spirits. I believe in this apparition of the departed Samuel, because the text positively calls the appearance Samuel."

In his Theological Institutes, a standard work embraced in the course of study for ministers, Dr. Watson says:

"This is the doctrine of revelation; and if the evidence of that revelation can be disproved, it may be rejected; if not, it must be admitted, whether any argumentative proof can be offered in its favor or not. That it is not unreasonable may be first established. That God who made us and who is a pure spirit, can not have immediate access to our thoughts, our affections, and our will, it would certainly be much more reasonable to deny than to admit; and if the great and universal Spirit possesses power, every physical objection at least, to the doctrine in question is removed, and finite, unbodied spirits may have the same kind of access to the mind of man, though not in so perfect and intimate degree. Before any natural impossibility can be urged against this intercourse of spirit with spirit, we must know what no philosopher, however deep his researches into the courses of the phenomena of the mind, has ever professed to know - the laws of perception, memory and association. We can suggest thoughts and reason, to each other, and thus mutually influence our wills and affections. We employ, for this purpose, the media of signs and words; but to contend that these are the only media through which thought can be conveyed to thought, or that spiritual beings cannot produce the same effects immediately, is to found an objection wholly upon our ignorance. All the reason which the case, considered in itself, affords, is certainly in favor of this opinion. We have access to each other's minds; we can suggest thoughts, raise affections, influence the wills of others; and analogy, therefore, favors the conclusion that, though by different and latent means, unbodied spirits have the same access to each other, and us."

Dr. Watson related a remarkable instance which serves to illustrate the views so forcibly expressed, which was published many years ago in the Methodist Magazine, and later in the Baltimore Methodist Magazine. A man and his wife by the name of James, both of whom died very suddenly, leaving a large estate, as was supposed without a will. There arose serious difficulty among the heirs about the property. James and his Wife came back (in the day time) and informed a lady where the will was, in a secret drawer, in a secretary. She informed the circuit preacher (a Mr. Mills), who went and found the will, and reconciled the parties.

Bishop Simpson said it seemed to him "as though he were walking on one side of the veil, and his departed son on the other. It is only a veil. These friends will be the first to greet you, their faces the first to flash upon you, as you pass into the invisible world. This takes away the fear of death. Departed spirits are not far above the earth, in some distant clime, but right upon the confines of this world."

Dr. Wilber Fisk says: "God has use or employment for all the creatures he has made - for every saint on earth, for every angel in heaven. Oh consoling doctrine! Angels are around us. The spirits of the departed good encamp about our pathway."

Indeed it is a happy thought, a belief that must keep the soul anchored by faith near to God, a realization that is worth all else in a dying hour. How many of us have stood by the bedside of a loved and sainted friend, when the shadows were falling, watching every change of expression as they marked the features with the light of joy, while the veil was being drawn, affording a glimpse of the beautiful beyond, and heard the sweet feeble voice utter exclamations of rapturous praise for a vision too sublime to be described? And have we not felt a sanctifying awe pervading the heart as if conscious that the atmosphere was full of ministering spirits? Ah! "I would not live always." These are serious thoughts and impression that the living delight to cling to, no matter what may be our opinions concerning the spiritual world.

How anxiously we inquire after the last faint expressions from the lips of dying saints, in the hope of more evidence confirming the faith in a blessed abode, where the soul shall live forever in ecstasy. Can any one doubt that Bishop McKendree recognized ministering spirits around his dying bed when he exclaimed:

"Bright angels are from glory come,

They are around my bed,

They are in my room,

They wait to waft my spirit home."

Can any one read the last days and the last hour, yea, the last minute of John Wesley's life, as recorded by Tyerman in his Life and Times of Wesley, vol. iii., beginning on page 651, without feeling enthused by rapturous joy expressed by the great man, or doubt that the same ministering spirits that he claimed attended him all through his most wonderful and eventful career, directing his course and warning him daily of some new persecution that was coming, were present, and beheld by him during the last moments as the veil was drawn, when he exclaimed, "I'll praise! I'll praise!" and then cried, "Farewell!" the last word he uttered. Then as Joseph Bradford was saying, "Lift up your heads, 0 ye gates; and be ye lifted up, ye everlasting doors, and this heir of glory shall come in!" Wesley gathered up his feet in the presence of his brethren, and without a groan and without a sigh was gone.

Indeed there must be something exceedingly comforting in this simple childlike fairly, and it does appear that no one need go astray as long as such faith is well poised in God, looking to Him always for spiritual guidance, rather than relying directly on apparitions, premonitions, and spiritual communications; a kind of self-righteousness, forgetting that God has any hand in the matter, and may permit bad spirits unrestrained, to deceive the believer.

Recurring once more to Saul, who had in his great zeal for God's cause, (or rather his own conceit) "put away those that had familiar spirits and the wizards out of the land," and would have slain the witch of Endor had he known of her, as she greatly feared, and cried with a loud voice when Samuel appeared, Saying, "Why hast thou deceived me? For thou art Saul," he was conscious of having disobeyed the voice of the Lord, in not executing His fierce wrath upon Amalek, and knew that God was angry and had withdrawn from him; and yet, in his sore distress, when the Philistines were upon him, he did not humble himself in the sight of God, imploring pardon and Divine aid.

He simply "inquired of the Lord, and the Lord answered him not, neither by dreams, nor by Urim, nor by prophets." Saul no doubt thought it was God's business to direct him in saving Israel, and was sulky, and in his own strength, went in disguise to the witch he would have slain, "Wherefore then dost thou ask of me, seeing the Lord has departed from thee, and is become thine enemy," answered Samuel. Now mark two expressions in this chapter, Samuel xxiii. "What sawest thou?" inquired Saul. "And the woman said unto Saul, I saw gods ascending out of the earth." "An old man cometh up; he is covered with a mantle." It appears from this that the spirit of Samuel ascended out of the earth and came not from above. Again, Samuel said to Saul, "Moreover, the Lord will also deliver Israel with thee into the hands of the Philistines; and tomorrow shalt, thou and thy sons be with me." The question: Where was Samuel that Saul should be with him on "tomorrow" when he fell upon his own sword and was slain as prophesied? Samuel came up out of the earth and Saul was certainly not in favor with God, to warrant any belief in his ascension to heaven, if Samuel was.

Another reference, Daniel v., gives an account of the handwriting on the wall. Nebuchadnezzar, to whom God had given majesty and glory and honor, but when his heart was lifted up, and his mind hardened in pride, he was deposed and his glory taken from him, and he was driven from the sons of men and become as a beast fed with grass like oxen, till he knew that the most high God ruled in the kingdom of men. Belshazzar, his son and successor, knowing this, humbled not his heart, but made a great feast, drank wine and praised the gods of gold, and of silver, of brass, of iron, of wood, and of stone. This was not all; he had the consecrated vessels which his father Nebuchadnezzar had taken out of the Temple at Jerusalem and desecrated them in use in his drunken revelry. "In the same hour came forth fingers of a man's hand, and wrote over against the candlestick upon the plaster of the wall of the King's palace; and the king saw the part of the hand that wrote: "Then the King's' countenance was changed, and his thoughts troubled him, so that the joints of his loins were loosed, and his knees smote one against the other." None of the astrologers, the Chaldeans, soothsayers, or wise men of Babylon, could read or interpret the hand writing, and Daniel of the captivity who had an excellent spirit and knowledge, was brought before the king and read the hand writing, "Mene, mene, tekel, upharisin."

The interpretation, "Thou are weighed in the balances and art found wanting." "In that night was Belshazzar the king of the Chaldeans slain." Again the question recurs, whose hand was this that wrote upon the wall? Many believe it was the hand of God, but the Bible says it was "fingers of man's hand." Daniel says "the part of the hand sent by Him," (God) and Daniel certainly knew, for he was the only one who could read and interpret, the writing. Then it was a man's hand and God sent it. Here again it is claimed that the doctrine of spiritual communication is sustained, and the laws of God being immutable, just what was done then can be done now; and therefore people cannot understand the many mysterious things that occur. But the moral: Belshazzar was not so much frightened by the hand writing on the wall, as he was by that inward conscience smiting on the wall of his heart, which awakened him to a sense of his guilt and condemnation, which caused his knees to tremble and smite each other. The handwriting was the warning of his doom, and that was what he wanted to know. There is not a wrong doer or sinner in this enlightened age, who has not felt this same smiting of the heart. Conscience is an all-powerful spirit that cannot be resisted though it may not be heeded until the handwriting appears off the wall.

We learn also from reading the Bible that there was another class of extremist, religious bigots, who believed that all spiritual communications were works of the devil, and they made laws to put mediums or witches to death. II. Kings xxiii, informs us of the great zeal of Josiah for the house of the Lord. In the eighteenth year of King Josiah the greatest Passover known in all the history of the Jews was held to the Lord.

"Moreover, the workers with familiar spirits and the wizards, and the images and the idols, and all the abominations that were spied in the land of Judah, and in Jerusalem, did Josiah put away, that he might perform the words of the law which were written in the book that Hilkiah the priest found in the house of the Lord. Notwithstanding, the Lord turned not from the fierceness of His great wrath, wherewith his anger was kindled against Judah."

This kind of zeal to please God in some other way than by the sacrifice of a contrite heart, and free communion with the spirit of the Most High, has characterized all ages, and down to the present time we find men who have come in possession of great fortunes by stealth and advantage, by which thousands have been impoverished, giving munificent gifts to charitable institutions in the hope of winning favor with God and gaining the praise of religious people, and whose funeral orations team with glowing accounts of their goodness in life. This was the kind of opposition that John Wesley had to contend with. He was reviled, hounded and vilified by the ablest ministers of the Church of England, books and pamphlets by the score were written, and newspapers engaged in ridiculing his religion. But the great man with a heart overflowing with the love of God and humanity, by a single mild utterance or the dash of his pen, turned all of their anathemas against them.

Witches were burnt at the stake in the name of the church, even in this country. The laws of Massachusetts made witchcraft an offense punishable by death, and the Puritans found no trouble in procuring the evidence to convict the accused. The first execution took place in Charlestown, Mass., in 1648; Margaret Jones was the victim, and John Winthrop, Governor of the State, presided at the condemning trial. Witchcraft was considered a crime against the laws of God, and the persecution continued, and many were put to death all along, but the great crusade occurred in February, 1692, at Salem, when the excitement reached its highest tension. Thirty women were convicted that year on the testimony of children, who claimed that they were tormented by the women; twenty of the number were executed.

Out of such intolerance came the necessity for religious liberty, a division of sentiment on Bible doctrines, and the formation of many sects or denominations into churches, and religious liberty has continued to broaden into a mighty spread of the gospel of Christ through the rivalry of denominations, or rather a spirit of emulation, each striving to do the most for the advancement of pure Christianity. But for these divisions and religious liberty, zealots would have been burning witches until yet. And if our churches could all be united into one, under one universal creed and laws of control, as some people desire, we would return to witch burning within fifty years. The world, and the churches as they are organized, are full of religious bigots, who have no patience with that class professing close communion with God through the medium of the spirit, because they themselves know nothing of such religion.

The Bible has much to say about evil spirits as well as good spirits, and all through Acts we find that Paul often came in contact with those having evil spirits and those who practiced witchcraft, sorcery, etc., but this the reader is familiar with, while there are many authenticated phenomena of later days that serve better for the present purpose. No one now doubts the authenticity of the Epworth ghost – "Jeffry." Rev. John Wesley published the whole story himself in the Arminian Magazine for October, November and December, 1784.

THE BELL WITCH PROJECT

The demonstrations commenced very much like the Bell Witch, by knocking and other noise just by Mr. Wesley's bed. For some time the Wesley family hooted at the idea of the supernatural, but investigation finally settled them in this conclusion beyond a doubt. It continued to gather force just as did the Bell Witch but never to the extent of talking or speaking. When spoken to, the answers were in groans and squeaks, but no intelligent utterance. It was seen several times and looked like a badger. The man servant chased it out of the dining room once, when it ran into the kitchen, and was like a white rabbit. Miss Susannah Wesley relates details which point to the presence of a disembodied Jacobite, the knocking being more violent at the words "our most Gracious Sovereign Lord," when applied to King George I, as generally used by Mr. Wesley in his prayers. This being noticed, when Mr. Wesley omitted prayer for the royal family no knocking occurred, which Mr. Wesley considered good evidence.

The Review of Reviews, New Year's extra number for 1892, which is devoted entirely to the scientific investigations of the Psychical Research Society, contains in its wide scope of investigations more than one hundred phenomena. The story of a haunted parsonage in the north of England in which the phenomena occurred in 1891, the spirit was more demonstrative than the Epsworth ghost. The demonstrations consisted in the rocking of Dr. William Smith's cradle, which occurred in 1840 in Lynchburg, Va., is a most remarkable and well authenticated phenomena. Dr. Smith was pastor of the Lynchburg church and many people called to witness the strange action of the cradle, which commenced rocking of its own accord, and rocked one hour every day for thirty days. A committee was appointed to investigate the cause, and the cradle was taken to pieces and examined, every part and put together again, and transferred to different rooms, and it rocked all the same without any hand touching it. Rev. Dr. Penn undertook to hold it still, and it wrenched itself from his hands, the timber cracking as if it would break in his firm grasp.

Thousands of such phenomena, premonitions, etc., well authenticated, might be cited, but there is nothing on record, or in all history of phenomena outside of the Bible, that equals the deeply mysterious demonstrations of the Bell Witch - seemingly a thing of life, like that of a human being, endowed with mind, speech, and superior knowledge, knowing all things, all men, and their inmost thoughts and secret deeds, a thing of physical power and force superior to that of the stoutest man - action as swift as the lightning, and yet invisible and incomprehensible.

Spiritualists undertake to account for such mysteries, but theirs is a very dangerous doctrine for the ordinary mind to tamper with. One is liable to lose sight of God and repose faith in the medium, who is but a human being, and if possessed with power to communicate with spirits, may communicate with evil as well as good spirits. Moreover, it is destructive to an unbalanced mind. All people possess more or less animal electricity or magnetism, which is more largely developed in one than in another, and always more in the medium, whose will power overbalances the other. This force, however, is developed in the practice of methods of communication, and involves the whole mind and will power, convulsing the mind into an abnormal state, subjected to the electric force.

Persons who will sit for one hour daily, with their hands on a table, giving all attention to spiritual manifestations, will, on rising, feel a tingling nervous sensation in their arms, and all through the system, which should not be cultivated. It is better that such investigations be left to the Society of Psychological Research, scientific men of strong minds who have nothing else to do but to demonstrate, if they can, the theory that all such mysteries are hidden in the yet mysterious electrical force that permeates the atmosphere, the earth and all animal nature, and which is being brought into use, developing some new power or force every day, and prove that we are nearing a spiritual kingdom where the disembodied are to be seen and conversed with.

Man is constituted a worshipping being, consequently all men are superstitious, notwithstanding that, nine out of ten will deny most emphatically holding to any kind of superstition. Yet when put to the test not one of common intelligence can be found who has not seen something, or heard something, dreamed something, or experienced premonitions, that left an impress of the mysterious. For instance, a gentleman familiar with the history of the Bell Witch, discussing it with the writer, declared that those old people were superstitious, and he did not believe a word of it; that there was not a particle of superstition in his composition; "yet," said he, "there was something unaccountable at Bell's, no doubt about that." Did he believe it? Why certainly. Another instance: A very able, pious minister, discussing the same subject in connection with the Wesley haunt, said he did not believe a word of such things; it was all spiritualism, misleading and dangerous, and Wesley, great man as he was, was liable to such mistakes in an abnormal state of mind. Then he related an incident in the early settlement of the country, when our fathers came among the red men. Said he: "My grandfather belonged to the Nashville settlement; he dreamed that the Indians had attacked the little fort in Sumner county, while the inmates were asleep, and killed every one. He was awakened by the force of the presentment, yet thought nothing of it, and fell asleep again, and dreamed the same thing, the premonition coming the second time with still more force. He was greatly agitated, and mounted his best horse, as quick as he could, running the horse every jump of the way to the little fort. Arriving he found everybody sound asleep, and aroused the people in great haste, shouting in the camp that Indians were marching on the fort, and the settlers had barely made ready when the enemy attacked.

The citizens won the victory, routing the Indians without loss. But for the dream and grandfather's prompt action, the last one in the fort would have been slain." Is this excellent gentleman, believing his grandfather's story, as he certainly does, free from superstition? Summing up the whole matter, it is useless and silly to condemn that which we know nothing about and cannot understand or explain. It is an assumption of wisdom that discredits our intelligence, and the best way to treat ghosts is to let them alone, never go spook hunting, but if a spirit comes to us, receive it just as a spirit deserves to be treated, and observe the warning on the wall, whether it be written by the hand of a spectre, or indicted by the finger of conscience.

THE BELL WITCH PROJECT

Chapter 8

Our Family Trouble: The Story of the Bell Witch as Detailed by Richard Williams Bell

The reader is already familiar with the motives that inspired Richard Williams Bell to write this sketch of "Our Family Trouble," a phenomenal mystery that continued to be a living sensation long after John Bell's death, the mention of which in any Robertson County family, even to this good day, leads to a recital of events as they have been handed down through tradition.

After a brief biography of his parents and the family, which is more fully recorded elsewhere, Mr. Bell goes on writing:

After settling on Red River in Robertson County, Tenn., my father prospered beyond his own expectations. He was a good manager, and hard worker himself, making a regular hand on the farm. He indulged no idleness around him, and brought up his children to work, endeavoring to make their employment pleasurable. Mother was equally frugal and careful in her domestic affairs, and was greatly devoted to the proper moral training of children, keeping a restless watch over every one, making sacrifices for their pleasure and well being, and both were steadfast in their religious faith, being members of the Baptist church, and set Christian examples before their children. Father was always forehanded, paid as he went, was never in his life served with a warrant or any legal process, and never had occasion to fear the sheriff or any officer of the law, and was equally faithful in bearing his share of whatever burden was necessary to advance morality and good society.

In the meanwhile he gave all of his children the best education the schools of the country could afford, Zadok being educated for a lawyer, while the other boys chose to follow agriculture. Jesse and Esther had both married, settled, and everything seemed to be going smoothly, when our trouble commenced. I was a

THE BELL WITCH PROJECT

boy when the incidents, which I am about to record, known as the Bell Witch took place. In fact, strange appearances and uncommon sounds had been seen and heard by different members of the family at times, some year or two before I knew anything about it, because they indicated nothing of a serious character, gave no one any concern, and would have passed unnoticed but for after developments. Even the knocking on the door, and the outer walls of the house, had been going on for some time before I knew of it, generally being asleep, and father, believing that it was some mischievous person trying to frighten the family, never discussed the matter in the presence of the younger children, hoping to catch the prankster. Then, after the demonstrations became known to all of us, father enjoined secrecy upon every member of the family, and it was kept a profound secret until it became intolerable. Therefore no notes were made of these demonstrations or the exact dates.

The importance of a diary at that time did not occur to any one, for we were all subjected to the most intense and painful excitement from day to day, and week to week, to the end, not knowing from whence came the disturber, the object of the visitation, what would follow next, how long it would continue, nor the probable result. Therefore I write from memory, such things as came under my own observations, impressing my mind, and incidents known by other members of the family and near neighbors to have taken place, and are absolutely true. However, I do not pretend to record the half that did take place, for that would be impossible without daily notes, but will note a sufficient number of incidents to give the reader a general idea of the phenomena and the afflictions endured by our family.

As before stated, the knocking at the door, and scratching noise on the outer wall, which continued so long, never disturbed me, nor was I the least frightened until the demonstrations within became unendurable. This I think was in May, 1818. Father and mother occupied a room on the first floor, Elizabeth had the room above, and the boys occupied another room on the second floor; John and Drewry had a bed together, and Joel and myself slept in another bed. As I remember it was on Sunday night, just after the family had retired, a noise commenced in our room like a rat gnawing vigorously on the bed post. John and Drew got up to kill the rat. But the moment they were out of bed the noise ceased. They examined the bedstead, but discovered no marks made by a rat. As soon as they returned to bed the noise commenced again, and thus it continued until a late hour or some time after midnight, and we were all up a half dozen times or more searching the room all over, every nook and corner, for the rat, turning over everything, and could find nothing, not even a crevice by which a rat could possibly enter. This kind of noise continued from night to night, and week after week, and all of our investigations were in vain.

The room was overhauled several times, everything moved and carefully examined, with the same result. Finally when we would search for the rat in our room, the same noise would appear in sister Elizabeth's chamber, disturbing her, and arousing all the family. And so it continued going from room to room, stopping when we were all up, and commencing again as soon as we returned to bed, and was so exceedingly annoying that no one could sleep. The noise was, after a while, accompanied by a scratching sound, like a dog clawing on the floor, and increased in force until it became evidently too strong for a rat. Then every room in the house was torn up, the furniture, beds and clothing carefully examined, and still nothing irregular could be found, nor was there a hole or crevice by which a rat could enter, and nothing was accomplished beyond the increase of our confusion and evil forebodings. The demonstrations continued to increase, and finally the bed covering commenced slipping off at the foot of the beds as if gradually drawn by some one, and occasionally a noise like the smacking of lips, then a gulping sound, like some one choking or strangling, while the vicious gnawing at the bed post continued, and there was no such thing as sleep to be thought of until the noise ceased, which was generally between one and three o'clock in the morning.

Some new performance was added nearly every night, and it troubled Elizabeth more than anyone else. Occasionally the sound was like heavy stones falling on the floor, then like trace chains dragging, and chairs falling over. I call to mind my first lively experience, something a boy is not likely to forget. We bad become somewhat used to the mysterious noise, and tried to dismiss it from mind, taking every opportunity for a nap. The family had all retired early, and I had just fallen into a sweet doze, when I felt my hair beginning to twist, and then a sudden jerk, which raised me. It felt like the top of my head had been taken off. Immediately Joel yelled out in great fright, and next Elizabeth was screaming in her room, and ever after that something was continually pulling at her hair after she retired to bed. This transaction frightened us so badly that father and mother remained up nearly all night. After this, the main feature in the phenomenon was that of pulling the cover off the beds as fast as we could replace it, also continuing other demonstrations. Failing in all efforts to discover the source of the annoyance, and becoming convinced that it was something out of the natural course of events, continually on the increase in force, father finally determined to solicit the cooperation of Mr. James Johnson, who was his nearest neighbor and most intimate friend, in trying to detect the mystery, which had been kept a secret within the family up to this time. So Mr. Johnson and wife, at father's request, came over to spend a night in the investigation.

THE BELL WITCH PROJECT

At the usual hour for retiring, Mr. Johnson, who was a very devout Christian, led in family worship, as was his custom, reading a chapter in the Bible, singing and praying. He prayed fervently, and very earnestly for our deliverance from the frightful disturbance, or that its origin, cause and purpose might be revealed. Soon after we had all retired, the disturbance commenced as usual; gnawing, scratching, knocking on the wall, overturning chairs, pulling the cover off of beds, etc., every act being exhibited as if on purpose to show Mr. Johnson what could he done, appearing in his room, as in other rooms, and so soon as a light would appear, the noise would cease, and the trouble begin in another room. Mr. Johnson listened attentively to all of the sounds and capers, and that which appeared like some one sucking air through the teeth, and smacking of lips, indicated to him that some intelligent agency gave force to the movements, and he determined to try speaking to it, which he did, inquiring, "In the name of the Lord, what or who are you? What do you want and why are you here?" This appeared to silence the noise for considerable time, but it finally commenced again with increased vigor, pulling the cover from the beds in spite of all resistance, repeating other demonstrations, going from one room to another, becoming fearful. The persecutions of Elizabeth were increased to an extent that excited serious apprehensions. Her cheeks were frequently crimsoned as by a hard blow from an open hand, and her hair pulled until she would scream with pain. Mr. Johnson said the phenomenon was beyond his comprehension; it was evidently preternatural or supernatural, of an intelligent character. He arrived at this conclusion from the fact that it ceased action when spoken to, and certainly understood language. He advised father to invite other friends into the investigation, and try all means for detecting the mystery, to which he consented, and from this time on, it became public.

All of our neighbors were invited and committees formed, experiments tried, and a close watch kept, in and out, every night, but all of their wits were stifled, the demon and kind to her in this trying ordeal. It was suggested that sister should spend the nights with some one of the neighbors to get rid of the trouble, and all were very kind to invite her. In fact our neighbors were all touched with generous sympathy and were unremitting in their efforts to alleviate our distress, for it had become a calamity, and they came every night to sit and watch with us. The suggestion of sending Elizabeth from home was acted upon. She went to different places, James Johnson's, John Johnson's, Jesse Bell's, and Bennett Porter's, but it made no difference, the trouble followed her with the same severity, disturbing the family where she went as it did at home, nor were we in anywise relieved. This gave rise to a suspicion in the minds of some persons that the mystery was some device or stratagem originated by sister, from the fact that it appeared wherever she went, and this clue was followed to a logical demonstration of the phenomena was gradually developed, proving to be an intelligent character.

THE BELL WITCH PROJECT

When asked a question in a way, that it could be answered by numbers, for instance, "How many persons present? How many horses in the barn? How many miles to a certain place?" The answers would come in raps, like a man knocking on the wall, the bureau or the bedpost with his fist, or by so many scratches on the wall like the noise of a nail or claws, and the answers were invariably correct. During the time, it was not uncommon to see lights like a candle or lamp flitting across the yard and through the field, and frequently when father, the boys and hands were coming in late from work, chunks of wood and stones would fall along the way as if tossed by some one, but we could never discover from whence, or what direction they came. In addition to the demonstrations already described, it took to slapping people on the face, especially those who resisted the action of pulling the cover from the bed, and those who came as detectives to expose the trick. The blows were heard distinctly, like the open palm of a heavy hand, while the sting was keenly felt, and it did not neglect to pull my hair, and make Joel squall as often.

The Witch Commenced Whispering

The phenomena continued to develop force, and visitors persisted in urging the witch to talk, and tell what was wanted, and finally it commenced whistling when spoken to, in a low broken sound, as if trying to speak in a whistling voice, and in this way it progressed, developing until the whistling sound was changed to a weak faltering whisper uttering indistinct words. The voice, however, gradually gained strength in articulating, and soon the utterances became distinct in a low whisper, so as to be understood in the absence of any other noise. I do not remember the first intelligent utterance, which, however, was of no significance, but the voice soon developed sufficient strength to be distinctly heard by every one in the room.

A Disturbed Spirit

This new development added to the sensation already created. The news spread, and people came in larger numbers, and the great anxiety concerning the mystery prompted many questions in the effort to induce the witch to disclose its own identity and purpose. Finally, in answer to the question, "Who are you and what do you want?" the reply came, "I am a spirit; I was once very happy but have been disturbed." This was uttered in a very feeble voice, but sufficiently distinct to be understood by all present, and this was all the information that could be elicited for the time.

THE BELL WITCH PROJECT

The Seer's Prophecy

The next utterance of any note that I remember, occurred on a Sunday night, when the voice appeared stronger, and the witch talking more freely, in fact speaking voluntarily, and appeared to be exercised over a matter that was being discussed by the family. Brother John Bell had for some time contemplated a trip to North Carolina to look after father's share of an estate that was being Wound up, and was to start next morning (Monday) on horseback, and this was the matter that interested the family and was being discussed, the long tiresome journey, his probable long absence, the situation of affairs, concerning Which father was giving him instructions. Several neighbors were present, taking an interest, volunteering some good natured advice to John, when the witch put in, remonstrating against the trip, dissuading John from going, predicting bad luck, telling him that he would have a hard trip for nothing, that the estate had not been wound up and could not be for some time, and he would get no money, but return empty handed. As a further argument to dissuade John, the witch told him that an elegant young lady from Virginia was then on her way to visit friends in Robertson county, who would please him, and he could win her if he would stay; that she was wealthy, possessing forty Negroes and considerable money. John laughed at the revelation as supremely ridiculous, and left on the following morning as contemplated, and was absent six months or more, returning empty handed as predicted. Very soon after his departure, the young lady in question arrived, and left before his return, and John never met her.

A Spirit Hunting a Lost Tooth

The witch continued, to develop the power of articulation, talking freely, and those who engaged in conversation with the invisible persevered in plying questions to draw out an explanation of the mystery, and again the question was pressed, inquiring, "Who are you and what do you want?" and the witch replied, stating the second time, "I am a spirit who was once very happy, but have been disturbed and made unhappy? Then followed the question, "How were you disturbed, and what makes you unhappy?" The reply to this question was, "I am the spirit of a person who was buried in the woods near by, and the grave has been disturbed, my bones disinterred and scattered, and one of my teeth was lost under this house, and I am here looking for that tooth."

This statement revived the memory of a circumstance that occurred some three or four years previously, and had been entirely forgotten. The farm hands while engaged in clearing a plot of land, discovered a small mound of graves, which father supposed to be an Indian burying ground, and worked around it without obliterating the marks. Several days later Corban Hall, a young man of the neighborhood, came to our place, and was told by Drew the circumstance of finding the Indian graves. Hall thought the graves probably contained some relics which Indians commonly buried with their dead, and proposed to open one and see, to which 'Drew agreed, and they proceeded to disinter the bones. Finding nothing else, Hall brought the jawbone to the house, and while sitting in the passage he threw it against the opposite wall, and the jarring knocked out a loose tooth, which dropped through a crack in the floor.

Father passed through the hall in the mean while, and reprimanded the boys severely for their action, and made one of the Negro men take the jawbone back, replacing all the disinterred bones, and filling in the grave. This was evidently the circumstance referred to by the "spirit," so long forgotten, and to be reminded of the fact so mysteriously was very perplexing, and troubled father no little. He examined the floor just where the bone dropped when it struck the wall, as the boys had left it, and there was the crack referred to, and he was pestered, and decided to take up a portion of the floor and see if the tooth could be found. The dirt underneath was raked up, sifted and thoroughly examined, but the tooth was not found. The witch then laughed at father, declaring that it was all a joke to fool "Old Jack."

The Buried Treasure

The excitement in the country increased as the phenomena developed, The fame of the witch had become widely spread, and people came from all quarters to hear the strange and unaccountable voice. Some were detectives, confident of exposing the mystery. Various opinions were formed and expressed; some credited its own story, and believed it an Indian spirit; some thought it was an evil spirit, others declared it was witchcraft, and a few unkindly charged that it was magic art and trickery gotten up by the Bell family to draw crowds and make money. These same people had stayed as long as they wished, enjoyed father's hospitality, and paid not a cent for it, nor did it ever cost any one a half shilling. The house was open to every one that came; father and mother gave them the best they had, their horses were fed, and no one allowed to go away hungry; many offered pay and urged father to receive it, insisting that he could not keep up entertaining so many without pay, but he persistently declined remuneration, and not one of the family ever received a cent for entertaining.

Father regarded the phenomena as an affliction, a calamity, and such accusations were very galling, but were endured. Inquisitive people continued to exercise all of their wits in plying the witch with questions concerning, its personality or character, but elicited no further information until the question was put by James Gunn, then came the reply: "I am the spirit of an early emigrant, who brought a large sum of money and buried my treasure for safe keeping until needed. In the meanwhile I died without divulging the secret, and I have returned in the spirit for the purpose of making known the hiding place, and I want Betsy Bell to have the money." The spirit was then urged to tell where the money was concealed. This was refused and the secret withheld until certain pledges were made that the conditions would be complied with. The conditions were that Drew Bell and Bennett Porter would agree to exhume the money and give every dollar to Betsy, and that "Old Sugar Mouth" (Mr. James Johnson) would go with them and see that the injunction was fairly discharged, and that he should count the money and take charge of it for Betsy.

The story was questioned and laughed at, and then discussed. The witch had made some remarkable revelations, and it was thought possible there might be something in it, and the proposition was acceded to. Drew and Bennett agreed to do the work, and Mr. Johnson consented to become the guardian and see that the right thing was done. The spirit then went on to state that the money was under a large flat rock at the mouth of the spring on the southwest corner of the farm, on Red River, describing the surroundings so minutely that there could be no mistake. Every one was acquainted with the spring, having frequented the place, but no one could have described it so minutely, and this all tended to strengthen faith in the revelation. The spirit insisted that the committee selected should start very early the next morning at the dawn of day, lest the secret should get out, and some fiend should beat them to the place and get the money. This was also agreed to, and by the break of day next morning all hands met and proceeded to the spring.

They found everything as described, the huge stone intact, and were sure they were on time. They observed that it was an excellent place for hiding money where no human being would ever dream of looking for a treasure, or care to move the great stone for any purpose, and yet susceptible of such a minute description that no one could be mistaken in the revelation. They carried along an axe and mattock, and were pretty soon at work, devising ways and means for moving the big rock, which was so firmly imbedded in the ground. It was no light job, but they cut poles, made levers and fixed prizes, after first removing much dirt from around the stone, so as to get under it. Then Drew and Porter prized and tugged, Mr. Johnson occasionally lending a helping hand, and after a half day's very hard work, the stone was raised and moved from its bedding, but no money appeared. Then followed a consultation and discussion of the situation. They reasoned that the glittering treasure was possibly sunk in the earth, and the stone imbedded over it to elude suspicion, and they decided to dig for it, and went to work in earnest, Porter digging, and Drew scratching the loosened dirt out with his hands, and so on they progressed until they had opened a hole about six feet square and nearly as many feet deep, and still no money was found. Exhausted and very hungry, they gave up the job, returning to the house late in the afternoon much disgusted and chagrined.

That night the "spirit" appeared in great glee laughing and tantalizing the men for being so easily duped, describing everything that occurred at the spring in the most ludicrous way, telling how they tugged at the big stone, and repeating what was said by each one. Bennett Porter staved the mattock in up to the eye every pop, and oh how it made him sweat. It told how "Old Sugar Mouth" looked on prayerfully, encouraging the boys. The dirt taken out was mixed with small stones, gravel, sand, etc., leaves and sticks, all of which indicated that the earth had been removed and put back. Drew, the witch said, could handle a sight of dirt, his hands were made for that purpose, and were better than a shovel; no gold could slip through his fingers. The witch's description of the affair kept the house in an uproar of laughter, and it was repeated with equal zest to all new comers for a month.

Priest Craft and Scriptural Knowledge

There were but very few churches in the country at this period of the century, nevertheless, ours was a very religious community. Most of those coming from the older States brought their religion with them, and inculcated the principle in their families. The influence of Revs. James and Thomas Gunn, Rev. Sugg Fort, Mr. James Johnson, and other good men, swayed mightily. Every man erected an altar in his own home, and it was common for neighbors to meet during the week at one or another's house for prayer and exhortation, and Bible study. In the absence of the preachers, Mr. James Johnson was the principal leader in these exercises, and the meetings were held alternately at his house and father's, and occasionally at one or the other of the Gunn's. There was no spirit of denominational jealousy existing, and all Christians mingled in these meetings like brethren of the same faith. The witch, as it accumulated force, dissembled this spirit, giving wonderful exhibitions of a thorough knowledge of the Bible and Christian faith. The voice was not confined to darkness, as were the physical demonstrations. The talking was heard in lighted rooms, as in the dark; and finally in the day at any hour.

The first exhibition of a religious nature was the assimilation of Mr. James Johnson's character and worship, repeating the song and prayer, uttering precisely the same petition made by the old gentleman the night himself and wife came for the purpose of investigation, and the impersonation of Mr. Johnson was so perfect that it appeared like himself present. It was not uncommon after this for the witch to introduce worship, by lining a hymn, as was the custom, singing it through, and then repeat Mr. Johnson's prayer, or the petitions of some one of the ministers. It could sing any song in the hymn hooks of that time, and quote any passage of Scripture in the Bible from Genesis to Revelations.

The propensity for religious discussion was strongly manifested, and in quoting Scripture the text was invariably correctly cited, and if any one misquoted a verse, they would be promptly corrected. It could quote Scripture as fast as it could talk, one text after another, citing the book, chapter, and number of the verse. It was a common test to open the Bible at any chapter, and call on the spirit to repeat a certain verse, and this was done accurately, as fast as the leaves were turned from one chapter of the book to another. It delighted in taking issue on religious subjects, with those well versed in Scripture, and was sure to get the best of the argument, being always quick with a passage to sustain its point. This manifest knowledge of Scripture on the part of the witch was unmistakable, and was the most mystifying of all the developments, and strangers who came from a long distance were eager to engage the seer in religious discussions, and were is often confounded; and they were no less astounded when the witch would remind them of events and circumstances in their history in a way that was marvelous.

Just here one circumstance I call to mind. The discussion had turned on the command against covetousness and theft. A man, whose name I will call John, put in remarking that he did not believe there was any sin in stealing something to eat when one was reduced to hunger, and could not obtain food for his labor. Instantly the witch perniciously inquired of John "if he ate that sheepskin." This settled John. He was dumb as an oyster, and as soon as the subject was changed he left the company, and was conspicuously absent after that. The result was the revival of an old scandal, so long past that it had been forgotten, in which John was accused of stealing a sheepskin. This warlock was indeed a great tattler, and made mischief in the community. Some people very much feared the garrulity of its loquacious meddling and were extremely cautious, and it was this class who the invisible delighted in torturing most. Nothing of moment occurred in the country or in any family, which was not reported by the witch at night. The development of this characteristic led the people to inquire after the news and converse with the witch as they would with a person, very often inquiring what was then transpiring at a certain place or house in the neighborhood. Sometimes the answer would be, "I don't know, wait a minute and I will go and see," and in less than five minutes it would report, and the report was generally verified. This feature of the phenomena was discovered in this way: Brother Jesse Bell lived within one mile of the homestead. He had been absent several days on a trip, and was expected home on a certain evening.

After supper mother entered the room, inquiring if any of us knew whether Jesse had returned or not. No one had heard, or could inform her. The witch manifested much regard for mother on all occasions, and never afflicted her in any way. On this occasion it spoke promptly, saying: "Wait a minute Luce, I will go and see for you." Scarcely a minute had elapsed when the voice reported that Jesse was at home, describing his position, sitting at table reading by the light of a candle. The next morning Jesse came to see us, and when told the circumstance, he said it was true, and just at that time there was a distinct rap on his door, and before he could move the door opened and closed immediately. His wife, he said, noticed it also, and asked me what caused it, and I replied that I reckoned it was the witch. Every Sabbath service that occurred within the bounds was reported at night, the text, hymn, etc., and the preacher also criticized, and everything of peculiar note was described. The company was treated one night to a repetition of one of Rev. James Gunn's best sermons, preached in the vicinity, the witch personating Mr. Gunn, lining the hymn, quoting his text and prayer, and preaching so much like Mr. Gunn, that it appeared the minister himself was present.

A number of persons were present who attended the meeting that day, and recognized the declamation as the same sermon. Shortly after this, Rev. James Gunn preached on Sunday at Bethel Methodist Church, six miles southeast, and Rev. Sugg Fort filled his appointment at Drake's Pond Baptist Church, seven miles northwest, thirteen miles apart, both preaching at the same hour, eleven o'clock. It so happened that both ministers came to visit our family that evening, finding quite a crowd of people gathered in, as was the case every day during the excitement. Directly after supper the witch commenced talking as usual, directing the conversation to Brother Gunn, discussing some points in his sermon that day. Mr. Gunn asked the witch how it knew what he had preached about?

The answer was, "I was present and heard you." This statement being questioned, the "vociferator" began, quoted the text and repeated the sermon verbatim, and the closing prayer, all of which the preacher said was correct. Some one suggested that Brother Fort had the advantage of the witch this time, that having attended Brother Gunn's service, it could tell nothing about Brother Fort's discourse at Drake's Pond. "Yes I can," was the prompt reply. How do you know? was the inquiry. "I was there and heard him." Then assimilating Rev. Fort's style, it proceeded to quote his text and repeated his sermon, greatly delighting the company. There was no one present who had heard either sermon, but both ministers admitted that their sermons had been accurately reproduced, and no one could doubt the fact, or were more greatly surprised than themselves.

The Afflictions of Betsy and Father

The reader will understand that no feature of the exhibitions already introduced was ever abandoned, but continued developing virulence, or beneficence and felicity. The practice of pulling the cover off the beds was a favorite pastime, and frequently the sheets would be pulled from under the sleepers, or the pillows jerked from under their heads, and other new performances added to the exhibitions. The most serious consequence, however, was the afflictions of Elizabeth and father. Notwithstanding the invisible agency feigned a tender regard at times for Betsy, as it affectionately called her, it did not cease tormenting in many ways, increasing her punishment. The feint pretext for this was a manifest opposition to the attention paid her by a certain young gentleman, who was much esteemed by the family, often interposing impertinent objections, urging that these mutual relations be severed. At least there was no other cause manifested, or this would not be mentioned. Sister was now subjected to fainting spells, followed by prostration, characterized by shortness of breath and smothering sensations, panting as it were for life, and becoming entirely exhausted and lifeless, losing her breath for nearly a minute between gasps, and was rendered unconscious. She would revive and then relapse, and it appeared that her suffering was prolonged by the greater exertions used for her restoration. These spells lasted from thirty to forty minutes, and passed off suddenly, leaving her perfectly restored after a few minutes in which she recovered from the exhaustion.

There is no positive evidence that these spells were produced by the witch. However, that was the conclusion, from the fact that there was no other apparent cause. She was a very stout girl, and with this exception, the personification of robust health, and was never subject to hysteria or anything of the kind. Moreover, the spells came on at regular hours in the evening, just at the time the witch usually appeared, and immediately after the spells passed off the mysterious voice commenced talking, but never uttered a word during the time of her prostration. In the meanwhile father was strangely afflicted, which should have been mentioned in the outset, but he had never regarded his trouble as of any consequence until after sister recovered from the attacks just described. In fact his ailment commenced with the incipiency of the witch demonstration, or before he recognized the phenomenal disturbance. He complained of a curious sensational feeling in his mouth, a stiffness of the tongue, and something like a stick crosswise, punching each side of his jaws.

This sensation did not last long, did not recur very often, or cause pain, and therefore gave him but little concern. But as the phenomena developed, this affliction increased, his tongue swelling from the sides and pressing against his jaws, so that he could neither talk nor eat for ten or fifteen hours. In the meanwhile the witch manifested a pernicious dislike for father, using the most vile and malignant epithets toward him, declaring that it would torment "Old Jack Bell" to the end of his life. As father's trouble increased, Elizabeth was gradually relieved from her severe spells, and soon recovered entirely from the affliction, and never had another symptom of the kind. But father was seized with another malady that caused him much trouble and suffering. This was contortions of the face, a twitching and dancing of his flesh, which laid him up for the time. These spells gradually increased, and undoubtedly carried him to his grave, of which I will have more to say further on.

The Witch Named "Kate"

People continued to ply our loquacious visitor with shrewd eager questions, trying to elicit some information concerning the mystery, which were with equal dexterity evaded, or a misleading answer given. First, it was a disturbed spirit hunting a lost tooth; next, a spirit that had returned to reveal the hiding place of a buried treasure. Then it told Calvin Johnson that it was the spirit of a child buried in North Carolina, and told John Johnson that it was his step mother's witch. At last Rev. James Gunn manifested a very inquisitive desire to penetrate the greatest of all secrets, and put the question very earnestly. The witch replied, saying that Brother Gunn had put the question in a way that it could no longer be evaded, and it would not do to tell the preacher a flat lie, and if the plain truth must be known, it was nobody else and nothing but "Old Kate Batts' witch," determined to torment "Old Jack Bell" out of his life. This was a startling announcement and most unfortunate under the circumstances, because too many were willing to believe it, and it created a profound sensation.

Mrs. Kate Batts was the wife of Frederick Batts, who was terribly afflicted, and she had become the head of the family, taking charge of her husband's affairs. She was very eccentric and sensitive. Some people were disposed to shun her, which was still more irritating to her sensitive nature. No harm could be said of Mrs. Batts. She was kind hearted, and a good neighbor toward those she liked. Mr. Gunn, of course, did not believe the witch's statement, but many did, or professed to, and the matter made Mrs. Batts very mad, causing a lively sensation in the community. Ever after this the goblin was called "Kate," and answered readily when addressed by that name, and for convenience sake I shall hereafter call the witch Kate, though not out of any disregard for the memory of Mrs. Batts, for after all she was a clever lady, and did not deserve the cruel appellation of "witch."

THE BELL WITCH PROJECT

The Witch Family — Blackdog, Mathematics, Cypocryphy, and Jerusalem

The next development was the introduction of four characters, assuming the above names, purporting to be a witch family, each one acting a part making night hideous in their high carnivals, using the most offensive language and uttering vile threats. Up to this time the strange visitor had spoken in the same soft delicate voice, except when personating some individual. Now there were four distinct voices. Blackdog assumed to be the head of the family, and spoke in a harsh feminine tone. The voices of Mathematics and Cypocryphy were different, but both of a more delicate feminine tone. Jerusalem spoke like a boy. These exhibitions were opened like a drunken carousal, and became perfect pandemoniums, frightful to the extreme, from which there was no escape.

Father would most gladly have abandoned home and everything and fled with his family to some far away scene to have escaped this intolerable persecution, but there was no hope, no escape. The awful thing had sworn vengeance, and for what cause it never named, nor could any one ever surmise. Nevertheless, when the question of moving was discussed, it declared it would follow "Old Jack" to the remotest part of the earth, and father believed it. The family was frightened into consternation, apprehending that a terrible crisis was rapidly approaching. Many of our neighbors were frightened away, fearing they would become involved in a tragic termination. Others, however, drew nearer, and never forsook us in this most trying ordeal. James Johnson and his two sons, John and Calvin, the Gunn families, the Fort's, Gooch, William Porter, Frank Miles, Jerry Batts, Major Bartlett, Squire Byrns and Major Picketing were faithful and unremitting in their sympathy, and attentions, and consolations, making many sacrifices for our comfort, and not a night passed that four or more were not present to engage the witch in conversation, and relieve father of the necessary attention to strangers, giving him much rest.

These demoniac councils were introduced by singing songs of every character, followed by quarreling with each other, employing obscene language and blasphemous oaths, making a noise like a lot of drunken men fighting. At this stage of the proceedings Blackdog would appear as peacemaker, denouncing the others with vehemence and scurrility, uttering bitter curses and threats of murder unless the belligerents should desist and behave themselves, and sometimes would apparently thrash Jerusalem unmercifully for disobeying orders. These carousals were ended only by the command of Blackdog, professedly sending the family away on different errands of deviltry, one or two remaining to keep up the usual disturbance in different rooms at the same time. On one occasion all four appeared almost beastly drunk, talking in a maudlin sentimental strain, fuming the house with the scent of whiskey. Blackdog said they got the whiskey at John Gardner's still house, which was some four miles distant. At other times the unity appeared more civil, and would treat our company to some delightful singing, a regular concert of rich feminine voices, modulated to the sweetest cadence and intonation, singing any hymn called for with solemnity and wonderful effect.

The carousals did not continue long, much to the gratification of the family and friends, and our serious apprehensions were relieved. These concerts were agreeable closing exercises of this series of meetings, and after they were suspended the four demons or unity never, apparently, met again. It was plain old Kate from that time on who assumed all characters, good or bad, sometimes very pious and then extremely wicked.

The Witch and the Negroes

Kate manifested a strong aversion for the Negro, often remarking, "I despise to smell a nigger, the scent makes me sick," and this no doubt accounts for the fact that the Negroes were never molested in their cabins after night, but away from their quarters they encountered a sight of trouble. Kate's repugnance was mutual; the Negroes disliked the witch, and were careful to evade all contacts possible by staying in after night, augmenting that natural odor peculiar to the race that was now worth something. They were afraid of the witch, and it was difficult to get one out for an emergency.

This fear was increased by the miraculous stories told by Dean, who was a kind of autocrat among the darkies, and by the way, was a good Negro, father's main reliance for heavy work, and noted for his skill with the axe and maul and wedge. He was worth two ordinary men in a forest clearing. Dean could see the witch any time when alone, or on his way to visit his wife, who belonged to Alex. Gunn. It appeared to him, he said, in the form of a black dog, and sometimes had two heads, and at other times no head. The Negroes would stand around him with eyes and mouth wide open to hear his description of the witch, his encounters and hair breadth escapes. He always carried his axe and a witch ball made by his wife, according to Uncle Zeke's directions, to keep the witch from harming him. He came up one morning, however, rather worsted, with his head badly bruised and bloody, and always declared that the witch inflicted the wound with a stick. Dean's stories are not to be quoted as altogether reliable; he was allowed a wide range for his vivid imagination.

Harry, the houseboy, however, had cause for believing every word Dean told. It was Harry's business to make the morning fires before daylight. He became negligent in this duty, and father scolded and threatened him several times. Finally Kate took the matter in hand, speaking to father, "Never mind, old Jack, don't fret. I will attend to the rascal the next time he is belated." This passed off like much of such gab, but a few mornings after, Harry was later than ever and father commenced scolding harshly, when the witch spoke again, "Hold on old Jack, didn't I tell you not to pester; I will attend to this nigger." Harry had just laid the kindling wood down, and was on his knees blowing the coals to a blaze; when some unseen force apparently seized him by the neck and flailed him unmercifully. Harry yelled and begged piteously, and when let up the witch spoke, promising to repeat the operation if he was ever derelict again. Father said he heard the blows as they fell with force, sounding like a paddle or strip of wood, but could see nothing but the boy on his knees yelling for life. Harry was never late after that.

A rather funny trick was played on Phillis, a twelve year old girl who waited in the house and assisted her mother in the kitchen. We had a log rolling on our place, as was the custom in the country. After the work was over, the youngsters, while waiting for supper, engaged in some gymnastic exercises, trying the difficult feat of locking their heels over the back of their neck. Phillis observed these exercises, and the next day stole away up stairs to test her athletic capacity. After several unsuccessful attempts, she suddenly realized that her feet had forcibly gone over her head and were securely locked. Time and again Aunt Lucy, her mother, called and Phillis as often answered up stairs, but never came. Finally Aunt Lucy got her dander up, and picking up a switch started, saying, "Bound I fetch that gal down them stairs." Pretty soon there was a racket upstairs, and Aunt Lucy had worn out the switch before Phillis could explain that the witch had her.

The case of Anky, however, lends more zest to the witch's characteristic antipathy for the Negro. Mother had taken notice of the fact that Kate never made any demonstrations in the cabins, and conceived the reason why, accepting the witch's own statement. She exercised her genius and hit upon a scheme to outwit Kate, which was rather novel in its purpose. However, she turned the matter over in her own mind carefully, and spoke not a word about it, not even to father, for the reason, perhaps, that she was afraid of the thing, and believed she fared best by cultivating the regard it manifested for her; consequently no one knew a breath of her plans until the outcome of the scheme was developed. Anky was a well-developed, buxom African girl, some eighteen years of age — a real Negro, so to speak, exuberant with that pungent aromatic which was so obnoxious to Kate's olfactory.

Mother had determined to cautiously test her plan for getting rid of the witch, telling Anky, in her gentle patronizing way, that she wanted her for a house girl and desired that she should sleep in her room. The girl manifested some misgivings, but felt complimented by the distinction implied, and enquired of mother if she reckoned the old witch would not pester her? Being assured that there was not much danger, that Kate would be too busy entertaining the company to take any notice of her, her fears gave way to her plucked up courage and she followed mother's directions to the letter, keeping the whole matter a secret from the other Negroes and all the family until the test was made as to whether the witch would trouble her or not. So one evening after supper Anky quietly slipped in the room with her pallet and spread it under mother's bed, fixing herself comfortably on it, to await the coming in of visitors and the witch and hear the talking. It was a high bedstead, with a white-fringed counterpane hanging to the floor, hiding Anky completely.

She was delighted, and not a soul except mother knew she was there. Very soon the room was filled with visitors, keeping up a lively chit-chat while waiting the coming of Kate, and mother had taken a seat with the company anxiously waiting to see the outcome of her scheme. Presently the voice of the witch angrily rang out above the din of conversation with the exclamation, "There is a damn nigger in the house, it's Ank; I smell her under the bed and she's got to get out." In an instant a noise was heard under the bed like that of a man clearing his throat, hawking and spitting vehemently, and Anky came rolling out like a log starting down hill, her face and head literally covered with foam like white spittle. She sprang to her feet with wonderful agility, frantically exclaiming, "Oh missus, missus, it's going to spit me to death. Let me out, let me out," and she went yelling all the way to the cabin, "Let me in, let me in." The witch then addressed mother, "Say Luce, did you bring that nigger in here?" "Yes," replied mother, "I told Anky that she might go under my bed, where she would be out of the way, to hear you talk and sing." "I thought so," replied Kate, "I guess she heard me. Nobody but you, Luce, would have thought of such a smart trick as that, and if anybody else had done it I would have killed the damn nigger. Lord Jesus I won't get over that smell in a month!"

The Mysterious Hand Shaking

The Johnson brothers, John and Calvin, perhaps had more intercourse with the witch than any other two men who visited our place during the excitement. That is they talked more with the invisible, entered more earnestly into the investigation by cultivating friendly and intimate relations. They were both very honorable men, of high standing in the community, but were very dissimilar in character. Calvin was a plain unassuming man of strict integrity, free from deception, faithful in everything he pretended, and would not swerve from the truth or break a promise knowingly and willfully under any circumstances. John was more dexterous, of a shrewd investigating turn of mind, guided by policy, and would make use of all legitimate means at hand to gain a point or accomplish a purpose, and he cultivated the witch more than any one else for the purpose of facilitating his investigations.

Kate was very fond of gab, and John Johnson made use of every opportunity to engage the mage in conversation, hoping to draw out something that would give a clue to the mystery, but it appears that all of his wits were baffled, and that the seer was all the while aware of his purpose. The question arose as to the character of the blows received by so many persons on the cheek after retiring. The sound was like a slap of an open hand, and every one to testified that it left a sting like that of a hand, even to the prints of the fingers being felt. Calvin Johnson conceived the idea of asking the witch to shake hands with him. After much persuasion Kate agreed to comply with the request, on one condition, that Calvin would first promise not to try to grasp or hold the hand that would be laid in his.

This he agreed to, and then holding out his hand, in an instant he felt the pressure of the invisible. Mr. Johnson testified that he felt it very sensibly, and that the touch was soft and delicate like the hand of a lady, and no one ever doubted his statement. John Johnson begged Kate to shake hands with him, persisting that he was as good a friend as his brother, but the witch refused, telling John "No, you only want a chance to catch me." John vowed that he would not attempt anything of the kind. Kate still refused, replying, "I know you, Jack Johnson; you are a grand rascal, trying to find me out, and I won't trust you." Two or three other persons claimed to have shaken hands with the witch, which I don't know about, though many testified to the force of the hand as felt on the cheek.

He Stole His Wife

It was not uncommon for Kate to recognize strangers the moment they entered the house, speaking to them on familiar terms. Here is one instance I will note. Four strangers who had traveled a long distance (whose names I cannot now remember, there were so many unknown callers), arrived late — on a dark night, and knocking at the door, and were admitted.

They were unknown to any one in the house or on the place, but the moment they entered the door, and before they could speak to introduce themselves, Kate announced one by name, exclaiming, "He is the grand rascal who stole his wife. He pulled her out of her father's house through a window, and hurt her arm, making her cry; then he whispered to her, 'Hush honey don't cry, it will soon get well.'" The strangers were greatly confused. They stood dumbfounded, pausing some time before they could speak. The gentleman was asked before leaving if the witch had stated the facts in regard to his matrimonial escapade. He said yes, the circumstance occurred just as stated.

Detective Williams

A good looking stranger arrived who introduced himself as Mr. Williams, a professional detective, stating that he had heard much of the witch mystery, which no one could explain, and having considerable experience in unraveling tangled affairs and mysteries, he had traveled a long distance for the purpose of investigating this matter, if he should be permitted to do so; further stating that he did not believe in either preternatural or supernatural things, and professed to be an ex pert in detecting jugglery, sleight-of-hand performances, illusions, etc., and would certainly expose these manifestations, so much talked of if given a fair chance. Father bid the gentleman a hearty welcome, telling him that he was just the man that was wanted. "Make my house your home, and make free with everything here as if your own, as long as you think proper to stay," said father, and Mr. Williams politely accepted the invitation and hung up his hat. Mr. Williams was rather a portly, strong-muscled, well dressed, handsome gentleman. He was no less self-possessed, and wise in his own conceit, full of gab, letting his tongue run continually, detailing to the company his wonderful exploits in the detective business, and was very sure he would bring Kate to grief before leaving.

A day and night passed and Kate, for some cause best known to the witch, kept silent, making no show except a little scratching on the walls and thumping about the room, just enough to let the company know that the spirit was present. Mr. Williams became very impatient, appearing disgruntled, and spoke his mind more freely. He said to a coterie of gentlemen who were discussing the witch, that he was convinced that the whole thing was a family affair, an invention gotten up for a sensation to draw people and make money, and the actors were afraid to make any demonstrations while he was present, knowing his profession and business, and that he would most assuredly expose the trick. One of the gentlemen told father what Williams had said, and it made him very indignant. He felt outraged that such a charge should be made without the evidence, by a man professing to be a gentleman, to whom he had extended every courtesy and hospitality, and had proffered any assistance he might call for, and in a rage he threatened to order Williams from the place immediately. Just at this juncture Kate spoke, "No you don't, old Jack, let him stay; I will attend to the gentleman and satisfy him that he is not so smart as he thinks." Father said no more, nor did he take any action in the matter, but treated Mr. Williams gentlemanly as he did the others, nor was anything more heard from Kate. The house was crowded with visitors that night, all expectantly and anxious to hear the witch talk, and sat till late bed time awaiting the sound of the mystifying voice, but not a word or single demonstration of any kind was heard from Kate. This confirmed the detective in his conjectures, and he repeated to several visitors his conclusions, declaring that the witch would not appear again as long as he remained.

After they were all tired out, mother had straw mattresses spread over the floor to accommodate the company. Mr. Williams, being the largest gentleman present, selected one of these pallets to himself. All retired and the light was extinguished, and a night of quiet rest was promising. As soon as perfect quiet prevailed, and every one appeared to be in a dose of sleep, Mr. Williams found himself pinioned, as it were, to the floor by some irresistible force from which he was utterly powerless to extricate himself, stout as he was, and the witch scratching and pounding him with vengeance. He yelled out to the top of his voice calling for help and mercy. Kate held up long enough to inquire of the detective, which one of the family he thought had him, and then let in again, giving him an unmerciful beating, while the man plead for life. All of this occurred in less than two minutes, and before a candle could be lighted, and as soon as the light appeared the pounding ceased, but Kate did a good deal of talking, more than Mr. Williams cared to hear.

The detective was badly used up and the worst scared man that ever came to our house. He sat up on a chair the balance of the night, with a burning candle by his side, subjected to the witch's tantalizing sarcasm, ridicule and derision, questioning him as to which of the family was carrying on the devilment, how he liked the result of his investigations, how long he intended to stay, etc. As soon as day dawned, Mr. Williams ordered his horse, and could not be prevailed upon to remain until after breakfast.

Kate Gets in Bed With William Porter

William Porter was a very prominent citizen of the community, a gentleman of high integrity, regarded for his strict veracity. He was also a good friend to our family, and spent many nights with us during the trouble, taking his turn with others in entertaining Kate, which was necessary to have any peace at all, and also agreeable to those of an investigating turn of mind who were not afraid, and this was Mr. Porter's character; like John Johnson, he rather cultivated the spirit, and said he was fond of gabbing with Kate. This seemed to please the witch, and they got along on good terms. William Porter was at this time a bachelor, occupying

THE BELL WITCH PROJECT

his house alone. The building was a large hewn log house, with a partition dividing it into two rooms. There was one chimney having a very large fireplace, and the other end was used for a bedroom — entered by a door in the partition. I give this as related by Mr. Porter himself, to a large company at Father's, and as he has often repeated the same to many persons, and no one doubted his truthfulness.

William Porter Attempts to Burn the Witch

"It was a cold night and I made a big log fire before retiring to keep the house warm. As soon as I got in bed I heard scratching and thumping about the bed, just like Kate's tricks, as I thought, but was not long in doubt as to the fact. Presently I felt the cover drawling to the backside, and immediately the witch spoke, when I recognized the unmistakable voice of Kate. 'Billy, I have come to sleep with you and keep you warm.' I replied, 'Well Kate if you are going to sleep with me, you must behave yourself.' I clung to the cover, feeling that it was drawing from me, as it appeared to be raised from the bed on the other side, and something snake-like crawling under. I was never afraid of the witch, or apprehended that it would do me any harm but somehow this produced a kind of chilly sensation that was simply awful. The cover continued to slip in spite of my tenacious grasp, and was twisted into a roll on the back side of the bed, just like a boy would roll himself in a quilt, and not a strip was left on me.

I jumped out of bed in a second, and observing that Kate had rolled up in the cover, the thought struck me, 'I have got you now, you rascal, and will burn you up.' In an instant I grabbed the roll of cover in my arms and started to the fire, intending to throw the cover, witch and all in the blaze. I discovered that it was very weighty, and smelt awful. I had not gone half way across the room before the luggage got so heavy and became so offensive that I was compelled to drop it on the floor and rush out of doors for a breath of fresh air. The odor emitted from the roll was the most offensive stench I ever smelt. It was absolutely stifling and I could not have endured it another second. After being refreshed I returned to the room, and gathered up the roll of bed clothing shook them out, but Kate had departed, and there was no unusual weight or offensive odor remaining, and this is just how near I came catching the witch."

Our School Day Experience

Major Garaldus Pickering, who was a distinguished man of that day, kept a large school near by, which Joel and myself attended, and had many little experiences with Kate along the way. The custom was to take in school as soon as the teacher could get there, a little after sunrise, and dismiss about thirty minutes before sunset. Our route was through the woods, and some briar patches and hazel thickets by the wayside. Passing these thickets, returning home, sticks of wood and rocks were often tossed at us, but never with much force, and we soon learned not to fear any harm from this pastime, and frequently cut notches on the sticks, casting them back into the thicket from whence they came, and invariably the same sticks would be hurled back at us. After night Kate would recount everything that occurred along the way. Even if one of us stumped a toe, falling over, the witch claimed to have caused it, and would describe how it appeared in the form of a rabbit or something else at certain places. Our most serious trouble, however, was experienced at home, the witch continually pulling the cover off, and twisting our hair, and it was hard for a tired boy to get any sleep.

Joel Severely Whipped

It happened that Joel and myself were left to occupy a room alone one night, and were troubled less than usual in the early part of the night, but Kate put in good time just before day. It was quite a cold morning, and rather too early to get up, but Kate continued pulling the cover off and jerking my hair, and I got out of bed and dressed myself. Joel, however, was much vexed, and said some ugly things about "Old Kate," and gathering up the cover from the floor, he rolled himself up in it for another nap. Directly the witch snatched it from him again. Joel became enraged, pulling at the cover while Kate seemed to be hawking and spitting in his face, and he had to turn loose the cover. This made Joel raving mad, and he laid flat on his back, kicking with all his might, calling old Kate the meanest kind of names. "Go away from here, you nasty old thing," he exclaimed. Kate became furious also, exclaiming, "You little rascal, I'll let you know who you are talking to."

That moment Joel felt the blows falling fast and heavy, and no boy ever received such a spanking as he got that morning, and he never forgot it. It was absolutely frightful. I could do nothing for his relief. He yelled frantically with all of his might, arousing the whole house, nor did his punisher cease spanking until father entered the door with a light, finding him almost lifeless. The blows sounded like the spanking of an open heavy hand, and certainly there was no one in the room but Joel and myself, and if there had been, there was no way of escaping except by the door which father entered, and that would have been impossible unobserved.

Chasing the Shakers

The Shakertown People at that time kept their trading men on the road continually, traveling through the country, dealing with the people. They went in two's, generally on horseback, and could be distinguished from other people at a distance by their broad brim hats and peculiarity in dress. The two who traveled through our section always made it convenient to call at our house for dinner or a night's lodging. It was about the regular time for these gentlemen to come around, and near the dinner hour one of the servants came in announcing to mother that the Shakers were coming down the lane. This was a notice to increase the contents of the dinner Pot.

The Witch Chases the Shakers

Kate spoke up immediately, exclaiming, "Them damn Shakers shan't stop this time." Father was troubled a good deal by breachy [sic] stock on the outside pushing the fences down, and generally sent Harry, a Negro boy, around every day to drive away stock and see that the fences were up. There were three large dogs on the place that the boy always carried along, and he had them well trained and always eager for a chase, and would start at his call, yelping furiously. Harry was nowhere about. He was out on the farm with the other hands. But instantly after Kate spoke Harry's voice was heard in the front yard calling the dogs, "Here Caesar, here Tiger, here Bulger, here, here, sic, sic," slapping his hands. Not a soul but the Shakers coming down the lane could be seen.

The dogs, however, responded with savage yelping, going in a fury, following the voice that left the way egging them on, and just as the Shakers were nearing the turning in gate, the dogs leaped the fence at their horses' heels, and Harry's voice was there too, hollering, "Sic, sic, take 'em." The Shakers put whip to their horses and the dogs after them, and Kate vehemently urging the dogs on and hilariously enjoying the sport. It was a lively chase, and broke the Shakers from coming that way again. The witch enjoyed the sport greatly, laughing and repeating the affair to visitors, injecting many funny expressions in describing the chase, and how the Shakers held on to their big hats.

Mother Bell's Illness—The Witch Sings Sweet Songs and Brings Her Hazelnuts and Grapes

The story of the hazelnuts and grapes brought to mother during her illness was hard for many to believe, and it may prove a severe strain on the credulity of the reader, but it is nevertheless true, and will be verified by several worthy persons who witnessed the facts and have stated the same to many people. Kate had all along manifested a high regard for mother, often remarking, "Old Luce is a good woman." This was very gratifying to the family; we were all much devoted to her, and this earnest expression of tender respect for her; so often repeated, was to a great extent an assurance that whatever might befall other members of the family, mother would be spared personal affliction. She was fearful of the thing, and could not see any good sense or policy in antagonizing what was now evidently a powerful, intelligent and incomprehensible agency, and therefore she conceived it to be the best policy to cultivate the kind manifestations of the witch, and she exercised all the gentleness of her nature toward Kate, as she did her tender affections for her children.

This proved to be the best policy, for it is evident that she appeased the seer's malice in many instances, except in father's case, toward whom the malignity was unrelenting and beyond control. About the middle of September, 1820, mother was taken down with a spell of pleurisy, and then it was that Kate manifested a sorrowful nature, growing more plaintive every day as the disease progressed, giving utterance to woeful expressions that were full of touching sympathy. "Luce, poor Luce, I am so sorry you are sick. Don't you feel better, Luce? What can I do for you, Luce?"

These and many other expressions of sympathy and anxious inquiries were given vent by the saddened voice, that now appeared to remain constantly in mother's room prattling all through the day, changing to a more joyful tone when she indicated any temporary relief. The persistent jabbering and disquietude was enough to craze a well person, but mother bore it all patiently, frequently replying to questions. Sometimes she would reply, "Oh Kate, I am too sick to talk to you." Then the voice would hush for some time, as if choking expression. When anything was wanted or called for that was needed for mother's comfort, the witch would speak promptly, telling precisely, where the article could be found. And so the strange voice continued from day to day, mystifying everyone who came to visit and minister to mother's wants, and it was utterly impossible to distinguish from whence it came, and yet so pathetic as to affect the sympathy of everyone who came within hearing.

It was noticeable also that Kate kept quiet when mother was apparently at rest or sleeping. She rested better in the latter part of the night, and was somewhat refreshed for the morning, and as soon as she was aroused Kate was heard inquiring, "How do you feel this morning, Luce? Did you rest well through the night? Don't you want to hear a song, Luce?" Mother was very fond of vocal music, in which Kate excelled, and it was her pleasure to reply, "Yes Kate, sing something sweet." While the witch sung a number of beautiful stanzas, the following was the favorite, which was sung every day:

THE BELL WITCH PROJECT

Come my heart and let us try

For a little season

Every burden to lay by

Come and let us reason.

What is this that casts you down?

Who are those that grieve you?

Speak and let the worst be known,

Speaking may relieve you.

Christ by faith I sometimes see

And He doth relieve me,

But my fears return again,

These are they that grieve me.

Troubled like the restless Sea,

Feeble, faint and fearful,

Plagued with every sore disease,

How can I be cheerful?

No rhythmical sound or melody ever fell upon the ear with sweeter pathos, coming as it did like a volume of symphony from a bursting heart. I have seen the tears trickle down mother's fevered cheeks, while friends would turn away to hide repressed weeping. Sick as she was, mother never neglected to compliment the song. "Thank you Kate, that was so sweet and beautiful, it makes me feel better," which the witch seemed to appreciate. Mother gradually grew worse, the disease reaching a serious stage. The doctor was still very hopeful, but the family and our good neighbors were feeling the deepest concern. Father became very restless and apprehensive of the worst.

THE BELL WITCH PROJECT

Her appetite failed entirely, and this distressed Kate woefully. The neighbors brought all sorts of tempting good things to induce her to eat, and this example the observing witch imitated, conceiving the idea, no doubt, that the most important thing was the discovery of something agreeable to her appetite, and this was the circumstance that seemed to have inspired the action of the witch in bringing the nuts and grapes. Wild fruits were plentiful in the bottoms and woods around the place, and were then ripening. Tim first instance was the appearance of the hazelnuts. The same plaintive voice was heard exclaiming, "Luce, poor Luce, how do you feel now? Hold out your hands, Luce, and I will give you something." Mother stretched her arms, holding her hands together open, and the hazelnuts were dropped from above into her hands. This was witnessed by several ladies who had called in to see mother, and it was so incredible that the floor above was examined to see if there was not a loose plank or some kind of opening through which they were dropped, hut it was found to be perfectly secure, and not even a crevice through which a pin could pass.

After some time the amazement was increased by the same voice inquiring, "Say, Luce, why don't you eat the hazelnuts?" Mother replied that she could not crack them. Then the exclamation, "Well I will crack some for you," and instantly the sound of the cracking was heard, and the cracked nuts dropped on her bed within hand's reach, and the same passionate voice continued insisting on mother's eating the nuts, that they would do her good. Next came the grapes in the same way, the voice importuning her to eat them, that they would do her good. Mother was thoughtful in expressing her thanks, remarking, "You are so kind, Kate, but I am too sick to eat them."

From this time on mother steadily improved, coming out of a severe spell that held her down some twenty days, and no one could express more joy and gladness than Kate, who also praised Dr. Hopson, the good physician who brought her through safely. As soon as mother was convalescent, Kate devoted more attention to the entertainment of the large number of visitors who were constantly coming to hear the mysterious voice. One evening the room was full of company, all deeply interested in discussing the phenomena of the grapes, etc., when the presence of the witch was announced by the voice exclaiming, "Who wants some grapes?" and before any one could answer, a large bunch of luscious wild grapes fell out on Elizabeth's lap. The bunch was passed around and all tasted of the fruit, and were satisfied that it was no illusion. Kate evinced remarkable knowledge of the forest, and would tell us where to find plenty of grapes, hazelnuts, herbs of every kind, good hickory for axe handles, or tough sticks for a maul.

THE BELL WITCH PROJECT

Mrs. Martha Bell's Stockings

Kate, as before intimated, visited the family of Brother Jesse Bell quite often, making demonstrations, but never to the extent of the manifestations at home. Jesse's wife, whom the witch called "Pots," observed mother's policy in humoring the warlock, paying kindly attention to its gabble, incurring favor or kindly relations, and she too was treated with such consideration as to relieve her fears of any immediate harm. Jesse Bell and Bennett Porter had determined to move with their families to Panola county, Mississippi, and were shaping their affairs to that end, as soon as circumstances would admit.

This phenomena I give as related by Martha herself, there being no other witnesses to the circumstance, but I can not doubt her statement, which is borne out by other facts. Late in the afternoon she was sitting out some ten steps on the east side in the shade of the house, engaged in pealing apples for drying. She heard a kind of buzzing or indistinct whispering in her ear, and recognized at once that it was the voice of the witch, and spoke to it, inquiring, "What do you want, Kate? Speak out so I can understand you." Then the witch spoke plainly, saying, "Pots, I have brought you a present to keep in remembrance of me when you go to your far away new home. Will you accept it?" She replied, "Certainly Kate, I will gladly accept any present you may bring. What is it?"

Just then a small roll, neatly wrapped in paper, fell on her lap. She looked up and around in every direction, but no one was near, nor could she discover from whence it came. In her confusion the witch spoke again, saying, "I brought it, Pots; see what a nice pair of stockings. I want you to keep them for your burial, to remember me, and never wear them." She then stripped off the paper and found a pair of elegant black silk hose, for which she thanked Kate, promising to keep them as requested. Martha said she discovered an ugly splotch on one of the hose, which she was eyeing with much curiosity, when the witch spoke very promptly, remarking, "That is blood. They killed a beef at Kate Batts' this morning, and the blood spattered on the stocking." Martha said she was so disconcerted and perplexed that she could not speak, and Kate departed, or said nothing more.

Jesse Bell came in from the field very soon, and when made acquainted with all the facts as above stated, determined to go at once to the Batts home and ascertain the facts regarding the witch's story of the butchering that morning. He did not mention the circumstance, but very soon Mrs. Batts expressed herself as very glad that he had called, stating that they had killed a fine young beef that morning, and intended sending Patsy (his wife) a piece, but had had no opportunity, and wished him to take it, which he did. So this part of the witch's story was confirmed, and Jesse further ascertained from Mrs. Batts that it had been a very busy day, and not one of the family had left the place during the day, or but for the pressing engagement she would have sent the beef to his house. Moreover, Martha Bell had not left the premises, nor had any visitor been on the place.

Dr. Mize, the Wizard

During the period of these exciting demonstrations, ever so many detectives, wise men, witch doctors, or conjurers, came to exercise their skill on Kate, and were permitted to practice schemes and magic arts to their heart's content, and all were brought to grief in some way, confessing that the phenomena was something beyond comprehension. One notable instance was that of Dr. Mize, of Simpson County, Ky., some thirty-five miles away, whose fame as a magician had been widely spread, and many brought word to father of his genius, urging him to send for the noted conjurer. The truth is, father had become alarmed about his own condition. His spells of contortions of the face, twitching of the flesh and stiffness of the tongue, were gradually growing more frequent and severe.

His friends observed this, and also that the animosity of the witch toward him was increasing in vehemence, every word spoken to him being a blast of calumnious aspersions, and threatenings of some dire evil which was horrifying. He had also become convinced from his observations, that this terrible thing had the power, as it claimed, to so afflict him, and that the purpose was to torture his life out, as it also declared; and under these circumstances he yielded to the many persuasions to exhaust all means and efforts to free himself and family from the pestilence. He consulted with Mr. James Johnson about the matter, who thought it would be well to give Dr. Mize a trial, and farther proposed to go with Drew after the famous wizard. So it was agreed that Mr. Johnson and Drew were to start on the hunt for Dr. Mize after three o'clock in the morning, while Kate was not about, and clear the neighborhood before the morning hour for the witch's appearance.

The whole matter was to be kept a profound secret, and no one was let into the understanding. Drew made ready to accompany Mr. Johnson on a business trip, to be absent two or three days, and that was all that was known about it. They got off according to the arrangement in good time, and had perhaps passed Springfield before day. Kate came as usual that morning, observing first Drew's absence, setting up an anxious inquiry for him. Not one of the family could give any information concerning him, and the witch seemed baffled and disappeared, and was not heard again during the day, but returned that night in great glee, having discovered the whole secret, telling all about Drew and Mr. Johnson's trip. Kate went on to say, "I got on their track and overtook them twenty miles on the way, and followed along some distance, and when I hopped in the road before them, looking like a poor old sick rabbit, 'Old Sugar Mouth' said, 'There is your witch, Drew; take her up in your lap. Don't you see how tired she is?'" Kate continued to gossip about the trip in a hilarious way, manifesting much satisfaction in discovering the deep laid scheme, but no one knew how true the story was until Mr. Johnson and Drew returned the following evening, when they confirmed everything that Kate had stated.

Mr. Johnson said that he did not really believe at the time of calling Drew's attention to the rabbit, that it was the witch, but spoke of its peculiar action in a jocular way, as a mere matter of pastime, nor did Drew think otherwise of it. They found Dr. Mize at his home east of Franklin, Ky., told him the story of our trouble, and the information received concerning his power to dispel witchery, etc. The Doctor said it was out of the ordinary line of phenomena, but he had no doubt of his ability to remove the spell and expose the craft that had brought it on, and he set the time, some ten days ahead, when he would be ready to begin the experiment. Accordingly, the wise man put in his appearance, having studied the question, and was prepared for business, making boasts of his knowledge of spirits and skill in casting out devils, much to the disgust of father, who had about sized him up on sight. However, like others, Mize was treated courteously and allowed to pursue his own plans. The wizard stayed three or four days, hearing not a breath from Kate.

In the meanwhile he found an old shotgun that had been out of repair some time, and he at once discovered that the witch had put a spell on it. He soon cleaned the old gun, readjusted the lock and trigger, performed some conjurations, making the gun shoot as well as ever. This much, taken in consideration with the fact that the witch had kept perfectly quiet since his arrival, he considered as remarkable progress, and he doubted the return of Kate. Certain he was that the witch would hardly show up as long as he remained; witches, he said, were always shy of him. So Mize continued, working sorcery, making curious mixtures, performing incantations, etc., to the amusement of those who observed his actions. Finally Kate put in, questioning the conjurer impertinently as to what he was doing, and the object of his sorcery. Mize was nonplussed by the mysterious voice, which he had not before heard, recognizing that the witch had come to keep company with him. He tried to be reticent and evasive, intimating that a witch had no business prying into his affairs.

Kate, however, continued to ply him with hard questions, and finally suggested to Dr. Mize that he had omitted some very important ingredients for his charm mixture. "What is that?" inquired Mize with astonishment. "If you were a witch doctor you would know how to aerify that mess, so as to pass into the aeriform state, and see the spirit that talks to you, without asking silly questions," replied Kate. "What do you know about this business, anyhow?" again inquired the bewildered conjurer. Kate then told him that he was an old fool and didn't know what he was doing, and then started in to cursing Mize like blue blazes. Such a string of blasting oaths was never heard, and Dr. Mize was frightened out of his wits, and was anxious to get away. "That thing," he said, knew so much more about witchcraft than he did, that he could do nothing with it.

Mize arranged for an early start home the next morning. Somehow his horse refused to go off kindly, rearing and kicking up. Finally Kate came to the rescue, proposing to make the horse go, and accompany the Doctor home. Immediately the horse started with a rush, kicking and snorting, and went off at full speed with the Doctor hanging on to the mane. The witch came that night in great glee, describing the trip home with the "old fraud," and the tricks played on him along the way, just as Mize described the affair to his neighbors.

The Doubles or Apparitions

Much has been talked about Bennett Porter shooting at the witch. Porter, according to his own statement, did shoot at an object that appeared to his wife and Elizabeth, as described by them, but saw nothing himself, except the bent saplings in motion. This circumstance occurred during the time the witch family appeared on scene. Elizabeth was there on a visit to her sister. Bennett Porter was absent during the day, filling an engagement at Fort's mill, which was in course of construction, and returned home late in the afternoon. The hens were laying about the stables, which were located on the opposite side of the lane from the house.

Esther started across the lane that afternoon to gather up the eggs. Just as she passed from the yard into road, she observed a woman walking slowly up the lane toward the house, and she hurried on her mission and returned just in time to meet the lady at the front entrance. She recognized the person as one of her neighbors, and spoke to her pleasantly, to which the woman made no reply. She repeated the salutation, which again failed to elicit any response. The woman appeared to have taken off her bonnet and let her hair down, and was engaged in combing out her hair as she walked, and stopped just opposite the house, where Esther met her, continuing the combing, and appeared deeply absorbed or troubled. Esther said she invited the lady in the house, repeating the solicitation several times, to which the woman paid no attention.

THE BELL WITCH PROJECT

She felt much chagrined by the strange conduct of her neighbor, and concluded that something was wrong with the lady or that she had become offended towards her, and she passed in, leaving the woman standing in the lane, combing her hair. She called Elizabeth's attention to the woman and her conduct, and they both observed her still in the same attitude. Presently she climbed on the yard fence, sitting there some five minutes, still combing her hair, and then she tucked it up in the usual way and left the fence, crossing over into the stable lot, where she could not have possibly had any business. The lot enclosed some three or four acres, a grove mostly of young saplings on the further side, ill the midst of which was a large knotty log.

The woman walked across the lot, passing around the log, when there appeared three other persons, two younger women or girls, and a boy. Each one bent down a sapling, sitting upon them and riding up and down, giving motion to the spring afforded by the bush. While this exercise still continued, Bennett Porter returned home, finding Esther and Elisabeth excited over the strange demonstrations that they tried to point out to him. He said he could see the bushes in motion, but could not see the persons described. He suggested that they were the witch apparitions, and got his gun, insisting that Esther should shoot at one of the objects. While he was getting his rifle, the appearances let the saplings up and took positions behind the log, first one and then another showing a head above the log. Esther refused to shoot, but directed Porter to shoot near a large knot on the log, where one of the heads appeared. He fired and his bullet cut the bark on the log just where he aimed, but nothing more was seen of the four persons, nor could they, as Porter thought, have escaped from the lot without detection. They all three went to the log, and searched the lot over, and could discover no signs except the bent saplings, and the mark of the bullet on the log.

Now whether these were doubles, apparitions, witches, or real persons, the witch family in their carousal that night made much ado about it, declaring to the company present that Bennett Porter had shot at Jerusalem and had broken his arm with the bullet.

The Poisonous Vial — The Last Illness and Death of John Bell, Sr.

I have already written more about this abomination than contemplated in the outset, and still have not told the half; but have presented enough, to which others can testify, to enable the reader to form some idea of the heinous thing, and the horrors that our family had to endure during the early settlement of Robertson county, from an unknown enemy, and for an unknown cause. Whether it was witchery, such as afflicted people in past centuries and the darker ages, whether some gifted fiend of hellish nature, practicing sorcery for selfish enjoyment, or some more modern science akin to that of mesmerism, or some hobgoblin native to the wilds of the country, or a disembodied soul shut out from heaven, or an evil spirit like those Paul drove out of the man into the swine, setting them mad; or a demon let loose from hell, I am unable to decide; nor has any one yet divined its nature or cause for appearing, and I trust this description of the monster in all forms and shapes, and of many tongues, will lead experts who may come with a wiser generation, to a correct conclusion and satisfactory explanation.

However, no part of what I have written would be complete without the finale; the climax which I now approach with a shudder that fills my frame with horror, bringing fresh to memory scenes and events that chilled the blood in my young veins, cheating me out of twenty years of life. It hangs over me like the pall of death, and sends weary thoughts like fleeting shadows through my brain, reviving in memory those demoniac shrieks that came so oft from an invisible and mysterious source, rending the air with vile and hideous curses that drove me frantic with fear.

It is no ghastly dream of a fevered brain that comes to haunt one's thoughts, but a sad, fearful reality, a tremendous truth, that thrills the heart with an unspeakable fear that no word painting can portray on paper. Courageous men in battle line may rush upon bristling bayonets and blazing musketry, and face the roaring cannon's month, because they can see the enemy and know who and what they are fighting; but when it comes to meeting an unknown enemy of demonstrative power, with gall upon its tongue and venom in its bosom, heaving bitter curses and breathing threats of dire consequences, which one knows not of, nor can judge in what shape or form the calamity is to come, the stoutest heart will prove a coward, faltering and quivering with painful fear.

Why should my father, John Bell, be inflicted with such a terrible curse? Why should such a fate befall a man striving to live uprightly? I would be untrue to myself and my parentage, should I fail to state boldly that John Bell was a man every inch of him and in every sense of the term. No man was ever more faithful and swift in the discharge of every duty, to his family, to the church, to his neighbor's, to his fellow man, and to his God, in the fullness of his capacity and that faith which led him to love and accept Christ as a Savior. No mortal man ever brought a charge of delinquency or dishonor to his door. Not even the ghastly fiend that haunted him to his death, in all of its vile curses and evil threats, ever brought an accusation against him, or uttered a solitary word that reflected upon his honor, his character, his courage, or his integrity.

THE BELL WITCH PROJECT

He lived in peace, and in the enjoyment of the full confidence of his neighbors, and lacked not for scores of friends in his severest trials. Then why this affliction? Where the cause? Which no man, saint, angel from heaven, or demon from hell, has ever assigned. If there was any hidden or unknown cause why he should have thus suffered, or if it was in the providence of God a natural consequence, then why should the torments of a demon have been visited upon Elizabeth, who was a girl of tender years, brought up under the careful training of a Christian mother, and was free from guile and the wiles of the wicked world, and innocent of all offense? Yet this vile, heinous, unknown devil, torturer of human flesh, that preyed upon the fears of people like a ravenous vulture, spared not her, but rather chose her as a shining mark for an exhibition of its wicked stratagems and devilish tortures. And never did it cease to practice upon her fears, insult her modesty, stick pins in her body, pinching and bruising her flesh, slapping her cheeks, disheveling and tangling her hair, tormenting her in many ways, until she surrendered that most cherished hope which animates every young heart.

Was this the stratagem of a human genius skilled in the black art; was it an enchantment, a freak in destiny, or the natural consequence of disobedience to some law in nature? Let a wiser head than mine answer and explain the mystery. Another problem in the development of these mysterious manifestations, that has always puzzled my understanding: Why should the husband and father, the head of the family, and the daughter, the pet and pride of the household, the centre of all family affections, be selected to bear the invectives of this terrible visitation, while demonstrations of the tenderest love from the same source was bestowed upon the wife and mother? If it was a living, intelligent creature, what could have been the dominating faculty of its nature, which made this discrimination? Could it have been an intelligent human devotion springing from an emotional nature that could so love the wife and mother, and cherish such bitter enmity for her husband and offspring, both of whom she loved most devotedly? I think not; only a fiend of a hellish nature, with poisoned blood and seared conscience, if a conscience at all, could have possessed such attributes.

Yet we, who experienced or witnessed the demonstration, know that there was a wonderful power of intelligence, possessing knowledge of men and things, a spirit of divination, that could read minds, tell men's secrets, quote the Scriptures, repeat sermons, sing hymns and songs, assume bodily forms, and with all, an immense physical force behind the manifestations.

Father continued to suffer with spells as I have already described, the jerking and twitching of his face, and the swelling of his tongue, fearfully distorting his whole physiogamy. These spells would last from one to two days, and after passing off, he would be up and about his business, apparently in strong robust health. As time advanced the spells grew more frequent and severe, and there was no periodical time for their return, and along toward the last I stayed with him all the time, especially when he left the house, going with him wherever he went. The witch also grew more angry and virulent in disposition. Every word uttered to "Old Jack" was a blast of curses and heinous threats, while to mother, "Old Luce," it continued most tender, loving and kind. About the middle of October father had a very severe attack, which kept him confined to the house six or eight days.

The witch cursed and raved like a maniac for several days, and ceased not from troubling him. However, he temporarily overcome this attack, and was soon able to be out, though he would not venture far from the house. But it was not destined that he should enjoy a long respite. After a week's recuperation he felt much stronger, and called me very early one morning to go with him to the hog pen, some three hundred yards from the house, for the purpose of giving directions in separating the porkers intended for fattening from the stock hogs. We had not gone far before one of his shoes was jerked off. I replaced it on his foot, drawing the strings tight, tying a double hard knot. After going a few steps farther, the other shoe flew off in the same manner, which was replaced and tied as in the case of the first.

In no way that I could tie them would they hold, notwithstanding his shoes fitted close and were a little hard to put on, and we were walking over a smooth, dry road. This worried him prodigiously; nevertheless, he bore up strongly, and after much delay and worry we reached the place, and he gave directions, seeing the hogs properly separated as he desired, and the hands left for other work, and we started back for the house. We had not gone many steps before his shoes commenced jerking off as before, and presently he complained of a blow on his face, which felt like an open hand, that almost stunned him, and he sat down on a log that lay by the road side. Then his face commenced jerking with fearful contortions, soon his whole body, and then his shoes would fly off as fast as I could put them on. The situation was trying and made me shudder. I was terrified by the spectacle of the contortions that seized father, as if to convert him into a very demon to swallow me up. Having finished tying father's shoes, I raised myself up to hear the reviling sound of derisive songs piercing the air with terrorizing force. As the demoniac shrieks died away in triumphant rejoicing, the spell passed off, and I saw the tears chasing down father's yet quivering cheeks.

The trace of faltering courage marked every lineament of his face with a wearied expression of fading hope. He turned to me with an expression of tender,

THE BELL WITCH PROJECT

compassionate fatherly devotion, exclaiming in a woeful passionate tone, "Oh my son, my son, not long will you have a father to wait on so patiently. I cannot much longer survive the persecutions of this terrible thing. It is killing me by slow tortures, and I feel that the end is nigh." This expression sent a pang to my bosom which I had never felt before. Mingled sorrow and terror took possession of me and sent a tremor through my frame that I can never forget. If the earth could have opened and swallowed us up, it would have been a joyful deliverance. My heart bleeds now at every pore as I pen these lines, refreshing my memory with thoughts of the terror that possessed me then in anticipation of a fearful tragedy that might be enacted before father could move from his position. That moment he turned his eyes upward and lifted his soul to heaven in a burst of fervent passionate prayer, such as I had never heard him utter before. He prayed the Lord that if it were possible, to let this terrible affliction pass.

He beseeched God to forsake him not in the trying ordeal, but to give him courage to meet this unknown devastating enemy in the trying emergency, and faith to lift him to the confidence and love of a blessed Savior, and with all to relieve his family and loved ones from the terrible afflictions of this wicked, unknown, terrifying, blasphemous agency. It was in this strain that father prayed, pouring out his soul in a passionate force that seemed to take hold of Christ by a powerful faith that afforded fresh courage and renewed strength. After he had finished his prayer, a feeling of calmness and reconciliation seemed to possess him, and he appeared to have recovered from the severe shock. The reviling songster had disappeared, and he rose up remarking that he felt better and believed he could walk to the house, and he did, meeting with no more annoyance as we proceeded on the way. However, he took to his bed immediately on arriving at the house, and though able to be up and down for several weeks, he never left the house again, and seemed all the while perfectly reconciled to the terrible fate that awaited him. He gradually declined; nothing that friends could do brought any relief. Mother was almost constantly at his bedside with all the devotion of her nature.

Brother John attended closely in the room, ministering to him, and good neighbors were in constant attendance. The witch was carrying on its deviltry more or less all the while.

The crisis, however, came on the morning of December 19th. Father, sick as he was, had not up to this time failed to awake at his regular hour, according to his long custom, and arouse the family. That morning he appeared to be sleeping so soundly, mother quietly slipped, out of the room to superintend breakfast, while brothers John and Drew looked after the farm hands and feeding the stock, and would not allow him to be disturbed until after breakfast. Noticing then that he was sleeping unnaturally, it was thought best to awaken him, when it was discovered that he was in a deep stupor, and could not be aroused to any sensibility. Brother John attended to giving him medicine, and went immediately to the cupboard where he had carefully put away the medicines prescribed for him, but instead he found a smoky looking vial, which was about one-third full of dark colored liquid.

He set up an inquiry at once to know who had moved the medicine, and no one had touched it, and neither could any one on the place give any account of the vial. Dr. George Hopson, of Port Royal, was sent for in great haste and soon arrived; also neighbors John Johnson, Alex. Gunn and Frank Miles arrived early, and were there when the vial was found. Kate, the witch, in the meantime broke out with joyous exultation, exclaiming, "It's useless for you to try to relieve Old Jack, I have got him this time; he will never get up from that bed again." Kate was then asked about the vial of medicine found in the cupboard, and replied, "I put it there, and gave Old Jack a big dose out of it last night while he was asleep, which fixed him." This was all the in formation that could be drawn from the witch or any other source concerning the vial of medicine. Certain it was that no member of the family ever saw it before, or could tell anything about it. In fact no vial and no medicine of any kind had been brought to the house by any one else except by Dr. Hopson, and then it was handled carefully. Dr. Hopson, on arrival, examined the vial and said he did not leave it, and could not tell what it contained. It was then suggested that the contents be tested on something. Alex. Gunn caught a cat, and Brother John run a straw into the vial and drew it through the cat's mouth, wiping the straw on its tongue. The cat jumped and whirled over a few times, stretched out, kicked, and died very quick.

Deathbed of John Bell

Father lay all day and night in a deep stupor, as if under the influence of some opiate, and could not be aroused to take any medicine. The Doctor said he could detect something on his breath that smelt very much like the contents of the vial that he had examined. How father could have gotten it was a mystery that could not be explained in any other way except that testified by the witch. The vial and contents was thrown into the fire, and instantly a blue blaze shot up the chimney like a flash of powder. Father never revived or returned to consciousness for a single moment. He lingered along through the day and night, gradually wearing away, and on the morning of December 20th, 1820, breathed his last. Kate was around during the time, indulging in wild exultations and derisive songs.

THE BELL WITCH PROJECT

After father breathed his last nothing more was heard from Kate until after the burial was completed. It was a bright December day and a great crowd of people came to attend the funeral. Rev. Sugg Fort and Revs. James and Thomas Gunn conducted the services. After the grave was filled, and the friends turned to leave the sad scene, the witch broke out in a loud voice singing, "Row me up some brandy O," and continued singing this until the family and friends had all entered the house. And thus ended one chapter in the series of exciting and frightful events that kept the whole neighborhood so long in a frenzy, and worked upon our fears from day to day.

Kate's Departure and Return After Seven Years

After the death of John Bell, Sr., the fury of the witch was greatly abated. There were but two purposes, seemingly, developed in the visitation. One was the persecution of father to the end of his life. The other the vile purpose of destroying the anticipated happiness that thrilled the heart of Betsy. This latter purpose, however, was not so openly manifested as the first, and was of such a delicate nature that it was kept a secret as much as possible in the family and ignored when talked about. But it never ceased its tormenting until her young dream was destroyed.

The witch remained with us after father's death, through the Winter and Spring of 1821, all the while diminishing or becoming less demonstrative. Finally it took leave of the family, bidding mother, "Luce," an affectionate farewell, saying that it would be absent seven years, but would surely return to see us and would then visit every house in the neighborhood. This promise was fulfilled as regards the old homestead, but I do not know that it visited other homes in the vicinity.

It returned during February, 1828. The family was then nearly broken up. Mother, Joel and myself were the only occupants left at the old homestead, the other members of the family having settled off to themselves. The demonstrations announcing its return were precisely the same that characterized its first appearance. Joel occupied a bed in mother's room, and I slept in another apartment alone. After considerable scratching on the weatherboarding on the outside, it appeared in the same way on the inside, scratching on the bed post and pulling the cover from my bed as fast as I could replace it, keeping me up nearly all night. It went on in this way for several nights, and I spoke not a word about it, lest I should frighten mother.

However, one night later, after worrying me for some time, I heard a noise

THE BELL WITCH PROJECT

in mother's room, and knew at once what was to pay. Very soon mother and Joel came rushing into my room, much frightened, telling me about the disturbance and something pulling the cover off. We sat up till a late hour discussing the matter, satisfied that it was the same old Kate, and agreed not to talk to the witch, and that we would keep the matter a profound secret to ourselves, worrying with it the best we could, hoping that it would soon leave, as it did, after disturbing us in this way for some two weeks. This was my last experience with Kate. The witch came and went, hundreds of people witnessed its wonderful demonstrations, and many of the best people of Robertson and adjoining counties have testified to these facts, telling the story over and over to the younger generation, and for this and other reasons as before stated I have written this much of the details as correctly as it is possible to state the exciting events. So far no one has ever given any intelligent or comprehensive explanation of the great mystery. Those who came as experts were worse confounded than all others.

As I before stated, a few mendacious calumniators were mean enough to charge that it was tricks and inventions of the Bell family to make money, and I write for the purpose of branding this version as an infamous falsehood. It was well known in the vicinity and all over the county that every investigation confirmed the fact that the Bell family were the greatest, if not the only sufferers from the visitation, and that no one, or a dozen persons in collusion, could have so long, regularly and persistently practiced such a fraud without detection, nor could they have known the minds and secrets of strangers visiting the place, and detailed events that were then occurring or had just transpired in different localities. Moreover the visitation entailed great sacrifice. As to how long this palavering phenomenon continued in the vicinity, I am unable to state. It did not disturb the remaining members of the family at the old place anymore. Mother died shortly after this and the house was entirely deserted, the land and other property being divided among the heirs.

The old house stood for some years and was used for storing grain and other farm products, and was finally torn down and moved away. Many persons professed to have seen sights and heard strange sounds about the old house and in the vicinity all along up to this day. Several have described to me flitting lights along the old lane and through the farm, while others profess to have heard sounds of wonderfully sweet music and strange voices uttering indistinct word. And it is said that such things have been seen and heard at various places in the neighborhood, but I have no personal knowledge of the facts.

RICHARD WILLIAMS BELL

THE BELL WITCH PROJECT

Chapter 9

After John Bell's Death — The Lovers' Easter Monday — Prof. Powell's School - Uncle Zeke's Rectification of the Ghosts Disturbing the Fish – Several Weddings

The death of John Bell, Sr., left a shadow of impenetrable gloom hanging like the pall of darkness over the sorrow stricken family. They were as a ship without a rudder; no solace for anguish and no light penetrating the darkness of the future, or forecasting the end of this great family affliction, save that the witch was now less virulent in its demonstrations, ceasing to torment Betsy as it had before. The only way open was in pursuing the even tenor of life, awaiting the further developments of the unknown destroyer of the peace of the happy household. The death of Mr. Bell and the manner of his taking off awakened another sensation, one of a more serious and solemn import than all the events in the varied chapter of sensations that had so long kept the community in a state of frenzy, calling into exercise every faculty and all the stratagems of inventive genius, in the effort to detect the mysterious agency, only to be toiled and involved in still greater confusion.

The phenomena had progressed, developing new features, power and character from week to week, finally fulfilling that malignant purpose declared in the outset to be a part of its mission, that of tormenting "Old Jack Bell" out of his life by a slow process of mysterious torture, and now all eyes and thoughts centered on Betsy, curiously wondering and discussing with animation the probable effect of the death of the father upon the daughter, and the attitude of the witch towards her. The girl was then overwhelmed with grief for the loss of a devoted father, which in the course of time was to be overcome, but the forebodings of the horrible witch, whose caprice might chasten her through life, or burst at any moment in the malignity of volcanic wrath, hung over her like an impending calamity, menacing the happiness, of life with bitter anguish.

THE BELL WITCH PROJECT

The suspense was dreadful in the extreme, like a horrifying nightmare haunting a feverish dream, and was not to be contemplated without a shudder. However, days and weeks passed, and neighbors continued their good offices, visiting and ministering comfort to the distressed family, and much to the surprise and gratification of all, there appeared a remarkable change in the mordacity of Kate toward Betsy. The haunting sphinx ceased harassing and become a ministering spirit, manifesting more sympathy, and tender compassion than all the friends who sought her on that gracious mission, save perhaps one. Joshua Gardner was never remiss in his devotions, and he labored with all the earnestness of his soul to remove the cloud that shadowed her happiness, and his efforts were not without good effect, notwithstanding his presence was attended with the premonition of Kate's abhorrent augury. Betsy Bell was conscious that her heart, beat in unison of sympathy for that manly devotion so freely bestowed on her. But what would be the consequence if she should disregard the warnings of her wicked tormentor, whose inflictions were already as great as could be endured?

Might not the terrible freak execute its threats on her, as it had fulfilled the prophecy concerning her father, and destroy the peace and happiness of both herself and lover, rendering them miserable for life, should she yield to his entreaty and become his wife? Such were her thoughts and reasoning against the inclination of her cherished desire, and it was a most difficult problem to solve, in the struggle of the heart between love and fear. Kate had ceased meddling in the affair, never called Joshua's name to Betsy, nor spoke when he was present.

Betsy's and Joshua's Engagement

This relenting was encouraging to the lovers, and Joshua took advantage of the circumstance as evidence that the trouble was nearing the end, and pressed his suit, urging that the marriage should take place at an early date, when they might leave the haunted vale for their contemplated Western home, entering connubial life amid happier scenes full of new inspiration, and hearts thrilled with the joys they had so long anticipated. Betsy was disposed to yield to his persuasive reasoning; Joshua had drawn a different picture of the future from that which she had been looking upon. It was full of promise and stimulated renewed hope, and she gave her consent, conditionally, insisting that the matter be postponed a while longer, awaiting further developments in the witch's course, which were to be expected soon. There was, however, no more malevolent manifestations. Kate had almost ceased annoying the family, which served to give coloring to the rainbow of promise that Joshua painted so beautifully, and Betsy soon found her crushed hope reviving, animating her broken spirit. The flush returned to her paled cheeks, a brighter lustre filled her pretty blue eyes, while a mischievous smile returned to play in the light of those matchless orbs.

This change in Betsy was noticed by all comers and goers, and was the gossip of the neighborhood. The Fairy Queen of the Haunted Dale was herself again. The gloom of despond had passed away, and a happy heart revealed itself in her sparkling eyes and merry laughter, which seemed to defy Kate, and the witch had ceased to interpose any further impediment to the match, and the brilliant wedding long anticipated was conceded to be close at hand. The Bell home had resumed something of its former gayety and splendid hospitality, extending a hearty welcome to all who came, offering the greatest attraction to visitors known in the country, and Betsy's grace of manners, pleasing conversation and charming wit, combined with her personal beauty, was a source of pleasure that all, old and young, delighted in.

She was the joy of the home,

The pride of the vale;

Her presence like sunshine

That lights up the dale.

Easter Monday

Easter came in all the glory of ethereal April. Nature had put on its spring garb unusually early, and the day was like the resurrection morn, lending inspiration and vigor to all that was flush with life. The afternoon found a gay party of young people assembled at the Bell home, as by intuition, to arrange plans for the outing and pastime for the tomorrow, Easter Monday being a holiday observed by all people, even the servants being exempted from regular duty and allowed freedom to spend the day as they wished. A fishing excursion and a hunt for wild flowers along the river bluff seemed to promise the greatest diversion, and it was agreed upon to meet at Brown's for the sport.

The day dawned with a clear sky, and the sun rose in all of her splendor, sending forth gentle rays to kiss away the morning dew. The full blown orchard that almost surrounded the Bell residence presented a living bouquet of nature's beauty, white and pink blooms nestling amid the fresh young foliage of the trees, mingling their sweet perfumes on the gentle current that swept over the valley. Three interesting couples left the Bell place that morning for a stroll through the orchard and across the meadow to the river side, where the fishing party was expected to meet. The three couples were Betsy Bell and her lover, Joshua Gardner,

THE BELL WITCH PROJECT

Theny Thorn and Alex. Gooch, and Rebecca Porter and James Long. Three happier couples never started out for a glorious holiday.

Betsy had acceded to Joshua's proposition, dismissing all gloomy forebodings, and that morning for the first time wore a beautiful engagement ring, which Joshua placed on her finger Easter morning, while sitting beneath the favorite pear tree, and she started out with a light and joyous heart, full of mirthful sport, making merry the day.

"See there girls," exclaimed Betsy, "those beautiful pear trees, arrayed in white, representing the bride of the morning. They bow to us a hearty welcome this lovely holiday."

"Yes, I see," returned Theny Thorn, "they are perfectly lovely; but you overlook the peach trees on the other side of the path, dressed in pink. They represent the bridesmaids."

"Well," observed Becky Porter, "I should like to know what these pretty little violets represent which you all are unconsciously mashing under your big feet?"

"They are Cupid's arrows," answered Joshua Gardner. "They can not be crushed by trampling, Miss Becky; see how quick they rise up, smiling sweetly."

"Yes," exclaimed Betsy, "that is why I love them so much; break or bruise one, and it comes again as fresh as ever;"

Alex. Gooch presumed that these sentimental expressions were inspired by the invigorating morning breeze. "Please, Miss Betsy, what does this refreshing zephyr, which blows such a pleasant gale, represent in your beautiful Easter picture?"

"Oh, that is the breath of the bridegroom," laughingly answered Betsy.

"Then," observed James Long, "if we are to judge from the fragrance of his breath, the bridegroom must be a distiller, out gathering nectar from the myriads of sweet blossoms, that excites so much felicitous exultation."

"Yes, Mr. Long," replied Becky, "you have a correct appreciation of the work of nature's God; you observe that the sun beams come first, gathering dewdrops from the precious buds, giving off the perfume to the morning's breath; that is what Betsy refers to."

THE BELL WITCH PROJECT

"Oh, pshaw," ejaculated Alex. Gooch, "please all hold up a bit and find your equilibrium. We started out to go fishing, but you girls are about to turn to fairies and take wings on the morning air."

"Yes, yes," exclaimed Joshua, "lets go fishing; why linger here. Look yonder, see those majestic trees that line the river bank, lifting up their leafy boughs in solid phalanx like a bordering mountain range of evergreen, keeping sentry over this lovely valley. See how gracefully their waving tops beckon us on to catch the sweet strains of the warbling birds that are mingling their melody with the soft sighing winds and the murmuring waves that are surging by."

"Hold up, hold up two minutes, Joshua; catch your breath and take a fresh start," exclaimed. Alex. Gooch.

"Oh, no," interposed James Long, "let Josh gush. He is in ecstasy of mind this morning, which accounts for his poetical flights."

"Well, said Miss Theny, "I am not going to leave here without a bouquet of Cupid's arrows. Come Becky, let's you and I load up with violets and peach blossoms, while Josh and Betsy are taking down that pear tree."

Thus run the conversation in sallies of pleasantry and flights of fancy, as the three joyous couples wended their way through the orchard and across the green meadow to the river side, where many happy souls had already gathered and were making the best of the bright morning, entering fully into the frolicsome sports of the day.

Prof. Powell's School

Very soon Prof. Richard Powell put in an appearance, just out from Springfield on his first canvass for the Legislature. He had heard something about the fishing party, and could not resist the temptation to call by, and mingle a short while with the happy throng of youngsters who had grown up under his tutorage. His presence was the signal for a general rush to the circle that was gathering around the handsome teacher who, though a bachelor, maintained his youthful appearance, good humor and fascinating manners, extending hearty greetings and happy congratulations.

"How good it is to be here," exclaimed the Professor; "it carries me back to our joyous school days, when you were all happy rollicking children, and I was well — I was one of you."

THE BELL WITCH PROJECT

"We are all children yet," answered Joshua Gardner, "and I move that we open school right here and now."

"Good," said Alex. Gooch, "I am in for that."

"And we will have some fun turning out the teacher," remarked Jimmie Long.

"No you won't," returned Betsy, "we girls will take Mr. Powell's part and turn you boys in for the ducking. What say you girls? All in favor of that motion hold up your strong right hand."

"Both hands," exclaimed Theny, and all hands went up.

"There now boys," observed the Professor, "I have the advantage this time, and will not go into the river today. Betsy you are just the same sweet good girl you always were, taking my part against the boys, and you too, Theny, Becky, Betsy Gunn, Nicie Gooch, Mary Gotham, Sarah Batts; yes, and you too, Mahalia, Susan, Nancy, every one of those dear little hands; you are all my pets and sweethearts, and I am going to stand by you girls, as long as I live. If you should happen to marry these bad boys, and they don't treat you right, any of you, just call on me, and I will help to turn him out and put his head under the spring spout."

"Ha, ha," laughed Drew Bell, "I am going to be a girl today and help the Professor; put Calvin Johnson and Frank Miles under the spout, they have no business in this crowd anyway; they ought to be looking after some old girls."

"And where ought you to be, Drew? I just came down here thinking I would bait my hook with you for a catfish."

"No, no, Mr. Miles," exclaimed Betsy Gunn, "we can't spare Mr. Drew; he digs our fish bait; look at his hands."

"Hold up hands, Drew," cried Calvin Johnson; "if you are going to be a girl, hold up them hands."

"I shan't," said Drew.

"Oh yes, Drew," insisted the Professor, "you have elegant hands."

"You mean elephant hands, Mr. Powell," returned Frank Miles.

"No, grubbing hoes," said another.

THE BELL WITCH PROJECT

"Flatboat oars," put in Alex. Gunn."

"Call them what you please," spoke Becky Porter, "Mr. Drew can dig more fish bait than all of you, and we can't get along without him on Easter Monday."

"Why Becky," whispered Mary, "I guess you can get J. Long just as well."

"Now Mary, that's a good pun; what a witty Bell you might be," retorted Becky.

"Please, Professor, excuse brother Drew from holding up his hands, he hasn't washed them today," pleaded Betsy. "Drew you will be excused, now finish digging bait; go to the spring and wash your hands, and then come to books, and fetch your gun to keep bad boys like Frank Miles off."

Thus an hour passed in the exchange of pleasantry, witticisms, congratulations, repartee and general hilarity, recounting amusing events that occurred during school days, Mr. Powell declaring that it was the happiest hour he had spent since he had left the neighborhood, and he was very sorry that he could not spend the day in such pleasant company, but that he was obliged to leave, and wishing all much good luck in the catch of the day, he was off; not, however, without paying Betsy Bell some special compliments, telling her that she had grown up to be more beautiful and charming than he had ever dreamed of when he used to pet her so much.

"Just as I always told your mother, Miss Betsy, that you were the brightest and smartest girl in school, when she declared I would spoil you; but I did not, did I?"

"I think not, Professor; I hope I don't act like a spoilt girl," returned Betsy.

"No you do not, Josh will bear me out in that. And by the way, Josh is a fine fellow; I have heard that you and Josh were about to make a match, and I shall wish you much happiness and prosperity. That boy never could help loving you, and I never did blame him, as you were my little pet also, and I have waited almost as patiently as did Jacob for Rachel, hoping that you and Josh might forget that young school day love, but I have been disappointed, and now my request is to be at the wedding. I want to be present when you wed, my little pet. Good-bye, I wish you well."

"Professor, I shall let you know when that happens," answered Betsy.

THE BELL WITCH PROJECT

As soon as Mr. Powell left, the assembly broke up in couples, stringing out along the river bank wherever good places could be found to throw in their hooks.

The darkies in the country were all out early for the holiday, and had monopolized the river bank from Brown's ford up to Gorham's mill, and the young people respecting their rights too much to disturb their pleasure, sought places below the ford, the three couples from the Bell home being last to locate, Joshua and Betsy taking the last position, just opposite the enchanted spring where the treasure trove was said to be concealed, which was a fair open spot. Mr. Gardner soon baited the hooks and set the poles in the bank to await the coming of the fish, and he and Betsy seated themselves on a green sward back upon the hillside over looking the fishing tackle.

The sky continued clear, and the sun approached noontide, spreading bright rays over the valley, while a brisk wind heavily freighted with sweetest fragrance swept over, keeping the fresh green foliage of the tall trees along the river side in constant commotion. The modest little brook from the enchanted spring rippled down the riverbank in sweet consonance with the murmuring waves that rolled steadily by. The merry laughter of the gay throng strung out along the brink was caught up by the breeze in chorus with the music of the happy wildwood songsters that fluttered, chirped and twittered in the boughs overhead. It was indeed a real Easter day — the goddess of Spring restoring to nature that refreshing and renewal of life which so beautifully commemorates the resurrection of the world's Savior. Even the finny tribe seemed mindful of the commemorative event and were on a holiday frolic, coming to the top, jumping and flouncing on the bosom of the crystal-like waves, and didn't care a fig for the daintiest bait thrown out by eager fishermen.

"Keep less noise down there, you'll frighten the fish away," yelled a stentorian voice in a commanding tone.

"You are making more noise, Mr. Miles, than all of us," exclaimed Betsy Gunn.

"Yes, but I have got to roar to get you youngsters settled so I can catch fish. Now you and John Bell settle down to the business you came here for, like Josh and Betsy, I came to catch fish," returned Mr. Miles.

"So did we," observed John, "but we have no idea of scaring them to death."

"That is just what you are doing; see how they jump," replied William Porter; "Frank and I came here to catch some fish if you chaps will make less noise."

THE BELL WITCH PROJECT

"Then you will have to jump in and run them down, Brother Billy," exclaimed Becky Porter.

Uncle Zeke's Rectification On Dem Ghosts

Uncle Zeke, a consequential old darkie, who was very proud of the honor of being special valet to Rev. Thomas Gunn, occupied a position just above, to the right of Frank Miles, inquiringly put the question:

"Mars Frank, can I have the 'sumption to pose you a question?"

"Yes, Uncle Zeke, what is it?"

"Well sar, Ize bin wanting to know how dem fishes jumpin' up out der kin hear us talkin when they ain't got no ears?"

"I don't know, Uncle Zeke, but suppose it is by instinct or jar from the vibration of sound on the air; what do you think about it?"

"Well sar, Mars Frank, I was just lowin' da cud see fru dat water better dan da cud hear; den sar I was lowin' too dat dar war sumpen wrong wid dem fishes out dar, cause sir, you never seed fishes jump up dat way on holiday fo dis."

"What do you think is the matter, Uncle Zeke?"

"Well sar, an Injun spirit is out dar 'mong dem fish, dats what's der matter, an they ain't goin to bite today."

"Do you mean the old witch, Uncle Zeke?"

"Dats exactly what it is, sar."

"How do you know that it's an Indian spirit?"

"Well sar, dat is der ruction in der case. Do you know dat der Injuns fust had dis country and dis river, an dats why they named it Red River, cause it belonged to the red men?"

"Yes, but there is another story about the naming of this river which beats that. The story is that Moses Renfroe, who brought the first white settlement to this river, himself and all of his people were slaughtered by the Indians. The savage brutes dragged the men, women and children to the river, scalped their heads and cut their throats, throwing their bodies in, causing the water to run red with blood, and the stream was after that called Red River. That is what I understand about it, Uncle Zeke, but go on with your story, about the spirit."

"Well sar, dats all der same; cause I was goin to say, the Injuns was here fust, and we white fokes drove em out, all but dem what was dead and couldn't go, an they's here yet in der spirit. Ize had disconjection under consideration ever since I fust heard Mars Tom prayin fur der witch to abrogate, an it taint heard him yet, dats what. When Mars Tom Gunn prays against the spirits and hit don't abrogate, den it hain't got no connection with Heaven."

"I think you are about right on that," approvingly replied Mr. Miles.

"Well sar, dat is der rectification of dem ghostes in my mind. You neber heard tell of Injuns in hell then, did you, Mars Frank?"

"Never did, Uncle Zeke."

"Well den, you neber seed one in hell, did you?"

"No, Uncle Zeke, I have not," returned Miles.

"Needer did Mars Tom. Cause he don't pray for em; den where is they? Why sar, dem dead Injuns who lived here are here yet, cause dey ain't got nowhar to go, an dats what's der matter. I said soon as I heard about Corban Hall diggin up dem Injun bones over dar in the bottom, dar was goin to be trouble."

"Have you ever seen the spirit, Uncle Zeke?" enquired Miles.

"Dat spirit what you call der witch? Yes sar, ain't you seed dem lights that move over the bottom on dark nights like a ball of fire? Well, dats what it is, an you better not go about der except when you got a hair ball wid fox fire in it. That's der only way you kin fight dem spirits; jest like Dean does. Cause der Injun is like a black cat, he's got fire' in his eyes, fire in his back, an der devil in hiz neck, an you better let him alone. I said soon as I seed de Professor cum down here dis mornin, dat dar warn't goin to be no fish caught here today, an now you sees how dem fishes are jumpin up."

"Why, Uncle Zeke, what has the Professor got to do with it?" enquired Miles.

THE BELL WITCH PROJECT

"I tells you, Mars Frank, Ize a nigger and ain't got no business talkin', but I knows some things dat won't do to tell. Can't you see der spiritations in dat man's eyes? He didn't cum here for nuttin. I haint bin round here all dis time when der Professor kept school but know something, cause I've turned my witch ball on der phenomiter of dem ghostes, and seed dat man sperimentin' in der ruction of der spirits by der precunious instinction of der fungus, an every time he hit de Injun flint with the back of hiz knife he kotch der fire in hiz eyes; den when he looks on dat witch gal his eyes blazes, and den melts an dat put er spell on her."

Frank Miles laughed heartily at the idea, and told Uncle Zeke that his conclusions were no doubt correct.

During this interval, while time was swiftly passing, Joshua Gardner and Betsy Bell had not thought of their fishing tackle. They continued to occupy the velvety stratum first selected for a seat, oblivious to the merriment of their frolicsome friends, and all the passing events that lent gayety to the occasion. Prof. Powell had observed that Betsy was wearing an engagement ring, and it was no doubt the sight of this token of a betrothal that inspired his remarks on taking leave of his "pet" that morning; and this was the subject that absorbed the thoughts of the lovers. They were discussing the wedding day, the far away home in the West that should soon give them welcome; the new scene that the change would bring, and the joys that awaited to bless their union. They were given entirely to the revelry of their own sweet dreams, bestowing no attention upon the surrounding charms. They took no notice of the finny tribe that played upon the rolling waves in sight, nor to the rippling of the wandering brook that gushed wildly down the hill from the foaming fountain above. Nor were they attracted by the warbling strains of the birds in the rustling boughs overhead, or interested in any of those things that afforded so much pleasure to other members of the company. They longed for the holly, for love's own sweet home in the faraway West, where they had:

For Cupid built a flowery castle,

Stored with manna of pure love,

And strung Aeolian harps to sing

Songs of the turtle dove.

THE BELL WITCH PROJECT

The Phantom Fish

Presently the sound of a mighty splashing was heard upon the waters that attracted all attention. A great fish had seized Joshua Gardner's hook with such force that it jerked the pole from the bank, and dashed off up stream, slashing the waves furiously as it rose to the top, flouncing and fluttering with great rage, and then diving to the bottom, carrying the pole under also, and instantly rising with a spurt, rushing in wild confusion to the south bank, as if it meant to leap for the land, but just at the water's edge it darted under, bounding up stream with the pole trolling behind, between the bank and the hooks thrown out by the eager fishermen along the stream. Passing under Uncle Zeke's tackle, the big swimmer flounced again to the top, making a hurry-scurry circle, tangling the old darkies' lines with the pole, and taking another straight shoot up the river. Before Uncle Zeke could recover from the confusion, one of his poles had joined in the procession, and he was bewildered with excitement.

"Why don't you jump in, Uncle Zeke, and catch that fish and save your pole? Don't you see the fish is hung, and you are a good swimmer? Go quick, jump, plunge, and bring in the biggest fish ever caught in Red River," wildly shouted Frank Miles. This speech fired Uncle Zeke's courage to the highest pitch. He lost his head, and forgot all about the "Injun spirit" for the moment, and in less than a half minute had pulled off his coat and shoes and was in the act of jumping head-foremost into the river.

But a precaution struck him, and he called a halt, carefully stepping one foot in the water, which he quickly jerked back with a shudder, and exclaiming, "I aint goin in der; I've done had a sentment bout dat fish, cepen its goin to fool me."

"Oh go ahead, Uncle Zeke, don't be so cowardly; you belong to Parson Gunn, and what's the difference if you should drown, you will go straight to heaven," urged Mr. Miles.

"Dats so, Mars Frank, I ain't carin' nuffin bout drownin, but den whose goin to tend to Mars Tom's hoss like I does, and whose goin to brush his coat and hat an black hiz shoes? Cause their ain't nary another darkie that knows how to mix der lampblack; dats what pesters me by der sentment."

In the meanwhile a more youthful and daring darkie, a little higher up, heard Mr. Miles' suggestion and plunged in, swimming to the poles that were still bobbing up and down in the water, and as he grabbed the main pole, the fish made a circle, tightening the line, and whirling the Negro around in the water, as it made another dash for the bank, helping the darkie to swim with greater ease and speed.

THE BELL WITCH PROJECT

But just as he reached the shore, and the excited crowd had gathered to help land the catch, the great fish flounced to the top, releasing itself, and was gone dashing up stream, splitting the waves, amid the shouts of excited fishermen nearly up to Gorham's mill. Now an excited discussion turned upon the antics of the monster aquatic, its size, and to which family of the finny tribe it belonged.

One thought it was an "eel," another said "cat fish," another said a shark had wandered up the stream. Frank Miles declared that it was the biggest trout ever seen, but all agreed that the great finny was between two and three feet in length. William Porter observed that they had all better get to their places and bait their hooks; that the fish might return soon. The suggestion was sufficient, and pretty soon quiet was restored, every one giving strict attention to fishing. But Uncle Zeke could not suppress the inclination to whisper to Frank Miles, "I tole you so. I said sumptin war goin to happen."

Joshua and Betsy had been attracted from their delightful repose by the prevailing excitement, but as soon as the big finny made its escape, they returned to the beautiful sward, ostensibly to look after the remaining fishing tackle. Betsy, however, did not seem so gay and happy as she had appeared all the morning, and frankly confessed to her lover strange forebodings that depressed her feelings, but she could not explain the cause. Joshua then devoted his efforts to dispelling the gloom, as he had before done, and at the moment had quite well succeeded, when the reverberating sound of ecstatic voices above were heard in wild exclaim, "Look out, look out, its coming back!" The breaking waves and the furious lashing of the water told the story, that the playful fish was on its return down stream, riding upon the tide, as if to catch the sunbeams that glittered upon the foamy crest. It, however, quickly disappeared, and all was quiet, every fisherman anxiously watching for a bite.

The Lovers' Forebodings

The dying excitement of the last appearance left the lovers in a reverie of their own thoughts, deeply meditating upon their contemplated plans, as if trying to penetrate a shadow that seemed to hang heavily over their destiny, in spite of all efforts to rise above the crest of the cloud by looking all the while at the bright side. The suspense was painful, but nothing to compare with the sound of Kate's familiar voice which immediately pierced their ears like the bursting of a thunder cloud, pleading in that same old plaintive tone, "Please Betsy Bell, don't have Joshua Gardner," repeating the entreaty over and over, until the lovers were overwhelmed with dismay, when the melancholy voice died away gradually as the waves rolled by and were lost to sight with the passing current. The color faded from the poor girl's checks as quickly as if a dagger had pierced her bosom, and Joshua, though courageous as he had proven before on similar occasions, felt the pangs of a broken heart, and was powerless to soothe the anguish that told so plainly on his affianced.

They sat motionless and speechless for some minutes, as if awaiting an awful doom. At last Betsy broke the silence, proposing a walk up the hillside to the spring for a drink of water. There they drank and discoursed on the excellency of the cooling draught, the beauty of the foaming bubbles that broke away in diminutive billows rushing with the trickling stream down the craggy hillside, then gathering a few wild flowers, and thus they whiled away some twenty minutes in an effort to dispel the gloomy fore bodings and regain composure, but all was in vain.

Finally Betsy summoned the courage of her convictions, telling Joshua frankly that her mind was made up, and that she could not brook the storm which threatened all the fancied happiness which seemed to be in store for them; that she was now clearly convinced that her tormenter would follow her through life with an appalling destiny, should she resist its importunities and dire threatenings, just as it had already afflicted her, and brought her father to suffering and unto death. Even were she able to endure it all, her compliance with his wish would be an injustice to Joshua, and a wrong for which she could never expect forgiveness. Therefore she desired to with draw her promise and return to him the engagement ring that she prized so highly. Joshua Gardner was suffering the bitterest anguish that ever pierced a heart. He had never known before the strength of his passion for the queenly beauty who stood before him in the perfection of lovely young womanhood, conscious that the stern decision had cost her as much pain as it did him, and was rendered as a sacrifice for his own welfare, as she conceived.

He tried to plead his cause anew, but was so overwhelmed with the force of her reasoning and firmness of decision that he for the first time faltered, realizing that all hope was vain, and that every plea but added another sorrow to a bleeding heart, and a fresh pang to his own, and he gracefully accepted the inevitable, begging her to keep the ring in memory of one who loved her dearer than his own life. This she declined to do, telling him that the ring was a seal to her solemn vow, and the vow could not be broken in the sight of heaven, unless he would accept the return of the ring.

"I could not," she said, "retain it without retaining the thorn that now pierces my heart and I know Joshua that you are too generous not to accede to my wish."

THE BELL WITCH PROJECT

Slipping it from her finger as she held out her hand, Joshua Gardner in all the bitter anguish of a broken heart, exclaimed, "Betsy, my love, the adoration of my soul, the long hope of my life, this is the bitterest draught of all, but for your sake I drink to the dregs, releasing you from the promise which I know was earnest." Thus ended the affair in which the witch had manifested so much interest from the commencement of the "Family Trouble."

Very soon the three couples retraced their steps across the valley to the Bell home, amid the gay scenes of nature in the full flush of joyous Spring, but the walk was not attended by that levity and buoyancy of spirit which characterized the morning stroll. All were conscious of the shadow which hung so heavily over Betsy, depressing her happy spirit, and which had that day sent another poisonous shaft quivering to her bleeding heart, and the bowed form and dejected spirit of Joshua Gardner, which told plainly that he too carried a crushed heart in his manly bosom, and all hearts were touched too deep with burning sympathy to admit of any alacrity. It was more like going to a funeral, and the accompanying couples kept a respectful distance in the rear, discussing as they walked leisurely along the appalling sorrow which the return of the witch had brought that day.

The lovers separated that afternoon never to meet again. A few days later, as soon as he could arrange his affairs, Joshua Gardner took his departure, several days journey to the west, and settled in West Tennessee, the place now known as Gardner's Station, Obion county, where he passed a long and honorable career, esteemed by the people for his true manhood and moral worth. He died several years ago at the advanced age of eighty-four years.

The weird fiend, cast the scene,

Lurid with the seer's blight.

And hope forlorn, shadowed the morn

With the gloom of night.

Thus the sequel, young love unequal

To the wizard's subtle art.

And dreamers await, the hand of fate,

While despondency sears the heart.

THE BELL WITCH PROJECT

The lovers parted, weary, brokenhearted,

Cruel fate coming between.

The blasting frost, the appalling ghost,

Chilled the bower of green.

The flowers withered, the castle quivered

When Cupid fled the scene.

And the beautiful tower, lovers bower

Became a fading, crumbling sheen.

Seizing the wreck, scuttling the deck

Witches vaunted ghoulish spleen.

The vile freak, with exulting shriek

Cavorted the dale unseen.

The jack-o-lantern glare, flitted the air.

O'er the valley of doom.

And the pall of night, shadowed beacon light

Filling the vale with gloom.

Down the hill and o'er the rill

Horrid spirits delighted to prowl,

The piercing thrill, of whippoorwill,

Giving place to the hooting owl.

From the mill and old still

Came songs of the weird,

THE BELL WITCH PROJECT

Voices shrill, with horrible trill

Hushing the joyous mocking bird.

The old pear tree, hoary it be,

Still shadows the happy scene,

Spreading its boughs, over the vows

Witnessed beneath its green.

Where lovers plighted, hearts united,

The vows they would redeem.

And continues weeping, lovers sleeping,

For the return of the dream.

The witch exulted freely over the victory won, but troubled Betsy no more; rather tried to soothe and strengthen her depressed spirit, promising to leave soon, as it did, bidding the family goodbye.

Several Weddings

Some months later a brilliant wedding took place at the residence of James Johnson. The whole community gathered in to celebrate the nuptials that united Theny Thorn and Alex. Gooch. Six months after this affair, James Long and Rebecca Porter were happily wedded. Both couples settled in the Bell neighborhood, sharing the burdens of good citizenship, and their descendants still reside in that community, worthily sustaining the honored names inherited, ranking among the best people of the county. Next followed the marriage of John Bell, Jr., and Elizabeth Gunn, whose honorable career and success in life is recorded in the family biography.

It was a long while before Betsy Bell could overcome the shock of that notable Easter Monday in April 1821, which almost extinguished that effervescence which had characterized her girlhood. Vivacious as she was, it was difficult for her to conceal the depression that had so long menaced her young life and overwhelmed her on that memorial day. Some while after this, however, the Professor, Hon. Richard Powell, became her persistent suitor and was finally accepted, and in this she kept her promise that the Professor should be at the wedding. Richard Powell was many years her senior, but was a handsome gentleman of elegant manners, and bore all honorable name and reputation. He was in fact a leading character and politician, represented the county several times, or as long as he desired, in the State Legislature, which was then considered a very high honor. He was also prominent in all public affairs, and one of the most popular men in Robertson County.

Their married life was comparatively short, about seventeen years. Mr. Powell died, and Betsy remained a widow the balance of her life. About 1875 she moved to Mississippi, where one of her children and other relatives resided, and died in 1890 at the age of eighty-six years. She has grandchildren still living in Robertson county, who have inherited that vivacity and charming wit which characterized her young life. After mature years, Mrs. Powell became a large fleshy woman, and physically very stout. She was high spirited and noted through life for her industrious habits, good nature, and splendid social qualities, always entertaining in any circle. The fearful thing known as "The Family Trouble," so called to this day by the descendants, was the plague of her life.

She had borne with great fortitude and womanly courage the afflictions visited upon her, but the story set afloat by parties failing in their investigations, charging her with the authorship of the mystery, after she had submitted to all manner of tests, was crushing to her strong spirit, yet she murmured not, hoping to live down the misrepresentation, and that her innocence would be demonstrated to all intelligent reasonable people, and so it was to the people of Robertson County, acquainted with the facts, but a mischievous lie once set afloat travels far beyond the reach of truth. So it was in her case; wherever the story of the witch had gone among strangers, her name has been coupled with it as the author of those most wonderful demonstrations, and all through her long life the story was frequently revived, which to her was like a canker worm that never ceased torturing; and still she endured it patiently. However, the time came when patience ceased to be a virtue.

About 1849 the Saturday Evening Post, published either at Philadelphia or New York, printed a long sketch of the Bell Witch phenomenon, written by a reporter who made a strenuous effort in the details to connect her with the authorship of the demonstrations. Mrs. Powell was so outraged by the publication that she engaged a lawyer to institute suit for libel. The matter, however, was settled without litigation, the paper retracting the charges, explaining how this version of the story had gained credence, and the fact that at the time the demonstrations commenced Betsy Bell had scarcely advanced from the stage of childhood and was too young to have been capable of originating and practicing so great a deception. The fact also that after this report had gained circulation, she had submitted to any and every test that the wits of detectives could invent to prove the theory, and all the stratagems employed, served only to demonstrate her innocence and utter ignorance of the agency of the so-called witchery, and was herself the greatest sufferer from the affliction.

THE BELL WITCH PROJECT

THE BELL WITCH PROJECT

Chapter 10

NEGRO STORIES

The Experiences of Uncle Dean, the Rail Splitter

Rev. James Byrns, in his graphic sketch, intimates that the Negroes gave the most thrilling accounts of the witch operations, but he seems to regard Negro testimony as unreliable and declines to quote their sayings; on general principles no doubt. But in this the good man is mistaken. He has not studied the Negro character along this line. The colored brother may prevaricate in regard to a chicken roost; he may be extravagant in describing a coon fight; he may dilate humorously on his possum dog; he may spin fine yarns about the golden pavements in the New Jerusalem and the angels sopping possum gravy with ash cakes and "taters;" he may mislead one in regard to the contents of his gourd bottle; he may be weak on the subject of watermelons, and tell fine stories on Bre'r Rabbit sitting in the fence corner picking briars out of his feet, but when it comes to haunts, he is the most reliable witness on earth. The Negro may be off and crooked on some things, but under no circumstance will he tell a lie on a ghost, nor deviate a single hair's breadth from the truth in establishing the existence of the spooks. The purpose of the writer is to go to the bottom of this witch history and give all of the inside facts, and this cannot be done if Sambo is ignored.

No such a history would be complete without the stories of Uncle Dean, the famous rail-splitter, and trusty servant of John Bell, who had many contacts with the witch. Therefore the writer paid a special visit to Aunt Ibby Gunn, who was a servant of Alex. Gunn, and resides at Cedar Hill, Tenn., with her children, happy and cheerful, and at this writing is eighty-six years of age, as appears from the Gunn family record — born October 25, 1806. She was the younger sister of Dean's wife, Kate. They were daughters of Uncle Zeke, a pompous old darkie who belonged to Rev. Thomas Gunn, and felt elevated by the pious and dignified character of his master.

THE BELL WITCH PROJECT

Dean and the Two-Headed Dog Witch

Aunt Ibby is the only survivor of the Negro families who lived in that vicinity in the beginning of the Witch history.

Being approached on the subject she replied: "Course I members bout dar witch, cause it cum wid Dean to see hiz wife, fur she was my sister, an I done want no mo boderation by dem spirits nudder, I dont."

Aunt Ibby was disposed to stop at this. She did not care to discuss haunts, lest the demons might return to disturb her. Being assured, however, that the witch had become very rich and aristocratic, and had long since gone to Europe on a pleasure, trip, promising not to return during her life time, she consented to tell some things that Dean said about it.

"De fust time Dean seed der speritation he sed it appeared like a big black dog, jest trottin long afore him tipity tipity tip, to de door, an den banish. Dean sed how he warnt fraid, but I seed he ware mighty pale; den he tuck to fetchin hiz axe, kase dat dog cum wid him eber time, an den banish, sorter pericatin in der transfiction, jest gwine all ter pieces, risin like sparks when yer chunk der fire. Den hit got to pesterin old Mister Bell so bad, jabbin all der vitals outen hiz mouf wid a stick, Dean was sorter confuscated bout what ter do, cause dat sort uv carrication wuz pecteratin on der appetude, an spoilin er heap of good eatin. Den Kate she tuck and made Dean a witch ball outen her hair, an put in sum spunk, foxfire and such, and some brimstone an camfire, den wrapped hit all ober wid yarn an hair, an gave Dean der ball tu keep der dog frum hurtin him. So der nex night, cumin long der road whistlin he wuz, sumpen said, 'Dean what makes you whistle so lonesum, jest dar away."

Dean sez, "Kase ize gwinter see my wife.' Den hit sez, 'Dean what's dat yous got in yer pocket?' Dean sez, 'Nullin.' Den hit sez, 'Dean you knows dats er lie, kase yous got fox fire wrapped up in yer wife's hair tu pester me. I'll sho you Mr. Smarty you can't congergate me dat way,' jest so.

Dean he got down on hiz knees tu pray. Den hit sez, 'Lord Jesus, Dean, what er fool yer is; done yer know yer can't pray like ole Sugar Mouf? Git up frum dar an sho yer foxfire.' Sez Dean, sez he, just so 'In der name of der Lord what's yer gwine ter do tu me?' Den it sez, 'Cepen you give me dar ball Ise gwine ter turn you tu a hoss an ride you cross der river to der stillhouse.' Den Dean tuck der ball outen hiz pocket, an hit commenced swellin bigger an er fodder stack, an he had ter drap it, he did, an der ball busted an tuck fire, blazin up, an almost stunk hiz bref away, But dat warnt nuffin; dar wuz dar same black dog wid his mouf wide

THE BELL WITCH PROJECT

open grinin jest redy tu jump on im, an Dean he cum down wid hiz axe, he did, and split dar dogs head wide open, an staved der axe clear down in der ground so deep he couldn find it no more. De dog he turned ober an ober three times, kicked, an den jumped up mose outer sight an fell kerflop on dat fox fire, and der ball riz right up an shot off in er blaze like er star. Dean he lit out, he did, and he never stopped till he run agin der door an busted hit wide open, an fell on der floor, pale as er white sheet. For God! Dat nigger's eyes done come clean outen hiz head. Kate she tuck to rubin him wid cam fire an old berdildoc til he cum to his self an told all about this, and der next time Dean seed dat dog, it had two heads."

How Dean Was Turned into a Mule

Dean had another thrilling and most frightful experience with the witches, which he told to Alex. Gunn and others, after relating the same transaction described in Aunt Ibby's interview.

Said he, "I told Kate an Uncle Zeke bout how dat ball tuck fire shootin off wid dat dog after I split his head open, an sartin az your bawned, Mars Alex, but fur dat ball I'd been a gone nigger. Den Kate she tuck an made me a nudder ball an put some other spiritifications in it, cept them what wus in der first ball; some sort er Injun congerations jest like her fader said. Den she told me dat der witch couldn't do nuffin long as I kept dat ball in my pocket; an if I give it up any mo dar wud be der last of me, jest so. Den I tuck der ball in my pocket, I did, feelin pretty certain it was gwinter stay der dis time, an it did. Den sar, Mars Alex, der nex time I went by der wood pile an tuck my axe on my shoulder, cause I depends a heap on my axe, an went along outen der gate whistlin like I didn't care fur nuffin, an goin along up der lane, dar sat dat same black dog wid two heads an both moufs open grinnin at me, he wuz, showin his big white teeth. I sorter stopped, I did, Den sez I, 'In der name of der Lord what's dat?' Jest so, den sumpen sed, 'Dean you can't pass here cepten you give me dat ball in yo pocket,' Jest so, den I membered what Kate an Uncle Zeke said how der witch couldn't do nuffin cepen hit got my ball. Sez I, 'What's yo name?' 'My name is Black Dog; you knows me, you black rascal, cause you's done an split my head open wid yo axe,' Jest so, den sez I, 'I haut got no ball, yo tuck it tudder time.' Den it sez, 'You's a liar Dean, I knows you's done an got er hudder ball worsser dan der fust one, cause you is dun an fetched er whole heap of trouble on me.' Den sez I, 'If you won't lemme pass, I kin go back.' Jest so, den I sorter walked backwards, back, back, back, tel I got clean outen sight, an den turned round ter run. An befo God dar was dar same dog on tudder side wid his mouth wide open. I tells you, Mars Alex, I felt a heep wusser, like I wus kerflumuxed, but it warnt goin to give up, an I jest resolved in my mind to fight it out, cause dar warnt no udder choice. Den sez I, 'What you want?' Jest so, den it sez, 'Cepen you gimme dar ball Ise gwinter turn you to a hoss an ride you ober der river to der still-house.' Den I membered again what Kate an Uncle Zeke said, how dar want no dependence in what a Injun spirit said, an if I give up dat ball I'd be a dead nigger right dar, cause dat ghost ware mad. Den I solved to depend on dat ball and my axe, and sed, 'I aint goin ter give you my ball, an I'll split you clean open tu der tail cepen you git outen my way,' Jest so, den hit sez, 'Say yer prayers Dean, an I commenced gittin weak, an draped my axe, cause I felt er curious spell creepin on me. Den sumpen sed, 'Pick up your axe Dean,' and I stooped ober feelin fur der axe an cudden find it, an cudden git up no mo, an dar I stood on my hands an feet. Den sumpen sed, 'He's tu high behind to tote dubble.' Er hudder sed, 'Dats all right, level im down.' Den sumpen jerked my tail, an I kicked backwards wid one foot an hit fell kerflop in der road. Bout dis time der ole jack brayed an one witch sed, 'Dar, bad luck, dat spoilt der job; he's nuffin but er dam mule.' Tother one said, 'Well, you can't make nuffin but er mule outen er dam nigger, no how.' Den da commenced cussin an fussin bout which one was gwinter ride befo an behind. One says, 'Der mule hant got no main fur sturips an bridle ter hold to, an my arms are too short to catch his ears.' Den da both hopped up; de little witch got on behind an sed, 'Now les ride him to hell fur breakfast.' Den de big witch stretched both hands out an tuck me by der ears, an quicker dan da knowed nuffin, I tucked my head, jumped backwards, an kicked them clean over my back, an sat dem witches down ca-whallup on tudder side of der fence in der field, an I tuck out and went taren up der lane, an never stopped runnin tell I got to Kate's door an commenced pawin till I pawed der door open, an there sat Kate mendin my old britches, an seein her by der light it tuck der spell off, and I was myself again. I tells you, Mars Alex, but fur Kate's hair ball dem witches would of rid me all night, an where wud I be now? When I heard dem talkin bout ridin me to hell fur breakfast I was der most scared mule you eber seed, cause it appeared like a mighty long rocky road down hill for me ter tote double an skip in before sun up. Den I didn't know bout cumin back any mo. Den what wud I look like walkin round dar among gentlemen wid my ole rail-splitin clothes on? What would ole master say when he got up an found me missin? I tells you, Mars Alex, it ware a mighty solemn confusion what perigated round my prehension bout dat time."

How Dean Got His Head Busted

There are many persons still living in Robertson County who remember Uncle Dean. He lived to a very old age, and was noted throughout the surrounding country as the famous rail-splitter, a distinction which he was very proud of, though it did not elect him to the presidency of the United States. However, had he lived in later years, he might have walked Abraham Lincoln's log. The Negroes and children in the neighbor hood delighted in gathering around the old darkie to hear his hair-raising witch stories. Dean carried a prominent scar on his forehead, which gave his physiognomy a very conspicuous cast. A good lady connected with the Bell family, describing Dean to the writer, says he declared to the day of his death that this scar was caused by an unpleasant contact with "Kate," the witch, in which he was knocked in the head with a big stick.

Dean was a great possum hunter. Autumn came in all of its glory. The luscious persimmon was ripe, and possums fat and plentiful, and Dean's heart panted for the woods, as did his appetite long for "possum and taters." His mind was bent on a round with the "varmints," but a very serious dilemma was presented in the contemplation of the sport. His experience with "Black Dog" warned him of the danger in venturing out without his witch ball, and it was certain that no game could be found if he carried it; no dog could trail a possum after catching the scent of a witch ball. So it was, Dean turned the matter over and over in his mind, and kept a sharp lookout for "Kate."

He determined to make use of the first favorable opportunity that presented. Finally the time came. Hearing the Witch in the house carrying on at a great rate with the visitors, he concluded that was the opportunity to make a short round, and return before "Kate" adjourned the meeting. So he swung his axe over his shoulder, whistled to old Caesar and struck out. Next morning Dean was missing, and Mr. Bell was very uneasy for a time, but soon after breakfast he showed up with a great gash in his cranium and was very bloody.

"What's the matter now Dean?" inquired Mr. Bell.

"De witch dun had me for a fact, ole mars, an for God's sake, it liked ter killed me, it did. Cepten fur thinken bout whose gwinter split der rails, I specs that I'd of given up. Cause I knowed dar warn't gwinter be no mo rails split here cepten I done it. Dats all dat saved me sar, fur a fact it was."

"How did it happen Dean?" again inquired Mr. Bell.

"Well ole mars, Ise gwinter to tell der truf bout it, dar I iz. For God sake, it was jest dis way. I heard de ole witch in der house speakin wid de white folks bout religion. Den I concluded it was a mighty good time ter go out an kotch er possum fur dinner Sunday, supposin I cud git back before de witch knowed it. So I slips off round der field, an directly old Caesar he treed a big possum up on top of dat high stump side of der fence. I jest left him dar, cause I knowed he warn't gwinter git away from ole Caesar. Den I tuck an cut down a little saplin bout six foot long, an split one end of it, den tuck der possum down an pull his tail through der split, an layed him down ter git my axe. Den I hears sumpen cummin down other side of de fence, tipity tipity tip, tipity tipity tip, and der next ting I knowed, dar stood a great big ole rabbit, an Caesar he tuck out he did. Den I knowed sumpen war gwinter happen, cause dar dog neber lef me fo dis. Den de old rabbit said, 'Hello, Kernel Possum, what's all er dat ornamentation you got on yer tail?' Jest so, den der possum said, "Oh Kernel Rabbit, Ise so glad yous cum; dis aint no ornamentation, hit am er split stick Dean put on my tail to keep me from gittin away. Oh it am hurtin so bad. Please Kernel take hit off.' Den Kernel Rabbit, he said, 'Why aint you like me, Kernel Possum; don't hab no tail, den de niggers cant put split stick on yer.' Den Kernel Possum sed, 'If I done hab no tail like you, how's I gwinter hold on to der limbs an shake simmons down fur you? 'Dats so, sez Kernel Rabbit, jest take er way. 'Den Kernel Rabbit he commenced swellin like blowin up like a bladder, tell he got bigger den Mars Frank Miles an he tuck holt of dat stick and jerked der split wide open, he did, an told Kernel Possum to go on an shake dat simmon tree. Den he turned round to me, Kernel Rabbit did, an sez, 'Dean, I'll learn you sum sense bout puttin er poor possum's tail in der split stick. Next thing you'll be twisten all of my hide off tu get me outen de hollow.' Den he hit me kerwhack on der head wid dat stick, an I knowed nuffin mo til sun up."

This explanation satisfied "old mars," and he told Dean to go to Aunt Chloe and let her bandage his head, and lay up until he got well, and hereafter always wrap the possum's tail around his thumb and carry it in his hand, and never draw another one through the split of a stick. From that day to this, no one in this part of the country has been guilty of the barbarous act of drawing a "po" possum's tail through the split of a stick, or of twisting a rabbit out of a hole.

THE BELL WITCH PROJECT

Chapter 11

Gen. Andrew Jackson

Remarkable and Amusing Incidents Attending the Great Soldier and Statesman's Visit to the Witch, and Other Reminiscences

Col. Thomas L. Yancey, a prominent lawyer of the Clarksville, Tenn., bar, who is closely related to the Fort family, was raised in the Bell settlement, and has been familiar with the stories of the witch as told by different witnesses from his youth up, contributes the following interesting sketch from notes taken with a view to writing the history. In addition to the visit of Gen. Jackson and party, it will be observed that he confirms the statements of three other parties in regard to Dr. Sugg's experience:

CLARKSVILLE, TENN.

JAN. 1, 1894

M. E INGRAM - DEAR SIR:

In answer to your inquiry as to what I know about the Bell Witch excitement of many years ago, I will state that I was born within four miles of the John Bell home, where the witch is said to have disported itself to the terror of many good and pious souls. While quite a young man I became much interested in the stories my relatives and other people told in regard to the phenomenon, which I had heard repeated from my earliest recollection, and ambitious in my youth to discover the cause and write a history of the affair, I determined to enter into the investigation, and did some forty years ago undertake the matter, gathering many amusing and strange incidents, but not sufficiently connected and authenticated to justify my purpose. I soon learned that Williams Bell was the only person who had kept a diary of what transpired, and had written the facts, leaving the manuscript with his wife or some member of his family at his death. Of course I was anxious to get the paper, and not being acquainted with Williams Bell's widow, I applied to Squire John Bell, Jr., to know if such manuscript was in existence, and if it could be had for publication. He informed me that his brother had written the facts, etc., regarding the mystery, and that Washington Lowe, a lawyer of Springfield, had applied for it and been refused. He thought, however, he could induce his brother's family to let him have it, and promised to intercede for me. Some time after this he told me that he could not get it, that the family refused to let him or any one have it, and after this I gave up the purpose of writing a book and pursued the investigation no further.

However, I remember some very graphic stories told by the old people who visited the scene often, stated as having absolutely occurred, and told in all seriousness by persons whose veracity I could not doubt. My grandfather, Whitmel Fort, told me that he visited the place often during the excitement, meeting with many persons from a distance who came to investigate the witch. Grandfather said he could in no way account for the phenomena. There was no doubt of the fact that some thing persecuted Miss Betsy Bell terribly after she retired to bed. He went with others to her relief amid her outcries of agony, and they all could not hold the bed covering on her, so powerful was the unseen object in pulling it off. Even could this have been accounted for, the keen ringing sound like that of a hand slapping her jaws when she would scream with pain, and the deep red splotches left on her cheeks, were mysterious beyond comprehension.

Grandfather Fort also told me the story of Gen. Jackson's visit to the witch, which was quite amusing to me. The crowds that gathered at Bell's, many coming a long distance, were so large that the house would not accommodate the company. Mr. Bell would not accept any pay for entertaining, and the imposition on the family, being a constant thing, was so apparent, that parties were made up and went prepared for camping out. So Gen. Jackson's party came from Nashville with a wagon loaded with a tent, provisions, etc., bent on a good time and much fun investigating the witch. The men were riding on horseback and were following along in the rear of the wagon as they approached near the place, discussing the matter and planning how they were going to do up the witch, if it made an exhibition of such pranks as they had heard of. Just then, within a short distance of the house, traveling over a smooth level piece of road, the wagon halted and stuck fast.

The driver popped his whip, whooped and shouted to the team, and the horses pulled with all of their might, but could not move the wagon an inch. It was dead stuck as if welded to the earth. Gen. Jackson commanded all men to dismount and put their shoulders to the wheels and give the wagon a push. The order was promptly obeyed. The driver laid on the lash and the horses and men did their best, making repeated efforts, but all in vain; it was no go. The wheels were then taken off, one at a time, and examined and found to be all right, revolving easily on the axles. Another trial was made to get away, the driver whipping up the team while the men pushed at the wheels, and still it was no go. All stood off looking at the wagon in serious meditation, for they were "stuck." Gen. Jackson after a few moments thought, realizing that they were in a fix, threw up his hands exclaiming, "By the eternal, boys, it is the witch." Then came the sound of a sharp metallic voice from the bushes, saying, "All right General, let the wagon move on, I will see you again tonight." The men in bewildered astonishment looked in every direction to see if they could discover from whence came the strange voice, but could find no explanation to the mystery. Gen. Jackson exclaimed again, "By the eternal, boys, this is worse than fighting the British." The horses then started unexpectedly of their own accord, and the wagon rolled along as light and smoothly as ever. Jackson's party was in no good frame of mind for camping out that night, notwithstanding one of the party was a professional "witch layer," and boasted much of his power over evil spirits, and was taken along purposely to deal with Kate, as they called the witch. The whole party went to the house for quarters and comfort, and Mr. Bell, recognizing the distinguished character of the leader of the party, was lavishing in courtesies and entertainment. But Gen. Jackson was out with the boys for fun and "witch hunting" was one of them for the time. They were expecting Kate to put in an appearance according to promise, and they chose to set in a room by the light of a tallow candle waiting for the witch. The witch layer had a big flintlock army or horse pistol, loaded with a silver bullet, which he held steady in hand, keeping a close lookout for Kate.

He was a brawny man, with long hair, high cheekbones, hawk-bill nose and fiery eyes. He talked much, entertaining the company with details of his adventures, and exhibitions of undaunted courage and success in overcoming witches. He exhibited the tip of a black cat's tail, about two inches, telling how he shot the cat with a silver bullet while sitting on a bewitched woman's coffin, and by stroking that cat's tail on his nose it would flash a light on a witch the darkest night that ever come; the light, however, was not visible to any one but a magician. The party was highly entertained by the vain stories of this dolt. They flattered his vanity and encouraged his conceit, laughed at his stories, and called him sage, Apollo, oracle, wiseacre, etc. Yet there was an expectancy in the minds of all left from the wagon experience, which made the mage's stories go well, and all kept wide awake till a late hour, when they became weary and drowsy, and rather tired of hearing the warlock detail his exploits. Old Hickory was the first one to let off tension. He commenced yawning and twisting in his chair. Leaning over he whispered to the man nearest him, "Sam, I'll bet that fellow is an arrant coward. By the eternals, I do wish the thing would come, I want to see him run." The General did not have long to wait. Presently perfect quiet reigned, and then was heard a noise like dainty footsteps prancing over the floor, and quickly following, the same metallic voice heard in the bushes rang out from one corner of the room, exclaiming, "All right, General, I am on hand ready for business."

And then addressing the witch layer, "Now, Mr. Smarty, here I am, shoot." The seer stroked his nose with the cat's tail, leveled his pistol, and pulled the trigger, but it failed to fire. "Try again," exclaimed the witch, which he did with the same result. "Now its my turn; lookout, you old coward, hypocrite, fraud. I'll teach you a lesson." The next thing a sound was heard like that of boxing with the open hand, whack, whack, and the Oracle tumbled over like lightning had struck him, but he quickly recovered his feet and went capering around the room like a frightened steer, running over every one in his way, yelling, "Oh my nose, my nose, the devil has got me. Oh Lordy! He's got me by the nose." Suddenly, as if by its own accord, the door flew open and the witch layer dashed out, and made a beeline for the lane at full speed, yelling every jump. Everybody rushed out under the excitement, expecting the man would be killed, but as far as they could hear up the lane, he was still running and yelling, "Oh Lordy." Jackson, they say, dropped down on the ground and rolled over and over, laughing. "By the eternal, boys, I never saw so much fun in all my life. This beats fighting the British." Presently the witch was on hand and joined in the laugh. "Lord Jesus," it exclaimed, "How the old devil did run and beg; I'll bet he won't come here again with his old horse pistol to shoot me. I guess that's fun enough for tonight, General, and you can go to bed now. I will come tomorrow night and show you another rascal in this crowd." Old Hickory was anxious to stay a week, but his party had enough of that thing. No one knew whose turn would come next, and no inducements could keep them. They spent the next night in Springfield, and returned to Nashville the following day.

There was much talk about the witch shaking hands with one of the Johnson's, a near neighbor, and Patrick McGowin, a highly esteemed Irishman, who lived across the line in Montgomery County, and had refused to shake hands with all other persons, for the reason, as was stated the witch said, thee two men were honest and truthful and could be trusted when they promised not to try to hold or squeeze its hand. I knew Mr. McGowen well, who was then getting to be quite an old man, and knew he was cautious, prudent and perfectly reliable in all he said. This was his general character, and I went to see him expressly to hear his own statement about the mat ter. We discussed the witch and the many mysterious stories in regard to the occurrences at Bell's, which he could in no way account

THE BELL WITCH PROJECT

for. I asked him particularly about the handshaking.

The old gentleman talked about it with some reluctance. He said the witch did offer to shake hands with him, but he was not sure it could be called a handshaking. He held out his hand for that purpose, and felt something in his hand, which felt like a hairy substance. Calvin John son described that which he felt, like unto a woman's hand.

Dr. Henry Sugg was a man of great prominence in that community. He was quite a small boy during the reign of the witch, and of course never witnessed the early demonstration; and growing up skeptical, did not believe the stories told by the older people. He was disposed to ridicule the whole matter when spoken of, and he heard much about it in his practice among the sick. The old Bell house was torn down after the death of the old people, and moved to the place near Brown's ford, now owned by Levi Smith. It was also said that when the witch took its departure, it promised to return after a certain number of years and remain permanently, and this many people believed. This brings me to Dr. Sugg's statement which I had from his own lips. He was called to see a patient at this house, some thirty years after the witch first disappeared, or in the fifties. If I mistake not, he said Joel Bell lived there or owned the place. Anyway, the subject of the Bell Witch came up, and the man told about the strange noise heard and ridiculous things that had occurred the night before, and said he was sure that it was the Bell Witch. Dr. Sugg laughed at the man and told him it was all imagination, that the Bell Witch was a hoax and there never was anything in it, ridiculing his superstition. Just then he heard a terrible rattling of the vials in his medical bag, setting on the floor near the door, where he had placed the pocket as he entered the house, and immediately following the rattling noise came the sound of explosion, as if every bottle in the valise had burst or the corks all popped out.

He rushed immediately to the pockets to see what had happened, and found everything intact, just as it should be. Then it was the other man's turn to ridicule him. He, however, tried to explain the phenomena to the satisfaction of the superstitious man, and while doing so the same sound was repeated with still greater force, and the second examination discovered nothing wrong or out of place in the valise, and, said he, "I could find no explanation for the mystery, and never have; it was so remarkable and unmistakable that there could be no explanation."

Mrs. Wimberly, who was a daughter of Mat. Ligon, told me about the visit of Betsy Bell to her father's on the occasion when the witch followed and abused her dreadfully, boxing her jaws, pinching her arms and pulling her hair, calling her ugly names, for trying to run away from it. Ligon's family got no rest that night, and were terribly frightened. I could tell you many other stories in regard to this unexplained mystery, but no doubt you have them all from the statement of Williams Bell and others.

T. L. YANCEY

THE BELL WITCH PROJECT

Chapter 12

Theny Thorn

Reminiscences from the Girl Who Associated Most with Betsy Bell

Mrs. Lucinda E. Rawls, of Clarksville, Tenn., widow of the late J. J. Rawls, and daughter by the marriage of David Alexander Gooch and Partheny Thorn, contributes the following graphic interview from the reminiscences of her mother and other things connected with the exciting events of the Bell Witch history, and the effect and influence upon the community. Theny Thorn was born in 1803. Her parents lived in Stewart County, and died while she was quite a small child, too young to remember them. She was a niece of Jane Marvlin, who possessed considerable property, and became the second wife of James Johnson, father of John and Calvin by his first marriage. Mr. Johnson and second wife had no children, and they adopted Theny Thorn and raised her from a child, loving her as their own bestowing much care and devotion upon her, and she knew them only as father and mother, and Mrs. Rawls alluded to the old people most affectionately as grandfather and grandmother. Mrs. Rawls very cheerfully granted this interview, and said she was willing to state anything she knew personally or that which she had heard repeated by her mother, Grandfather James Johnson, John and Calvin Johnson, Dr. Ardra Gooch, John Bell, Jr., and many others concerning the Bell Witch.

It was, she says, a common subject of discussion in all family circles and neighborhood gatherings from her childhood up to the time she left the neighborhood in 1855, and she has rarely failed to hear the mystery spoken of on her visits to that vicinity since. "Yes," replied Mrs. Rawls, in answer to certain questions, "the Bell Witch was, and is still, a great scapegoat. Every circumstance out of the regular order of things is attributed to the witch. It has not been long since a man claiming to be the witch was waylaid and murdered by two men who were cleared, on the plea that the murdered man had bewitched them."

THE BELL WITCH PROJECT

"Mother was very intimate with Betsy Bell," continued Mrs. Rawls, "and sympathized deeply with her in the trouble and affliction brought upon her by the wicked thing. It not only punished her severely, but frightened the poor girl almost out of her life, and mother stayed with her the more on this account to relieve her fears; in fact, her parents were afraid to leave her in her room alone a single night, and mother stayed with her almost every night, except when Becky Porter was there. It was very cruel in some people, she said, to charge the awful thing against Betsy.

She was only twelve or thirteen years of age when the demonstrations commenced. She was a very tender, sweet girl, and was constantly under the gentle watch care of her mother, and never had an opportunity or any chance to learn such an art, if it were possible, and it was not in her nature to do so, nor could she have possibly escaped detection. Those who accused her could never state a reason or offer a shadow of evidence to that effect. The persecutions of the witch were enough for any frail mortal to bear, (more than her father could bear) without the slanderous charges of ignorant men who were incapable of discerning the cause, to crush her hope in life."

Question: Mrs. Rawls, did you ever hear your mother state in what particular way the witch annoyed Betsy?

Answer: "Yes, repeatedly; in every conceivable way and form imaginable. It would not let a bit of cover stay on the bed. It would pinch the girl till she would scream, slap her checks, pull her hair, stick pins in her body, and sometimes almost take her breath. Mother said it would seem to jerk the tucking comb out of her hair and dash it on the floor. You know that the girls in those days put up their hair with long tooth combs, instead of hair pins as now used. The combs were generally made of tortoise shell, which were ornamented and were pretty and costly, and easily broken by dropping on the floor, and strange as it appears, mother said Betsy never had one broken, though they struck the floor as if thrown with force. Mother said she had seen this trick performed often when looking directly at Betsy, and knew she did not move her hands and no visible hand or cause could be detected. Betsy had a fine suit of long flaxen hair, which hung in beautiful waves that made her appear most charming, and she was very proud of it. When the tuckers were pulled out, her hair would drop all about her neck and shoulders and become so tangled that it would require a full half hour's time to comb it out.

Then the witch would break out with hilarious laughter, 'Ha, ha, Betsy, if Josh could see you now he would envy me.' It carried on such mischief nearly all night, pulling the cover from the bed as fast as they could replace it, knocking over the chairs and keeping up a continual gabbing of nonsensical talk and laughter, and they were compelled to gas with the invisible thing through fear of something worse. Mother said she had spent many nights with no one else but Betsy and herself in the room, with doors and windows securely closed, and all efforts to detect the agency of these demonstrations or the source from whence came the remarkable voice, were in vain. Another favorite trick of the witch was that of tampering with Betsy's shoes. Mother said she had seen the strings tied so tight that the girl could not loose the knot, and the next minute the shoes would be unlaced and jerked from her feet. Sometimes when preparing to retire, the witch would exclaim, 'Betsy let me unlace your shoes and in a second her shoes would be pulled from her feet. Mother said she asked the witch why it would not unlace and remove her shoes, and the reply would come, 'I don't like you Theny, you are so silly; I don't want anything to do with you!'"

Question: Did you ever hear your mother repeat the circumstance of the four-leaf clover, which has been so generally spoken of?

Answer: "Yes, I have heard her tell it frequently to different persons. That occurred in this way. There were a number of young people in company, discussing the witch. Some one remarked that according to the saying, if any one could find a four-leaf clover they would be able to see the witch. Clover, you know, uniformly has three leaves, and it is very rare that four leaves are found. However, mother paid a visit to the Misses Pacely, daughters of Tanner Pacely, near Russellville, Ky. The girls were out one evening for a walk, and while strolling through a field, mother discovered a clover with four leaves, which she pulled, placing it in the front fold of her dress without calling any attention to it, intending carrying the clover home to try her luck, and not one discovered her action or purpose; nor did she mention the fact to a soul, lest people would think her superstitious, and silly. She returned home the next day with the clover in the bosom of her dress.

It was late in the afternoon when she arrived, and very soon 'Kate,' as they called the witch, exclaimed, 'Lord Jesus, Theny, what a fool you have made of yourself; you went all the way to old man Pacely's to hunt a four leaf clover and brought it home secretly in your bosom, believing that it would enable you to see me, but you will never be smart enough for that, ha, ha, ha,' and so it went on teasing mother, and telling the joke to every one who came in."

Question: Did the witch stay regularly at James Johnson's?

THE BELL WITCH PROJECT

Answer: "No, it only visited grandfather's occasionally, as it did several other places. Grandfather was a very devout Christian, and a very zealous worker in the Methodist Church. He made it a rule through life to hold family worship before retiring at night, and often the neighbors would gather in and have prayer meetings at his house. The witch was generally present on such occasions, and during prayers would thump and scratch on the chairs and do other mischief, and would tell the folks at Bell's, 'I went to hear "Old Sugar Mouth" pray last night; Lord Jesus, how good he did get.' It called grandfather 'Old Sugar Mouth.' It also visited the family at other times, and would talk about any and everything, discuss the Scriptures, and gossip about the affairs of the country. Grand father said it seemed to know everything that was transpiring. Uncle John Johnson was at Mr. Bell's during the last day of the old gentleman's illness.

I heard him tell the circumstances of finding a strange vial of medicine in the cupboard that no one could account for or tell what was in the vial. The witch said it put the vial there for Old Jack, and had given him a dose to kill him. There were several men present, who had called in to see Mr. Bell, and hearing this, some one advised John Bell, Jr., to test the medicine on a cat. He did so, giving the cat a very small portion, which threw it into convulsions instantly. The cat squalled, whirled around and died in a few minutes. Drew Bell had gone out before the vial was discovered, to direct the hands about some work on the place, and the first that Drew heard of the matter was from the witch. The very moment Drew returned, Kate commenced, 'Drew, John found that vial of medicine I put in the cupboard for Old Jack, and gave the cat some of it. Lord Jesus, how it did make that cat squall, jump up, turn over and die.'"

Question: Mrs. Rawls, did you ever hear your mother speak of the exploits of magicians or conjurers who came along?

Answer: "Yes, there were ever so many witch doctors during the time working incantations and magic arts, but with no avail. They were a great set of frauds. One or two I have in mind, and one who thought he had succeeded to a wonderful degree. One of these wizards notified the Bell family that he would be there on a certain day to kill the witch, and instructed that two silver dollars be concealed in a certain form or way, to make bullets, as he would be able to see the thing and shoot it with a silver bullet. The Bells tried everything suggested, no matter what it was, that looked to the discovery of the plague, and the money was hidden away in the cupboard as directed, and it was not suspected that the witch would know anything about it.

The conjurer, however, failed to come, and Kate then told them all about the arrangement, laughing heartily, and told them that they had better take that money out of the cupboard and put it to some better use. On another occasion a witch doctor insisted that he could relieve Betsy of the spell if she would take his medicine, and she readily agreed to take his prescription. Mother remonstrated with Betsy against taking the awful dose, but she persisted that she would take anything that anybody would give her, even if it was poison, to get rid of her excruciating pest, and so she did swallow it down. It very soon made her deathly sick, as the conjurer promised it would, and immediately a copious evacuation of the stomach followed.

The excrement was examined and found to be literally full of pins and needles, and Kate, the witch, fairly roared with laughter, and said that fellow was the only conjurer who had ever done any good. He had made Betsy throw up pins and needles enough to supply the whole community, and if he would give her another dose of that stuff, he would get enough to set up a pin and needle store. The witch doctor really believed that the pins and needles were ejected from the girl's stomach, and was astounded by the result of his own practice. There could be no mistake that they were real brass pins and needles. Mother gathered up a number and kept them as long as she lived. I have seen the pins and needles myself.

As a matter of course Betsy could not have lived with such a conglomeration in her stomach, and the only solution of the matter was that the witch dropped the pins and needles in the excrement unobserved; just as it pulled off her shoes, disheveled her hair, gave her and her mother hazelnuts, and many other miraculous performances that no one could ever account for."

Question: Mrs. Rawls, did you know Mrs. Kate Batts, or ever hear her name discussed in connection with the witchery?

Answer: "Yes, Mrs. Kate Batts lived many years after the death of John Bell and wife; after I was quite grown. She was very odd in her ways, original, having many funny sayings, and was the common talk of the neighborhood. I remember that she caused me to get an awful scolding from father for laughing at her on a certain occasion. It was during a protracted meeting at Red River Church. Rev. Thomas Felts had concluded a revival sermon that aroused the entire audience, and had called up the mourners, who were kneeling at the front seat as usual, praying, when Mrs. Batts came in and spread her riding skirt over Joe Edwards, who was a mourner, and sat down on him. The scene was so ludicrous that I could not restrain myself, and with several other girls, we got into a great titter.

THE BELL WITCH PROJECT

The efforts of the brethren to get her up, her refusal to rise, and quaint expressions, made the matter worse, and the whole house burst into laughter. It was enough to make an angel laugh, and I just had to tell father that he was too sanctimonious for heaven. Mrs. Batts had but three children. Mary, her only daughter, was a beautiful girl, very sprightly and lovely. Her sons, both mature men, were quite to the contrary. John was married; Calvin tall and very awkward. Mrs. Batts thought Calvin the finest young man in the country, and had a peculiar way of introducing and commending him to society, by pushing her self into company, remarking, 'Girls, keep your eyes on Calvin; he is all warp ready for the filling.'"

"You ask me what people thought of Mrs. Batts in connection with the witchery. The truth is some people firmly believed that she was the witch, and was afraid of her. Seventy-five years ago people were not very distantly removed from the age of witchcraft. Educational facilities were limited. People relied on the country school teacher and the preacher, and as a matter of fact superstition was abroad in the land. People accepted the teaching of the Scriptures literally, and those familiar with the Bible could quote freely in support of the doctrine of witchcraft. The whole country was excited by the wonderful performances of the Bell Witch, and people unable to discover any cause or agency for such exhibitions, naturally attributed it to witchery, and there was no better scapegoat than Mrs. Kate Batts, because it fitted her character so well. The witch, in the first instance, gave out the information that it was "Old Kate Batts' Witch." It was said that John Bell had a misunderstanding with Mrs. Batts in some trading between them soon after he came to the country. Mrs. Batts got very mad, said hard things, and made threats that she would get even with him.

Again it was said that Mrs. Batts was constantly on the pad from house to house, always wanting to buy wool rolls or sell something, and begged every woman she met with for a pin. These with many other circumstances led superstitious people to believe that she was a witch. Those who gave the matter intelligent consideration and investigation, though failing on every hypothesis for an explanation of the mystery, did not believe Mrs. Batts capable of performing such tricks. But to give you some idea of the extent and character of the superstition that prevailed, I will state two or three circumstances. The fact that Mrs. Batts was always begging pins was regarded as a direct circumstance against her, because the witch also had a weak ness for pins, and used them quite freely on Betsy Bell and the witch doctors, and pins were frequently found in the bed pillows, stuck from the inside of the pillow case with points out, and sometimes found in the chairs, and the saying was that the witch had power over any one who gave her pins. Again I remember, on the occasion of Mrs. Batts' death, the news soon spread all over the country, and it was difficult to find any lady who was willing to set up one night with the corpse, as was customary. Finally Fannie Sory volunteered to pay this respect to the dead if three or four other girls would join her and the company was then made up. After the burial next day, those girls told that they were beset with black cats and black dogs all night. One of them vowed to me that it was every word true, and she could prove it by the other girls.

Two of the girls went to the well during the night for fresh water, and said they had to fight dogs with sticks all the way from the house to the well —large black curly haired dogs. The yard was full, while the house was full of black cats, constantly jumping on the coffin. This was undoubtedly a bit of wicked mischief on the part of the girls, practicing on the superstition of people, and many believed every word of it. Doubtless there were one or two black dogs belonging to the place, and like as many black cats, as cats and dogs were generally plentiful about every place.

Another circumstance that occurred previous to the old lady's death: Emily Paine had the task of churning one morning. She was in a great hurry to get through, and after churning two hours, and the butter failing to come, her patience gave out, and she remarked that she just knew old Kate Batts had bewitched the milk, and she was going to burn her. She set the churn of milk aside and heated an iron poker red hot, and stuck it down in the churn, leaving it there, saying she was determined to find out if Mrs. Batts was burnt, and at once made some excuse for calling on the old lady. Sure enough Mrs. Batts was nursing a sore hand, which she said was burnt that morning. This confirmed the case beyond a doubt. I have heard Mrs. Paine, Emily's mother, tell this story and laugh. Emily Paine afterwards married Henry Calhoon."

The Murder

The murder referred to by Mrs. Rawls was the killing of a man named Smith, by Thomas Clinard and Richard Burgess; which occurred at a railroad crossing, between Springfield and Cedar Hill about 1875 or '76. Smith came into the community a stranger, and was employed by Mr. Fletcher, where Clinard and Burgess were also engaged on the farm. Smith professed to be something of a wizard, or rather boasted of his power to hypnotize and lay spells on people, subjecting any one who came under his influence to his will, and it was reported that he claimed to have derived this power from the mantle of the Bell Witch.

However, the writer interviewed Hon. John F. House, who was council for the defense, on the subject, who says that no such evidence was produced in the trial, but that the lawyers handled the Bell Witch affair for all that it was worth in the defense of their clients, presenting the analogy or similarity of circumstances with good effect on the jury. The evidence was overwhelming to the effect that Smith did practice hypnotism or some such art on the defendants, and had them completely under his control and practiced on their fears with dire threats, and made the them do many foolish things that they detested, and they could not escape his dogging influence that subjected them to ridicule. They tried to evade and shun Smith, and for this he chided and threatened them; consequently the animosity, and they planed his murder and waylaid and shot him to death, and then surrendered to the legal authorities, standing trial on a plea of self-defense and were cleared.

It was one of the most interesting cases that ever came before the courts of this country, and the entire community acquiesced in the decision of the court. No doubt that the young men owe their escape from the fearful rigor of the law to the powerful pleadings and matchless eloquence of Col. House, who has so often distinguished himself as a great orator, lawyer and philanthropist.

THE BELL WITCH PROJECT

Chapter 13

RECOLLECTIONS

HON. JOHN D. TYLER VISITED THE WITCH

Having heard the name of Hon. John D. Tyler mentioned as one of the investigators, the writer called on Judge Charles W. Tyler, of Clarksville, Tenn., to know if he ever heard his distinguished father speak of the mystery.

"Yes," said he, "I have heard my father tell many wonderful things that occurred at Bell's about the time he moved to this county from Virginia. I remember that he said reports concerning the mysterious affair reached Virginia before he left that State, and his friends laughed and ridiculed him for moving to a haunted country. But of course he paid no attention to such jeers and jests, for he did not believe the story. But when he arrived here, which was in the Fall of 1818, he found great excitement prevailing all over the country and he joined in with others, visiting the place to investigate the cause. I shall not undertake to detail any statements that my father made in regard to what he saw and heard on these occasions; but you can refer to me for the fact that he did state that he investigated the matter to his full satisfaction; having entered upon the investigation deeply impressed that the demonstrations were made by members of the family, and he pursued his inquiry along this line, making every test possible, and became thoroughly convinced that no member of the family had anything to do with it, and further than that, the mystery to him was never solved.

Judge Tyler is so well known in Tennessee, that the mention of his name is sufficient for home people. But for the information of those in other sections, we will state that he is a citizen of Clarksville, Tenn., County Financier, and Judge of the County and Criminal Court, which positions he has held eighteen years by the suffrage of the people. His father, Hon. John D. Tyler, was one of the most eminent educators known in this country in early days. He served one or two terms in the State Senate, and was prominent in all public affairs, as he was widely known as a man of high intelligence, and distinguished for his thoroughness in everything he undertook. There is no question that he entered upon the investigation with the determination to discover the cause if possible, but gave it up after satisfying himself of his mistake regarding the connection of any member of the family with the affair.

The writer made a special visit during July, 1892, to Cedar Hill, Tenn., for the purpose of interviewing Mrs. Mahala Darden, one of the most estimable ladies of Robertson county, then eighty-five of age. Mrs. Darden resides with her son, Charles Darden, a prosperous farmer, two miles from Cedar Hill. She is the pride and delight of the family, and a mother to be proud of. Mrs. Darden retains to a remarkable degree her physical strength and activity, while her memory is so clear and bright that she details incidents of her girlhood with the greatest accuracy, giving dates and circumstances, and altogether she is one of the most intelligent and entertaining ladies in the county, loved and venerated as mother by the entire community. After some pleasant conversation, the subject of the Bell Witch was broached.

"Yes," replied the good lady, "I have a very distinct recollection of the prevailing excitement during, the witch period. There never was any thing like it; people talked about nothing else, and a great many went to hear it; Mr. Bell's house was full of people almost constantly."

Did you witness any of the witch demonstrations, Mrs. Darden? "Oh, no; I was rather too young. Parents did not think it prudent to take their children, especially girls. Moreover, I had no desire to go at that time."

Will you tell what you know about John Bell and his family, and all about the witch, as you heard the story from the old people? "Certainly. John Bell was a fine looking gentleman, a man of distinguished appearance, and was one of the wealthiest men in the country. He always had plenty of money, and was very prosperous. He was also popular and highly respected by the people. I remember distinctly the first time I ever saw Mr. Bell, and how he impressed me. It was in 1817. My father, James Byrns, was a magistrate, living then several miles from John Bell's. Mr. Bell came to my father's one day with quite a number of men to attend a trial or some law business before my father. His commanding appearance was so marked as to distinguish him over all others, and impress me with his presence. I was then ten years old, and had learned to spin. Work was creditable to a girl in those days, and especially was it a mark of distinction for one of my years to become an expert in handling the cards and spinning wheel, and I was very proud of it. Well, I had the wheel out in the middle of the floor, making it fairly whiz. I had set in for a big day's work, expecting much praise from mother at night, and the men soon crowded the house so full that father told me I would have to move my wheel out and give up the spinning. I did so, and went to help mother about other things.

Dinner was prepared for the company, and when I went in to notify father that dinner was ready, I noticed that all rose up for the invitation except Mr. Bell, who shook his head declining. Father extended him the second invitation, which he still declined, shaking his head. Some remarks were made at the table about his refusal. He seemed depressed, confused and sullen. Mr. Bell returned on the following day, riding four or five miles, telling father that he came expressly to apologize and explain his conduct on the previous day, lest he (my father) should take offense for his refusal to dine. 'All of a sudden,' said he, 'my tongue became strangely affected. Some thing that felt like a fungus growth came on both sides, pressing against my jaws, filling my mouth so that I could not eat or talk.' It was said that Mr. Bell was affected in this way off and on to his death. Nothing, however, was known at this time of the Bell witch trouble; at least, was not known outside of the family. Soon after this my father moved to a farm near Mr. Bell's, and the two families became intimate.

The first I heard of the witch, was told as a secret, said to have leaked out through young John Bell, who told an intimate friend that something strange and very troublesome was disturbing the family. I was about twelve years old when the witch excitement reached its highest tension. My father went frequently to witness the mystery. The first time he heard it, the noise was like that of ducks fluttering and washing in a pond of water. He described many strange things which occurred after that. Mrs. Lucy Bell told me about the witch bringing her grapes and hazelnuts, and emptying the sugar out of the bowl on the hearth, and many other things. They were wonderful tricks, but I could not disbelieve Mrs. Bell. David Darden said he determined in his own mind one night to outdo the witch. He wrapped the cover of his bed around his hand, and held with all his might, but the witch stripped the bed in spite of him. When it visited Mr. Porter's it made a noise like a log of wood falling on the house. The witch told at Mr. Bells that it intended visiting every family in the neighborhood, and did visit many as reported, but never came to my father's that I know of, and I was in constant dread, fearing it would come. Mrs. Bartlett said she was there one night when many persons were waiting to hear the witch talk.

Finally a rapping or noise was heard just outside, and several went to the door to see what it was, when the witch laughed out, exclaiming, 'Oh it's nothing but Old Caesar lapping out of the bath tub.' Old Caesar was the dog. I heard a good deal of laughter about a trick it played on Drew Bell. Drew leaned his chair back against the bureau, which set against the wall, placing his feet on the rounds. Instantly the bureau was snatched from behind him and Drew tumbled down on the floor. The witch told him to get up, that he ought to have better sense than lean against the bureau. On one occasion a little unknown black dog came to the house, cutting some antics. Mr. Bell said he would shoot that dog, and started to get his gun. Mrs. Bell interfered, telling him he must not. The dog lay down on the floor and rolled over and over toward the door, and the minute the dog disappeared from the house the witch exclaimed, 'Look out, Old Jack, here comes Jerusalem.'"

Did you know Rev. Thomas and Rev. James Gunn, Mrs. Darden? "Indeed I did. They were the founders of Methodism in this community. Two nobler ministers never lived in this section, and I have never seen two men imbued with more spirituality, and have never heard any preacher with more inspiration. They preached all over the country for many miles around, after going a whole day's journey or more, and great revivals resulted from their preaching."

Did they visit Mr. Bell's or try to detect the witch? "My understanding was at the time that they did. Mr. Bell sent for them often and they tried faithfully to throw some light upon the mystery, but never could."

Did you know the Batts family? "Yes; there were two Batts families. Quite a number of the descendents of Jerry Batts are still living here, and they are mighty fine people. The other Batts family, descendants of Fred and Kate Batts, have disappeared."

What do you know, Mrs. Darden, of Mrs. Kate Batts? "Oh, Aunt Kate, as the young people all called her, was a good kind hearted old lady. She was very peculiar in her ways, and was mighty funny, which made people talk about her a great deal. But I always liked Aunt Kate, she was so cheerful and full of life I was glad to meet her. She was very sensitive. The witch told some one that it was 'Old Kate Batts,' and this is why the witch took the name of Kate. Some people were silly enough to believe it. She heard this and it made her very mad. She turned loose her tongue on people who talked about her in a way that made some really afraid of her. I did not blame her for getting mad at such foolishness. Of course she was no witch; if she had been she would have bewitched every one who talked bad about her. The witch gave itself many names, called itself Black Dog, Jerusalem and other names. People discussed all of these things, watched Mrs. Batts, and tried every way to detect the cause, but no discovery that I ever heard of that threw the least suspicion on Aunt Kate beyond the simple statement of the witch, which as a matter of course was false and intended to mislead. You know how people fly to extremes and jump at conclusions when trying to unravel or penetrate a great mystery. Some charged that it was John and Drew Bell practicing ventriloquism. Others thought it was Betsy Bell practicing some unknown art, but the more sensible people accepted none of these theories; in fact they would not support any kind of investigation. What on earth could possibly have induced the Bells to inflict so much distress and punishment on the family, even had they the power? Not money, for they had that, and refused to receive a cent from the many strangers and investigators calling. Not notoriety, for they kept the whole matter a secret as long as possible. Then it could not add anything to the good name Mr. Bell had earned for himself and family and cherished so much. No, it was simply a phenomenon which no one could explain."

Did you ever hear Jerry Batts express his opinion about the witch? "Yes; he discussed it a great deal with father and mother in my presence, but they never arrived at any satisfactory explanation. I remember distinctly one expression from Mr. Jerry Batts that impressed me. He remarked to father, 'The witch will never leave until John Bell's head is cut off,' meaning of course, not as long as the old gentleman lived. I suppose it was Mr. Bell's peculiar afflictions that led him to make the remark. The witch had declared its intention to kill him, and the old gentleman charged his affliction to that source. The witch did torment him to his grave, and reviled with ghoulish glee at his burying. A large crowd of people attended the funeral, and it was a very solemn occasion — every one seemed sadly depressed. After the grave was filled and the crowd of sorrowing friends started to leave, the witch commenced singing:

'Row me up some brandy, O,

Row row, row row,

Row me up some brandy, O,

Row me up some more.'"

Did you know Joshua Gardner, Mrs. Darden? "Yes. He was Betsy Bell's lover at the time, and it was generally believed that the sentiment was mutual. Betsy thought much of him. He came of a splendid family of people, was a handsome young man, full six feet tall, and weighed about one hundred and sixty pounds. He had dark hair and gray eyes, was intelligent and entertaining, and a man of good deportment, and very popular in the community."

Please, Mrs. Darden, describe Betsy Bell? "Betsy was a beautiful girl. She was of light complexion; what you would call a blonde. She was a little above medium height, presenting a graceful figure and elegant carriage. She possessed a rare suit of rich golden hair, soft gentle blue eyes and winning ways, and with all was an industrious, bright and interesting girl, who had more admirers than any girl in the country. I thought a great deal of Betsy; she was a sweet good girl, and I deeply sympathized with her in her disappointments and afflictions."

Then Betsy did not marry young Joshua Gardner? "No; she finally married Richard Powell, her school teacher, who was a very prominent man."

Do you know; Mrs. Darden, what broke up the love affair between Betsy and Gardner, and induced her to marry Powell? "Ah, now you ask me a hard question; I cannot tell. You may learn that from others. It was said that the witch had something to do with it but I do not know. I always thought Betsy loved Gardner best, that is she seemed happy in his company, and he was certainly greatly devoted to her when out in society. You know, however, that it has always been said that destiny controls the fortunes of men and women. You know also that women are counted as very fickle creatures, and there is no accounting for the change of a woman's mind in love affairs, and often the most desperate love cases come to naught. Don't you think I have told you enough?"

"Yes, Mrs. Darden, many thanks for this very entertaining interview."

REV. JAMES G. BYRNS'S STATEMENTS — FIRST APPEARANCE OF THE WITCH — ITS DOINGS AND SAYINGS — THE WITCH KILLER FROM THE EAST

Rev. James G. Byrns, one of the oldest and most highly esteemed citizens of Springfield, Tenn., a man whose years are full of good works, and whose integrity is above reproach of any kind, contributes the following interesting sketch, which goes to establish the character of the witnesses, giving a graphic account of the first appearance of the witch and its operations. The writer of this sketch is a son of Squire James Byrns, who was the good magistrate of the Bell district, a man of high moral character, noted for his intelligence and general usefulness as a citizen, and his impartiality and faithfulness in the dis charge of his official duties. Mr. Byrns, being requested to prepare a sketch, writes as follows:

Of course I am too young to know anything personally about the Bell Witch, but shall endeavor to state faithfully some of the facts impressed upon me, as I have so often heard them detailed by my father, James Byrns, Sr., John Johnson, Calvin Johnson, Alex. Gunn, Sr., William Porter, Frank R. Miles, Martin Pitman, Mrs. Rebecca Long, my wife's mother, who was Rebecca Porter, Mrs. Martha Bell, and many other citizens, and have also heard many miraculous statements by

THE BELL WITCH PROJECT

Negroes, which I will not repeat.

Old Mr. Bell told my father, also John Johnson and others, that the first unaccountable object that attracted his attention was a large, strange looking animal, resembling a dog. He walked out to the field to see if the fodder was ripe enough to gather. Before starting he cleaned his gun and loaded it to shoot squirrels and rabbits around the field. About the middle of the field, he said, he discovered the animal sitting in the row, looking intently at him. He approached nearer to it, and the dog, as he thought it was, did not move, which surprised him, and he then concluded to shoot it. At the fire of the gun the strange looking creature ran, and as soon as it moved, he discovered that it was an uncommon animal, and knew there was no dog in the country like it. However, this circumstance was without significance, and was forgotten until later developments connected it with other affairs.

Soon after this the trouble commenced. Something appeared scratching on the outside wall of the house, and occasionally a tap at the door. Mr. Bell said he frequently went out to see what was the matter, but could discover nothing. He said nothing about it, not even to the family, lest it might alarm them, and thinking too that it was some one playing pranks, and by watching he would be able to discover the intruder. Such demonstrations continued to increase, being heard two or three times during a week, and become so intolerable that Mr. Bell determined to lay some scheme to catch the offender. Finally the mysterious knocking appeared to be within the upper story of the house, and sometimes the noise would appear like trace chains or harness falling on the floor above him, but on investigation nothing could be found. From this on the demonstrations increased, and appeared like rats gnawing and dogs fighting in the house.

After carrying on at this rate for some time, it commenced troubling various members of the family, pulling the covers off of the beds, pinching and slapping the children, and became so frightful that the family could no longer conceal their distress, and neighbors were called in to witness the strange occurrences and detect the cause. But no one to this day has been able to explain or account for the mystery. The more people investigated, the more demonstrative it became, sounds like heavy stones and chunks of wood falling on the floor being heard. Finally the witch commenced talking and laughing, singing and praying. For some time it was very pious, and later became extremely wicked, using unchaste and most offensive language. The mystery deepened, and every one who undertook to explain it was covered with confusion. Some people thought it was two members of the Bell family practicing ventriloquism, but this theory soon exploded, by applying the strictest tests. The reader will remember that I am stating these things just as they were detailed to me by the parties above named, who were witnesses all through the troubles. The witch talked more freely to some parties than to others. It seemed to prefer talking with John Johnson and Bennett Porter more than any other persons, perhaps because they were more disposed to humor and gab with it than were others, Bennett Porter was Mr. Bell's son-in-law — married Esther Bell. The witch promised him one night to go home with him that the family might have some rest. Then it said, "Bennett, you will try to kill me if I visit your house." "No I won't," replied Porter. ",Oh, but I know you," replied the witch, "but I have been to your house. Do you remember that bird you thought sung so sweet the other morning?" "Yes," replied Porter. "Well that was me." Then continued the witch, "Bennett, didn't you see the biggest and poorest old rabbit that you ever saw in your life, as you came over here this evening?" "Yes," replied Mr. Porter. "Well that was me," said the witch, and who then burst into laughter. This was the kind of gossip it carried on constantly, and would tell what different people in the neighborhood had been doing during the day, or what was then transpiring.

It seemed to take special delight in afflicting and tormenting old Mr. Bell, and his young daughter Betsy. It often said that it had come to kill old Jack Bell and it was said that Mr. Bell died from strange afflictions visited on him by his tormentor. It interfered a great deal with Betsy's love affairs, and wanted her to marry a certain man in the neighborhood. Betsy complained of a painful, sensation like some one sticking pins in her body. It would fill her hair full of pins, jerk her tucking comb out, and laugh at its own wicked tricks and Betsy's discomfiture, and she was frequently sent from home for rest and freedom from the tortures inflicted by the witch.

It was very common for large crowds to gather at Mr. Bell's to hear the witch talk. One night when the house was full, there came an old gentleman by the name of Grizzard. The witch entered with the exclamation, "Here is old Grizzard; you all just ought to hear old Grizzard call his hogs. He begins, 'Pig, pig, pig.' The hogs come in a run, and Griz counts them and then begins hollering, 'Here, here, sic, sic, sowey, sowey.'

That's the way old Grizzard feeds his hogs." And Mr. Grizzard said the witch was correct. Next came the exclamation or inquiry, "Where is Jerusalem?" (Jerusalem was a member of the witch family.) No one replying, the same voice answered, "There he is on the wall." All eyes were at once turned to discover a large black bug crawling on the wall. Mr. Bell remarked, "Well, if that is Jerusalem, I will kill him," and he did kill the bug. The witch laughed heartily, exclaiming, "Lord Jesus, what a fool I did make of old Jack Bell."

THE BELL WITCH PROJECT

The Witch seemed to like old Mrs. Lucy Bell. It called her "Old Luce," and said Old Luce was a good woman, which was indeed her character throughout the country. Mrs. Bell had quite a spell of sickness, and one morning refused her breakfast. Very soon Mrs. Bell heard a soft pathetic voice, apparently just above her head, calling her name, "Luce, poor Luce, are you sick Luce?" "Yes," replied Mrs. Bell, "I am." "Well Luce, hold out your hands, and I will give you some hazelnuts I brought from the bottom; they will be good for you." Mrs. Bell held out her hands and received the hazelnuts as they dropped. Presently the same voice inquired, "Luce, poor Luce, why don't you eat the hazelnuts?" "Oh, you know that I can't crack them," replied Mrs. Bell. Then it told her to hold out her hands again, saying, "I will crack some for you." Instantly the sound of the cracking was heard, and the cracked nuts were dropped on her lap. Several ladies were there ministering to Mrs. Bell, and testified to this. That night the witch came in with the news that a baby had just been born to a family living in the bottom, which proved to be correct as stated. I understand that the baby was Mrs. Wash. Ayers, now living. The next day it visited Mrs. Bell again, bringing a bunch of wild grapes in the same manner as the hazelnuts came.

On another occasion the witch came in a jolly good mood, when quite a number of persons were sitting in the room engaged in social intercourse, announcing its presence with the inquiry, "Who wants some grapes," and that moment a bunch of large wild grapes dropped in Betsy Bell's lap. I heard John Bell, Jr., and others confirm this circumstance.

Calvin Johnson told me that after some persuasion the witch consented to shake hands with him if he would promise not to catch it. He promised and held out his hand, and instantly felt something like a soft delicate hand resting on his. The hand was placed lengthwise on his, so that he could not grasp it. John Johnson asked, the witch why it would not shake hands with him? The answer was, "You are a rascal, Jack; you want to catch me." John said that was just what he intended to do. The witch seemed to have more confidence in Calvin Johnson than any one. It said Calvin was an honest man, truthful and free from deceit, and this was true of the man.

John Johnson called in one night when the witch was in a great way talking, and addressing the witch said, "Well Kate, you can't tell what my wife has been doing today?" "Yes I can," it promptly replied, "she has been baking cakes for you to carry along to eat on your trip to Nashville, where you intend starting tomorrow." This Mr. Johnson said was true, and no one outside of the family could have known it.

THE BELL WITCH PROJECT

One night some one inquired of the witch what was going on over at Jesse Bells? "I don't know,'" it answered, "but will go and see." Five minutes later the witch returned and told what every member of the family was doing at that hour, which was confirmed the next day by Jesse Bell.

During the excitement the conjurers and experts in divining mysteries came along, and of course the Bell family were disposed to let them try their experiments. One of these was a smart fellow from the East, who claimed to be a witch killer, and said he could, by some sort of divination, see witches and shoot them. This smart gentleman conjured around several days with hair balls and foxfire, washed out his gun with his charm mixture, molded silver bullets and loaded for the witch, and set around day after day waiting for the goblin to put in its appearance, but Kate did not show up. He said the witch was afraid of him and would not come as long as he remained. The family had almost arrived at the conclusion that there was something in the man, and Mr. Bell was seriously contemplating the wisdom of hiring the gentleman from the East to stay about to keep the witch away. The family had not enjoyed so long a respite since the specter's first appeared. Finally the witch killer concluded that he would go home, and return very soon to stay longer, should Kate make any more trouble. But he was firmly impressed that nothing more would be heard of it.

His horse was brought to the front near the house, the witch man placed his saddle bags, stuffed with all kinds of conjurations, on the saddle, and bidding good-bye to Mr. Bell, the family and friends who came out to see him off, he mounted his horse to start, but the animal would not budge. He kicked, spurred and whipped, but it was no go. The horse would rear up, fall down and roll and kick. The witch man then turned to conjuring his horse, rubbed and petted the animal until it became quiet, and then mounted again, but the horse still refused to go. The witch killer was about to give up in despair, when the familiar voice of Kate was heard in the air, exclaiming, "I can make that horse go. Let me get on behind." Just then the horse dashed off, seemingly of its own accord, making a circle around the yard, kicking and squealing with wild rage, and the witch hollering, "Hold on old man, hold on." Finally the horse struck a bee line for the gate, and out he went, kicking and snorting, the rider hanging to the mane of the horse's neck, yelling for dear life, "Oh mercy." It appeared, however, that it was "Kate" and not mercy that had him. The witch laughed a week over that transaction. "Lord Jesus," it said, "I scared that old man nearly to death. I stuck him full of brass pins. He will spit brass pins and foxfire for the next six months. Lord Jesus, how he did beg. I told the old scoundrel that he came here to kill me, and I was not going to let him off easy. He said if I would let him alone he never would come here again. I broke him from trying that caper any more."

THE BELL WITCH PROJECT

The witch told various stories concerning itself, and said it could be anything, assume any form it desired; a dog, a rabbit, bird, or human form. It finally told the family that if Betsy would marry a certain gentleman, it would leave and not trouble them any more. The Negroes could tell the most wonderful stories, and narrate miraculous escapes.

The men and women whom I have mentioned as my authority for this statement are all dead, but their memories live and speak for their integrity and veracity. They were as pure and truthful people as I ever knew, and strange and mysterious as the story of the Bell Witch may seem, I could not, if I would, doubt the statements of these people. As to what it was, or who it was, I cannot form or express any opinion, but as to the truth of the trouble, I have not the shadow of a doubt. The evidence that James Byrns, Sr. was my father, is not to me a particle stronger or more convincing. There is no court in all of the land that would require one-half of the testimony to establish any fact, as can be produced in support of the story of these wonderful demonstrations, rather I should say history, for in fact it is a part of the early history of Robertson county, and will be handed down from generation to generation in this county, just as stirring events that transpired at the building of Solomon's Temple have come down through a certain channel to the present time.

Like the queen of Sheba when she heard the fame of Solomon concerning the name of the Lord, she came to prove him with hard questions, and confessed that the half had not been told her, people came from all quarters to see with their own eyes, or rather, hear with their own ears, and prove what they believed a cheap fraud and deception, but returned worse confounded than ever.

Though Mr. Bell was a man in good prosperous circumstances, strangers and visitors who came on the mission of divining the mystery almost ate him out of house and home. In conclusion, therefore, I must confess with the testimony before me, I believe as firmly as I can believe anything that I have not seen or felt, the truth of the existence of the Bell Witch.

JAMES G. BYRNS.

Some Thrilling Incidents Told by Mrs. Nancy Ayers, the Baby the Witch Spanked

Washington Ayers and wife are two happy old people living some two miles from the old Bell place, and about the same distance from Cedar Hill, Tenn. Mrs. Nancy Ayres is a daughter of John and Patsy Johnson, who had a most thrilling experience in trying to detect the authorship of the demoniac exhibitions, which disturbed the Bell family. She was born in 1819, and is still a very active lady for one at her ripe age. She is also intelligent and very entertaining, especially in describing the sensation which the Bell Witch left behind to live after the intensely exciting events of that period. Mrs. Ayres is greatly esteemed in the community. She inherited that rugged honesty which characterized the Johnson family, and is affectionately called "Aunt Nancy" by every one. The writer was told before visiting Mrs. Ayers, "You can rely on everything Aunt Nancy says as strictly correct."

Mrs. Ayers was asked if she was willing to tell all she knew about the Bell Witch? "Oh no, I could not tell the half I have heard in a week; strictly speaking, I know nothing. I was born in the middle of the most exciting events, and they say that the witch was the first to carry the news of my birth to the Bell family. All I know is hearsay from father, mother, Grandfather James Johnson, Uncle Calvin Johnson, Joel Bell, and everybody who lived in the neighborhood at that time, and, of course, I believe their statements as firmly as if I had witnessed the demonstrations."

It is said that the witch, whipped you when a baby. How is that, Mrs. Ayers? "Well, that is what father and mother told me repeatedly after I had grown up. It occurred in this way: Betsy Bell frequently came to our house to spend the night and get some rest if possible from the witch. In fact, father invited and urged her to come. He said he had two purposes in view; one was a desire to render any services possible that would relieve the family of the pest: even for a short time. His second reason was a determination to follow up every clue, or every line of investigation, that had been suggested or could be thought of, in an effort to elucidate the mystery.

This he was doing on his own account and in his own way, and proceeded in a way to elude all suspicion of his purpose. Several persons who had been trying the detect to cause of the remarkable exhibitions and failing, had arrived at the conclusion that Betsy Bell possessed some extraordinary gift akin to ventriloquism, and was practicing a deception in collusion with some other person, and that he had about arrived at this conclusion himself, but carefully concealed his convictions from her and all other persons, and he thought he would have a better opportunity of determining this matter if she were to come alone to spend a few nights at his house. As before stated, she did come, and the witch came with her, keeping up so much talking, scratching, knocking over the chairs, pulling the covering from the beds, and other vexatious disturbances that it was impossible for any one to sleep while it was there, and this all went to confirm his opinion.

So it happened one night when Betsy and the witch were there, that I was fretful and worried mother a great deal, she having to get up frequently to rock my cradle. Finally Kate, as they called the witch, spoke factiously, inquiring of mother, 'Patsy, why don't you slap that child and make it behave itself? If you won't I will.' Instantly they heard something like a hand spanking me, and I yelled to the top of my voice, as if something was taking my life, when both father and mother sprang out of bed to my rescue. They searched the room all over, but could find nothing irregular, no persons but themselves in the room, and no possible way that anyone could have gotten in and out without a noise or detection."

Did you behave after that? "Well, they said I did behave like a little lady the balance of the night."

Did your father's investigations satisfy him thoroughly that Betsy Bell was culpable in the witch demonstration? "Oh no. To the contrary he became thoroughly satisfied that Betsy was entirely innocent of the whole matter, and was a great sufferer from the affliction, as was her father. It was said by those who had been watching Betsy, that the witch never talked when her lips were closed. This was not true. He said it talked to him not only when her lips were closed, but when she was not near, not in talking or hearing distance, and in fact would talk at old man Bell's when neither Betsy, Drew or young John were on the place, and yet seemed to follow Betsy wherever she went, going with her to grandfather's, James Johnson, when she visited Theny Thorn, and at bedtime go through the form of reading a chapter in the Bible, singing grandfather's favorite song, and offer prayer, just as he would. Father said it did many things that would have been impossible for a young girl like Betsy, and told things that she could not possibly have known.

The witch talked almost incessantly, gabbing and spouting about everything that was going on in the country, seemed familiar with everybody's business, telling things that no one present knew anything about, called strangers by name and telling where they were from before they could introduce themselves. It would also quote Scripture, discuss doctrinal questions, sing songs, and pray eloquent prayers, and never failed to answer any question concerning any passage, verse or text in the Bible correctly, giving full references as to where it might be found. Then on the other hand it could be very wicked and out curse a sailor. Mr. Bell sometimes sent for father to set up and entertain Kate, that the family might get a little rest. He rather liked this, as it afforded him a better opportunity for prosecuting his investigations. The witch also seemed to like gossiping with him, and there was a peculiar excitement about it that interested him, and he would sit and talk to the thing just as patiently and earnestly as if he was discussing a very important matter with some person.

THE BELL WITCH PROJECT

Father said that one night after the witch had gone on for some time prattling about everything in the country, he concluded to change the topic and lead it out concerning itself, and beginning with flattery he said, 'Kate, I love to talk with you because you are so smart and can always learn me something. You and I have been good friends, and I want to know more about you. Now there is no person present but you and I; tell me confidentially something about yourself?' 'No Jack,' was the reply, 'I can't tell you that yet, but I will tell you before I leave.'

'How long before you will leave?' 'I won't tell you that neither, but I will not leave as long as old Jack Bell lives.' 'Have you really come to kill old Jack?' 'Yes, I have told him so over and often.' 'What has old Jack done that you want to kill him?' 'Oh, nothing particular; I just don't like him.' 'But everybody in the country likes him and regards him as a very fine old gentleman, don't they?' 'Yes, and that is the reason he needs killing.' 'But Kate, if you kill old Jack without giving a better reason than that, people will think very hard of you, and then according to law you will be hung for murder, won't you?' 'No, it's catching before hanging.'

'Yes, but isn't the maxim, "murder will out" equally true?' 'That may be Jack, but still its catching before hanging.' 'Well Kate, tell me why you hate Betsy; isn't she a sweet lovely girl?' 'How do you know Jack, that I hate Betsy?' 'Because you are always following and ding-donging after her.' 'Well, is that any evidence that I hate her?' 'But then you pull her hair, pinch her arms, stick pins in her.' 'Well, don't lovers play with each other that way sometimes?' 'No, I never did; no man who really loves a girl will serve her as you do Betsy,' 'How do you know that I am a man?' 'Because you get drunk and curse sometimes, and say and do things that no nice woman would do.' 'But Jack, why should I be a woman; may I not be a spirit or something else?' 'No Kate, you are no spirit. A spirit can't pull the cover from beds, slap people, pull hair, stick pins, scratch, and do such things like you.' 'Well, I will make you think I am a spirit before you get home.' 'How are you going to do that, Kate?' 'I am going to scare you.' 'You can't scare me, Kate; I know that you are too good a friend to do me any harm, and therefore I am not afraid of you.' 'Well, just wait until you start through the woods home, and see if I don't make you hump yourself.'

'Oh phsaw, Kate, you are just joking and gabbing now. Tell me where you live, and who and what you are, anyhow?' 'I live in the woods, in the air, in the water, in houses with people; I live in heaven and in hell; I am all things and anything I want to be; now don't you know what I am?' 'No, I don't; come and shake hands with me like you did with Calvin.' 'No, I can't trust you, Jack.' 'Why Kate, you trusted my brother Calvin and I am just as good as he is?' 'No you are not,' returned Kate, 'Calvin is a good Christian and a true man; he won't violate his promise for anything.' 'Neither will I.'

'Oh, but you are lying, Jack; I know you too well. You are smarter than Calvin, but you are a grand rascal, old Jack Johnson. You just want a chance to catch me; that is what you are here for, trying to find out who or what I am, and you want a chance to grasp my hand.' After much talking on this line, the conversation ended some time after midnight, and father started home.

Kate never would shake hands with him, though he importuned often, nor did he ever learn anything more about the witch than was manifested in this conversation, which I have heard him repeat so often that I remember it word by word. Father said as soon as he reached the woods, the bushes and trees commenced cracking, like they were all breaking down, and sticks and chunks of wood fell about him thick and fast, as if thrown by someone. He never would acknowledge that he run, but I always believed he did. Father said the witch seemed to know his mind and purpose as well as he did himself, and that he was fully determined to try to catch it by the hand if it had shaken hands with him."

Did you ever hear Calvin Johnson say it shook hands with him? "Yes, I have heard Uncle Calvin make the statement frequently. He said the Witch made him promise not to grasp or squeeze its hand before it consented, and he could not violate his Promise. He said he held out his hand, and very quick felt the pressure of another hand on his, which was laid lengthwise, and not across, in the common form of shaking hands, and that it felt very soft, like a woman's hand. But it never would trust father, though it showed a preference for talking with him. It told others as it told him, that old Jack Johnson was smart and cunning, that he was a grand rascal, always hatching plans and schemes to catch it, and he had to be watched."

Mrs. Ayres, your father, you say, addressed the witch as "Kate," did you ever hear him explain how it came by that name? "Yes; people continued their expostulations with overtures and importunities to reveal its name, purpose, etc. The witch had given many names and various explanations of its presence, but the biggest sensation of all came when it told that it was old Kate Batts' witch. Mrs. Batts was a very sensitive, peculiar, blustering kind of woman, whose eccentricities subjected her to much ridicule, and her original oddity was a kind of jesting stock, and common talk. So it was a popular hit, and started fresh gossip for all laughing tongues. It made the old lady very mad; she cut tall capers and said more funny things in her maledictions and imprecations than was ever heard, and naturally everybody took to calling the witch 'Kate.'"

Did anybody really believe that Mrs. Kate Batts was the witch? "Yes, some people did, and they were afraid of her. Father said the idea was the most absurd and preposterous that had been advanced; contrary to all reason. Mrs. Batts, he said could not have had any conception of such a thing, much less practice the art, eluding detection. On another occasion father said he was postulating with Kate, begging the witch to tell something about itself. Kate replied, 'Well Jack, if you will agree to keep it a secret, and not tell old "Sugar Mouth," (that was grandfather) I will tell you.' Of course father agreed to that. 'Now,' says Kate, 'I am your stepmother.' Father replied, 'Kate, you know you are lying; my step mother is a good woman, and the best friend I have. She would not do so many mean things as you are guilty of.' 'Now,' replied Kate, 'I can prove it to you.' Grandmother Johnson had an unruly servant who would go wrong, irritating her very much, and the old lady was constantly after Rachel, raising a sharp storm about her ears. Father said the witch at once assumed the voice and tone of his stepmother, and got after Rachel. 'Tut, tut, Rachel, what makes you do so,' imitating grandmother exactly."

Did your father ever speak of meeting the witch doctors and conjurers at Bell's? "Oh yes, ever so many came, and father used to tell many ridiculous and laughable incidents regarding the experiments of witch killers. The Bell's allowed every one who came along to experiment to his full satisfaction, and the witch always got the best of them. I remember one incident that amused him very much. This fellow put some silver, twelve dollars, in a bowl of water, performed his incantations, and set the bowl away, that the silver might remain in the water all night to work the enchantment when the witch came. Betsy Bell had to drink the enchanted water.

Next morning the money was gone, which caused a mighty stir. A Negro was charged with stealing the money, and Mr. Bell was threatening the servant with a whipping. This was one of the times that Kate came to the Negro's rescue. 'Hold on, old Jack,' spoke Kate, 'that Negro is innocent; I can tell you who got that money,' and did tell. Mr. Bell dropped the matter and said no more about it. Several evenings later father went over to entertain the witch while the family and visitors slept. After all had retired and everything was quiet, father said he sat leaning his chair against the wall, waiting for Kate. Presently he felt something touch him on the shoulder, and he was directly accosted by the voice of the witch. 'Say Jack, did you hear about that money scrape they had here the other evening?' 'Yes,' replied father, 'I heard something about it.' 'Well, it was funny; I saved that nigger from a good whipping by telling old Jack who got the money,' and then went on to state that the person who got the money went to Springfield yesterday and bought lots of nice things with it. 'Ha, ha, ha, I guess they will quit fooling with these witch doctors now.' Father had occasion to go to Springfield a day or two later, and inquired about the transactions of this person as told by Kate, and found that the witch had reported correctly."

Did you, Mrs. Ayers, ever hear Bennett Porter say anything about the witch? "No; Bennett Porter moved away while I was quite a child. I have, however, heard various persons say that Bennett Porter shot at the witch, and it made much ado about it, threatening something serious to him or his children. I have also heard it repeated by many that the witch was seen by Betsy swinging on the limb of a tree and looking like a little girl dressed in green."

Did you ever hear Williams or Joel Bell express any opinion in regard to the witch? "Nothing particular. They discussed it in a general way when asked questions regarding the demonstrations, but never seemed disposed to talk much about it. I suppose they had heard enough of it. However, Joel told me that the witch gave him the severest whipping he ever felt, and one that he would never forget as long as he lived."

Mrs. Ayers, did you ever hear anything detrimental in any way to the character of John Bell or his family? "Not a breath in the world. No man or family stood higher in the estimation of the people than John Bell. I have heard him spoken of as one of the leading men of the country, and father said the citizens had the utmost confidence in his integrity. More than that, he raised his children to be honorable men and women, and the family influence is felt in Robertson county to this day; even the grandchildren are men of the same substantial character."

Do you remember anything about Rev. Thomas and Rev. James Gunn? "Yes, certainly; they were the founders of Methodism in this section, and Rev. Sugg Fort was the leading Baptist. Their lives were full of good works and honors. I have heard it said many times that they visited Mr. Bell often and sympathized with him in his distress."

THE BELL WITCH PROJECT

THE BELL WITCH PROJECT

Chapter 14

TESTIMONIALS

The Bell Family, the Gunns, Forts, Johnsons, Porters, Frank Miles and Other Citizens Whose Statements Authenticate the History of the Bell Witch

Rev. Joshua W. Featherston, of Cedar Hill, Tenn., who after a long and useful career retired from the ministry and now lives happily, himself and wife, at his cottage, honored by all people, writes as follows:

CEDAR HILL, TENN, Dec. 23, 1891

In answer to the request to contribute what I know in regard to the characters or standing of Rev. Thomas Gunn, Rev. James Gunn, Rev. Sugg Fort, John and Calvin Johnson, W. B. Porter, Frank R. Miles, and the Bell family, I will state that they were among the early settlers of Robertson county, Tenn. I was intimately acquainted with each and every one of them except old Mr. John Bell, who died just before I settled in the neighborhood, and it is with pleasure that I can testify to their, high characters as men of worth and standing in the community. They were men of undoubted honor, possessing strong minds, and were not easily imposed upon.

As to the subject in hand, the Bell Witch, the history of which is made up from the detailed statements of these men, in connection with others, I can say that I have had many conversations with the parties in regard to the matter, and they all testified to very nearly the same facts and details, and I believe every word they told me respecting the demonstrations. As regards Rev. James and Rev. Thomas Gunn, they did more towards the establishment of the Methodist church in this country than any other men. In fact they were the founders of Methodism in this and surrounding counties, and their influence is felt to this day. They married at least two-thirds of the couples, and preached nearly all the funerals, in this and surrounding country during many years, and finally went down to their graves in peace, ripe with age and full of honors.

J. V. FEATHERSTON

About Frank R. Miles' Experience

The writer had an interesting interview with Rev. J. W. Featherston at his pleasant home, since the above letter was written. He repeats many thrilling incidents told him by the men above mentioned, all of which is found in other testimony. Mr. Featherston says he had more talk with Frank Miles in regard to the actions of the witch than any one else, and had implicit confidence in Miles as a man who would not exaggerate or misstate the truth. Miles weighed about two hundred and fifty pounds, was in the prime of life, vigorous and very stout. He was at John Bell's a great deal, going as other friends to relieve and comfort the family in their distress, just as he would have attended a sick neighbor. Mr. Miles had a lively experience with the witch, which required more courage than force to meet. He undertook to resist the playful frolics of the intruder, which rather excited the animus of the monster with resentment and pique for Miles, and it manifested special delight in snatching the cover from his bed and striking him heavy blows. Mr. Miles said he exercised all the strength in his arms in trying to retain the bed covering when the witch was pulling at it, but in vain; it was like tearing the whole fabric into shreds. Mr. Featherston further states that the witch sensation was the exciting theme of the whole community when he moved in, and continued so for years. It was the subject of discussion in every household, and is often talked of now, having a bearing upon other things.

One of the most remarkable features in the development of the witch character was its preeminent knowledge of men, an innate, tangible comprehension of every man's attributes of mind and nature. Every citizen or stranger that came in contact with the mystery found disparagement in trying to cope with it on any subject, and suffered, an exposure of the inmost purposes and secrets of the heart. Take for an example of its exposition of this supernatural gift, the Johnson brothers. There was no difference in their standing as men of high honor and integrity of character. John was perhaps considered the most intellectual and forcible man of the two, while Calvin was noted for his frankness, devotion to principle, and absolute freedom from all deceit and guile. These elements the witch observed, and while it manifested the highest pleasure in vociferating and palavering with John, it trusted Calvin implicitly, and assigned its reason for this distinction. Calvin, it said, was a pure, truthful, scrupulous, Christian man, and therefore it gave him its hand, which it refused John and every one else, trusting no man as it did Calvin

THE BELL WITCH PROJECT

Johnson. On the other hand it characterized John as a sharp, unscrupulous, tricky man, "whose inmost purpose was to catch it," and this, so far as the witch was concerned, John admitted to be true, and that he had pursued unawares every scheme, plan, stratagem, artifice or illusion he was capable of inventing in his efforts to detect the author of these most miraculous demonstrations, and at last gave it up in despair, as a matter beyond human power, knowledge or comprehension. This one instance of distinguishing the difference in the characters of the Johnson brothers would not be sufficient basis for a settled conclusion that the so-called witch was an agency above human genius or power, but the same wonderful intuition, instinct and archness [sic] was developed in hundreds of instances, and was a leading characteristic in all of its operations, and for this reason Mr. Featherston says he cannot believe that the demonstrations were the result of any human agency.

Dr. J. T. Mathews Testifies

Dr. J. T. Mathews, who has been a well established practicing physician of Cedar Hill for many years, writes as follows:

CEDAR HILL, TENN., Dec. 23, 1891

In answer to questions concerning the character of certain gentlemen among the older settlers, it gives me pleasure to testify to the high standing and stability of character concerning Frank R. Miles and W. B. Porter, whom I was personally acquainted with, but too young to remember the others. They were regarded as honorable gentle men, whose statements concerning any matter were to be relied upon implicitly without the least hesitation. They lived on Sturgeon Creek, were of the best families in their day and time, were known far and near, and no one who knew them would think of calling their veracity in question.

Respectfully,

J. T. MATHEWS

E. Newton Knew the Men

Mr. E. Newton, an old and respected citizen of Cedar Hill, writes under date of Dec. 23, 1891:

I was personally acquainted with Rev. Thomas Gunn, Rev. James Gunn, William Porter, John Johnson, Calvin Johnson, Alexander Gunn, and the Bell family. They were of the best families that ever lived in this country, men of the highest integrity and were honored by all people. They were among the pioneers of civilization: and Christianity, and were the leaders in the development of the county. They molded the character of the best element now in this section, and their influence will live to affect generations to come. No men contributed more to the advancement of Christianity than the two Gunns.

E. NEWTON

A Host of Good Citizens Testify

To Whom It May Concern:

We, the undersigned, affix our names to this, understanding its full purport and intent, which is to certify that the following named men, to wit: Rev. James Gunn, Rev. Thomas Gunn, Alexander Gunn, Rev. Sugg Fort, John Johnson, Calvin Johnson, Frank R. Miles, Wm. B. Porter and John Bell, Sr., were among the first settlers of the western part of Robertson county, Tenn. They were all men of prominence and great influence, and their memories are respected and revered to this day by the descendants of all who knew them. Many of their descendents are now among us, honored and respected citizens. The men above named all lived to a ripe old age, and left behind them honored names, and we consider anything emanating from any of them as entirely trustworthy. The post office address of the signers to this is Cedar Hill, Tenn.

This Dec. 23, 1891.

J. E. Ruffin

R. H. Bartlett

H. B. Spain

A. L. Bartlett

L. Batts

J. W. M. Gooch

Matt. Gooch

THE BELL WITCH PROJECT

Mrs. T. J. Ayers

W. R. Featherston

William Wvnn

E. S. Hawkins,

M. D. B. H. Sory, Sheriff

R. S. Draughon

B. S. Byrns

W. J. Barnes

J. H. Long, Jr.

G. W. Sherod

Levi Dunn

W. H. Menees

H. W. Williams

A. L. Batts.

A. J. Newton

William Soloman

R. B. Long

R. B. Morris

E. W. Gunn

J. T. Bartlett

Mary A. Bartlett

Nannie M. Morriss

THE BELL WITCH PROJECT

W. L. Melon

J. R. Rufffin

G. M. Darden

D. P. Ayres

Mrs. M. L. Ayers

J. H. Long, Sr.

W. J. Darden

J. C. Davis

M. J. Batts

T. B. Polk

J. H. Wynn

T. D. Morris

G. B. Fyke

C. B. Darden

Major Garaldus Pickering, the Man Who Kicked the Witch out of Bed

Mr. R, H. Pickering, an honored citizen of Clarksville, Tenn., who has been connected with the business interest of the city for forty years, also served as County Trustee, and is a prominent official in the Methodist Church, known throughout the Tennessee Conference, contributes the statement of his father, Major Garaldus Pickering, who was a distinguished citizen of his day, and visited the Bell family during the witch excitement. No testimony could be more reliable, Mr. Henry Pickering states:

I have heard my father, Garaldus Pickering, tell many wonderful things about the Bell Witch. He taught a large school in the Bell vicinity for a number of years, and educated two or three of the Bell boys. He visited the family and had some experience with the witch, as it was called, though he did not believe in witchcraft, and said he was never afraid of it. He had no idea as to what it was, but certainly it was an insoluble mystery, which has never been accounted for. A great many people went to hear it talk and witness its tricks; strangers came from North Carolina, Virginia and other States, and it was nothing uncommon to find the stables and lots full of horses, and a horse tied in every corner of the lane fence.

Father told me some remarkable experiences that Frank Miles had with the witch, but I will only repeat one or two things in his own personal experience and contact. He said: The family and company had all retired for the night in the usual way. Presently he felt the cover slipping off toward the foot of the bed, and he drew it up, holding it tightly. The next minute he felt something like a hand or fingers tickling him under the toes. He drew his feet up and kicked with all the power in him. He felt something weighty as his feet struck it, and heard it strike against the wall and fall to the floor, making a noise more like the falling of a side of heavy sole leather, than anything he could describe.

Another instance; while the family and guests were at supper, the subject of a wedding that was to take place at that hour came up. Father stated the names of the contracting parties, which I have forgotten, but remember the circumstance very distinctly, as it impressed me at the time. However, some one remarked that the hour for the marriage had about passed, and the parties were no doubt then man and wife. Another remarked that Rev. Gunn performed the ceremony. The witch then spoke, exclaiming, "No, he did not marry them." "Yes, but you are mistaken this time," replied one. "Brother Gunn was engaged to tie the knot, and he never fails." "He failed this time," returned the witch. "Brother Gunn was taken very sick and could not go, and the wedding was about to be a failure, but they sent off for Squire Byrns and he married them." No one present believed it possible for the witch to know the facts so soon, but this was ascertained on the following day to be the truth of the case in every particular. Regarding the authorship of these very singular exhibitions, father thought it absurd to charge it to any of the Bell family. They were the sufferers, and suffered greatly; moreover, they were every one afraid of it; that was clear to any observer. He was there one night when several strangers rode up and hallooed ever so long, and not one of the family could be induced to go out, because they were afraid, and he got out of bed, dressed, and went out himself.

John A. Gunn's Statement

CLARKSVILLE, TENN., May 16, 1893

To the Author — Dear Sir:

THE BELL WITCH PROJECT

In reply to your questions I will state that I am familiar with the Bell Witch story as written by Richard Williams Bell, and that I have heard the same things that are detailed by him, and many other incidents not recorded, repeated over and again by the old citizens who lived in the vicinity at that time. I have heard my father, Alexander Gunn, John Johnson and Frank Miles all repeat the circumstance of finding the vial of poison in the cupboard at the time of John Bell's death, the experiment in giving it to a cat, etc., just as told by the writer, all three being present and witnessed Mr. Bell's death and the circumstances. I have heard Calvin Johnson tell the circumstance of his shaking hands with the witch, and many other very strange things. I have heard my grandfathers, Rev. James Gunn and Rev. Thomas Gunn, repeat many of the demonstrations which came under their observation; also James Johnson related the same things; the story of the witch bringing Mrs. Lucy Bell grapes and hazelnuts. Mrs. Martha Bell, wife of Jesse Bell, who lived to be ninety-six years of age; told me the story regarding the stockings as written by Williams Bell. Also I have heard William Porter repeat the same circumstance of the witch's visit to his house and getting in bed with him. I have heard Alex. Gooch and wife, who was Theny Thorn, Jeff and James Gooch, Jerry Batts, Major Robert Bartlett, Prof. John D. Tyler, of Montgomery County, and many others who witnessed the demonstrations, relate the same events and discuss many other things observed.

I have also talked with Mrs. Betsy Powell regarding her troubles with the mysterious visitation. All of these people lived to a good old age, James John son passed his ninety-ninth year, John Johnson passed eighty, Grandfather Thomas Gunn ninety-six, and Rev. James Gunn seventy years. They were all honored citizens, whose statements were trustworthy in regard to any matter, and no one who ever knew them doubted the truth of the circumstances regarding the witch demonstrations at John Bell's and other places in the neighborhood. Moreover, these citizens followed every clue, exercised all of their wits, applied all manner of tests, placed unsuspected detectives in and around the house, acted upon all suggestions regarding the suspicion that had been lodged against certain members of the family, and with all, their investigations ended in confusion, leaving the affair shrouded in still deeper mystery, which no one to this day has ever been able to account for or explain in any intelligent or satisfactory way. Besides the names I have mentioned among the most prominent citizens of the community, hundreds of men from other communities and sections visited the place, remaining days and nights, for the same purpose, and all failed in the object of detecting the cause of the demonstrations.

John Johnson, perhaps, took more interest in the investigations than any other man; in fact, from all I could gather, he was the leader and inventor of most all the schemes resorted to. He was a man of splendid endowments, keen observation, quick perception, and close comprehension; self-willed, and self-possessed, sustaining an unsullied and intrepid character. Moreover, he was less given than most of men to the superstitious ideas that characterized the people in that age, and as he told me, he entered into the investigation believing that some human agency was at the bottom of the strange manifestations, and he was determined to find it out if possible.

Knowing Mr. Johnson and others who lived long years ago, as I did, together with the statements of my father and grandfather, I cannot at all question the appearance and existence of the unsolved mystery of the Bell Witch, nor do I doubt the actual occurrence of the incidents recorded by Richard Williams Bell, whom I knew to be one of the purest and best of men that ever lived in Robertson County.

Respectfully,

JOHN A. GUNN

David Thompson Porter's Testimony

Esquire Zopher Smith, a prominent Magistrate of Clarksville, Tenn., was raised in Keysburg, Ky., and gratefully remembers David Thompson Porter as the friend of his youth. Mr. Porter was a merchant of Keysburg, and was honored for his worth as a citizen of the highest integrity and force of character, enjoying at that day a reputation Similar to that sustained by his distinguished son, Dr. D. T. Porter, of Memphis, Tenn. Squire Smith was a young clerk in the store, and he says he has heard Mr. Porter state repeatedly that he spent many nights at John Bell's, acting in concert with other citizens in trying to detect the agency of those most mysterious and wonderful demonstrations, following up every clue, and exhausting all resources and stratagems to no purpose.

Squire Smith recounts many incidents stated by Mr. Porter, which impressed him at the time, especially the story of the witch carrying hazelnuts and grapes to Mrs. Bell, which Mr. Porter said was a positive fact. He described the knocking at the door like some one seeking admittance, and instantly the door would open of its own accord, and then the witch would begin talking. He also described the pulling of the cover off of the beds, and nearly all of the characteristic incidents recorded by Williams Bell, which need not be repeated. Such statements as this are of course hearsay, or second-handed testimony, but nevertheless reliable. The writer has several times observed Squire Smith as a witness in s higher court, testifying to the preliminary statements of certain witnesses in his court, which was accepted as valid testimony, and this is just the same kind of evidence.

THE BELL WITCH PROJECT

The men and Women of mature years who witnessed the demonstrations have all passed away, but we have the incidents recorded by Williams Bell, and approved by other members of the family, who were living witness to all of it, and these hearsay statements are simply repetitions of the same facts by other parties who never saw Williams Bell's manuscript, or knew that such a record was in existence, and the chain of evidence is as complete and strong as it is possible to make any kind of testimony. Squire Smith says Mr. Porter affirmed his statements with the same emphasis as if he had been qualified in a court of justice, and he could not disbelieve a word he said.

Dr. William Fort's Investigation

The writer is authorized by a highly reputable lady of the Fort connection to state that Dr. William Fort came all the way from his home, then in Missouri, to investigate the phenomena. Parties who had failed in all of their efforts to explain the mystery, gave publicity to the suspicion that the demonstrations had their origin in the practices of ventriloquism by certain members of the family (something that would have been impossible without the knowledge of the old people and intimate neighbors, and without easy detection). Dr. Fort determined to make a thorough test of this version, and had the accused members to sit by him, holding his hands over their mouths while the witch continued to talk uninterrupted and without change or modulation in the tone of voice.

Private Conversation Exposed

The same lady relates this incident: Jesse Herring and wife were two estimable old people who lived in the vicinity. They were extremely cautious and guarded in their conversation about other people, and never discussed the witch or spent any opinion about it away from their own fireside. One night with closed doors, and not a soul in the house except themselves, they discussed the mystery very freely, and not a word was spoken by either of them to any one in regard to this conversation, or the witch. On the following night the witch reported to be whole conversation to the company assembled at John Bell's.

Emptied the Milk Vessels

Mrs. Betsy Sugg called one morning to pay Mrs. Lucy Bell a visit. The subject of milk and butter came up, and Mrs. Bell spoke of her new dairy house and invited Mrs. Sugg out to show her how nicely it was arranged. She had just finished straining and setting the milk for cream, locked the door and put the key in her pocket. The milk was set in pewter basins, vessels then in common use for milk, with wooden covers. Mrs. Bell took the key from her pocket, unlocked and opened the door, and to her surprise and chagrin there was not a drop of milk there, and the basins were turned bottom up and the covers placed over them. "Some of Kate's mischief," exclaimed Mrs. Bell. "The witch is always playing some such prank as this."

Uncle to the Devil

The witch it is said always treated the preachers, the Gunns and Rev. Sugg Fort, with more respectful consideration than other people. It was inclined to be on intimate or jocular terms with Rev. Fort, calling him Uncle Suggie, always welcoming him at the door with a happy salutation, "Good morning," or "Good evening Uncle Suggie. How do you like to be called uncle to the devil?"

Frightened Jerry Stark's Horse

Mr. James Chapman, a good citizen of Keysburg, Ky., spent the prime of his life in Robertson County, and repeats many of the incidents herein noted, as he heard them stated by older citizens. He heard more from Jerry Stark than any other person, and says, knowing the upright character of the man, he could not question Mr. Stark's statements. Mr. Stark visited the Bell place frequently during the witch excitement, and the progress of the investigations, and generally stayed all night.

Mr. Stark, says Chapman, described a large tree that stood in the Bell lane, under which he had to pass, when leaving the Place the following morning, after staying over night, and invariably, as he approached near, a rustling sound was heard among the leaves of the tree, and immediately as he passed under the tree, something apparently the size of a rabbit would jump out of the tree behind him, and that instant his horse would dash off as fast as he could go, which Mr. Stark said he could not account for, and never saw anything more of the spectre after it jumped. Mr. Chapman further states that some time after the old Bell house had been torn away, he was there helping Williams Bell in the wheat harvest. The grain was very rank, and they had stopped under a pear tree to whet their scythes and rest, and while there he mentioned this circumstance as told him by Mr. Jerry Stark, and Williams Bell confirmed the statement, pointing to the tree which was still standing, remarking that Stark's horse always started in a run with him the moment he passed under that tree.

Esquire James I. Holman Writes

SPRINGFIELD, TENN., Nov. 4, 1893

THE BELL WITCH PROJECT

M. V. Ingram — My Dear Sir:

I see in the Nashville Banner of November 3d, a statement to the effect that you are writing a history of the Bell Witch for publication, and I write you to say that I want a copy as soon as it is out. I am now fifty-one years of age, and have as keen a relish for reading the full details of the great mystery as I did when a boy, and heard my grandfather, Irvin Polk, tell so much of the many wonderful things he had witnessed, known as the witch demonstrations. He lived near the Bell place, and was there on many occasions and witnessed strange things that he could in no way account for, and which, as I understand, has never been explained. I could not doubt the statements of grandfather, even had I never heard them confirmed by many others, and it certainly was a wonderfully mysterious thing.

The old Bell house in which the witch performed, if you do not know the fact, was many years ago torn down and moved to the place on the bluff of Brown's ford, now occupied by Levi Smith and family. I learn from my father, Col. D. D. Holman, that Major Wash. Lowe, who you re member as a prominent lawyer of Springfield, undertook to write up the facts, but for some reason never finished, and turned his writing over to Allen Bell, which you may get and learn something from.

Respectfully, your friend,

JAMES I. HOLMAN

The writer will state that he has all the notes written by Major Lowe, but it is so badly faded and colorless that very little of it is legible.

William Wall's Experience With the Witch

Esquire J. E. Ransdell, of the Fourteenth District of Montgomery County, Tenn., relates the experience of Uncle Billy Wall with the witch, as he heard the old gentleman tell it to many persons. Mr. Wall lived at Fredonia, in Montgomery County. He has been dead some ten years, but his story impressed Squire Ransdell in such a way that he has never forgotten it. Uncle Billy said he concluded to go over to Bell's and hear the mysterious talking that was exciting the country. He started late, on a good fat horse, that was remarkable for its good saddle qualities and gentleness. Nearing the place he was hailed by a voice, in the bushes calling him familiarly, "Hello, Billy Wall, you are going to see the witch?" "Yes", replied Uncle. Billy, "that is where I am going." The voice replied, "I am going there too, and believe I will ride behind you on that fat horse." "All right," returned Mr. Wall, "hop up." That moment he felt his horse squat, as if some heavy weight had fallen upon him, and then commenced wriggling, prancing and kicking up.

He threw one hand behind to feel what it was, and then the other hand, but found nothing, and yet, he said, "the damn thing kept up a continual palavering at my back, asking me all sorts of hell-fired questions, while my horse continued in a canter, squealing and kicking up, and every damn hair on my head stood straight up, reaching for the treetops. It wasn't any fun for me, but the damn thing kept on laughing and talking about my fine race horse, and how pleasant it was to ride behind on his broad fat back, telling me what a fine suit of hair I had, and how beautifully it stood up, making me look like a statesman. I let my horse out, and wasn't long in getting there.

As soon as I halted in front of the house, the damn thing politely invited me to 'light Mr. Wall, hitch your horse to the rack and go in; I will be in pretty soon and entertain you.' Just about an hour later the racket commenced, and it looked like hell was to pay. It came rattling like dried hazelnuts pouring down by showers on the floor; and all sorts of talking going on. That trip satisfied me; I got enough of the witch in one night and never went back."

Squire Ransdell says the way in which Mr. Wall told this story, giving emphasis to nearly every word, portraying in expression his own feelings at the time, was the most laughable thing he ever heard.

Joshua Gardner Testified to the Wonderful Phenomena

Among the many letters in answer to the advertisement for the Bell Witch, after it went into the hands of the publisher, the following from W. H. Gardner, a prominent business man of Union City, Tenn., and A. E. Gardner, of Dresden. Tenn., a gentleman favorably known throughout the State for his high integrity, presents evidence regarding Joshua Gardner's experience with the witch demonstrations:

UNION CITY, TENN., April 20, 1894

M. V. Ingram — Dear Sir:

When will your book, "History of the Bell Witch," be out? My uncle, Joshua Gardner, was a conspicuous figure in the remarkable affair, as Betsy Bell's lover, and of course I want to read your history. Truly, as you say, it is the most wonderful phenomenon that ever occurred in this or any other country, and which will no doubt ever remain a mystery. I can recall, perhaps, an hundred occasions since I was a boy that I heard Uncle Joshua relating the remarkable story, and strange: to say, in the latter years of his life, he was loath to speak of it, even when urged to recount the queer doings and sayings of the witch, and then, if one of his hearers manifested the least inclination to disbelieve, he would desist. He believed in it as strong as he held to his religion, and a more devoted, conscientious Christian man never lived than Joshua Gardner. He died a few years since at the age of eighty-four years. I remember that Uncle Joshua received a copy of the Philadelphia Saturday Evening Post of 1849, containing a long and interesting account of the witch, written by a reporter. We kept the paper until a few years since, but it has in some way been lost and cannot now be found. I understand that Mrs. Wade, living near here, who is now ninety years of age, was a witness to the stirring and exciting incidents. There are several persons in this vicinity who are familiar with the history of the witch, and agree perfectly as to the facts of the remarkable phenomenon.

Respectfully,

W. H. GARDNER

DRESDEN TENN., April 25, 1894

M. V. Ingram — Dear Sir:

I see notice of your intention to publish a history of the "Bell Witch." My uncle, Joshua Gardner, figured considerably in the life of the witch, and of course I have heard a great deal about it and feel anxious to see the history, and will ask you to put me down as one of your first subscribers.

Respectfully,

A. E. GARDNER

THE BELL WITCH PROJECT

Chapter 15

LATEST DEMONSTRATIONS

The Witch's Return After Seven Years

Williams Bell says when the witch took its departure in 1821, bidding adieu to the family, it promised to return in seven years. He also records the fact that it did return according to promise, remaining some two weeks, making the same demonstrations that characterized the first appearing, and that himself, Joel Bell and their mother, Mrs. Lucy Bell, were the only members of the family then remaining at the old homestead — John, Drew and Betsy, those accused of producing the demonstrations, having all gone away to themselves, and were not apprised of the reappearance, the three having agreed to keep the matter a profound secret, lest the old troubles should be renewed. This statement is substantiated by Joel, who in later years never hesitated to talk about the family troubles, detailing the circumstances to interested friends inquiring into the mystery.

He consulted with his brother in regard to the publication, read his manuscript, and knew everything that was in it. Williams Bell, however, does not vouch for the many reports of strange noises and varied sounds, and mysterious appearances, seen and heard about the place and at several other places in that end of the county, to which others testify; much of the testimony to these apparitions has been omitted. He heard no more of it up to the date of his writing, 1846. Later than this, however, there is some well substantiated evidence to demonstrations similar to the early manifestations.

After the death of Mrs. Lucy Bell, the land was divided, and Joel received the river plot, adjoining Williams on the north, on which he settled after his marriage.

THE BELL WITCH PROJECT

Dr. Henry H. Sugg's Statement

Dr. Henry H. Sugg's statement is first of importance, which the writer is authorized to repeat by three highly creditable persons, one a lady, and the others, Col. Thomas Trigg, of Montgomery County, Tenn., and Mr. John A. Gunn, to whom he made the statement at different times, and all repeat it precisely alike; also Col. Yancey narrates the same story. Dr. Sugg said he was called to Joel Bell's to see a sick child. This was about 1852. It was a cold day, and entering the house as usual he found a comfortable fire burning, and placing his medical pocket on the floor by the door as he entered, he seated himself by the fire to warm. Immediately he heard a rapping or rattling of glass in the valise, and instantly following this was an explosive sound like the popping of corks, and a crash of the vials. He was sure that every bottle in the valise had been smashed, and he jumped up excitedly to ascertain the cause, but on opening the valise, found nothing out of place and no harm done. Mr. Bell also observed the same thing, and remarked that such things were common, that he never paid any attention to them. This statement is further supported and given additional significance.

Reynolds Powell's Story

Reynolds Powell tells the story of a circumstance that occurred at the same place in 1861. Joel Bell sold this farm to his brother Williams, and after the death of Williams Bell, the place was allotted to his son, Allen Bell, who cultivated it several years before he was married.

The writer visited Mrs. Annie Powell, a daughter of the late Dr. Scott, of Barren Plains, Robertson County, and widow of DeWitt Powell, who now resides near Barren Plains, for the purpose of interviewing her on the subject in hand. We found her quite an interesting lady, familiar with the entire history of the Bell Witch, as she had heard it repeated by her father and mother, and mother-in-law, the Gunn family, and many others, rehearsing, as she did, many of the circumstances already recorded, remarking in the conversation, "Allen Bell could, tell you a very interesting circumstance if he would, but I have no idea that he will, as he has never spoken of it to any of us. Reynolds Powell, however, told all about the affair the next day after it happened. Allen Bell had about recovered from a hard spell of sickness. In fact he was discharged from the army soon after he joined on account of bad health, from which he was not expected to recover. Reynolds Powell went down to spend a night with him during his convalescence, and on his return home next morning he told how bad he and Allen were scared. Allen had been staying with his stepmother, but other company came in, and they went over to Allen's place to sleep, in order to make room.

THE BELL WITCH PROJECT

They retired, leaving the doors open for fresh air, and very soon, he said, the dog commenced barking furiously, and ran into the house greatly frightened, while a strange noise was heard without. The dog continued snarling, snapping and barking in a frightened way that indicated a close contest with something. They got up to see what was the matter, but could not discover anything unusual and put the dog out, closing the doors. The dog took to his feet and left the place, and all was quiet for the next hour, when they were awakened by the removal of the bolster from under their heads, and then followed the sheets, being jerked from under them. They arose to investigate the cause, but could find nothing out of the regular order of things.

They replaced the sheet and bolster, securely bolted the doors, and retired again, placing a light cover over them. After some while the same trick was repeated, the cover bolster and sheet all being snatched from the bed. They replaced the things, which were removed the third time. They then placed the bolster on the bed, and laid with their breasts across it, holding with their hands, determined to retain it, but it was immediately snatched away with great force., and the bolster was thrown on top of their heads, and this ended the contest. He said they didn't sleep much, and I suppose that was true. You ask Allen about it."

Reynolds Powell was killed in the Confederate army after this. The Writer interviewed Allen Bell in regard to the circumstance, and he admitted that it was substantially true, but he was surprised to learn that Reynolds Powell had ever told it to any one. He said, however, that the demonstrations were never repeated while he remained on the place. This demonstration was characteristic of the performances at John Bell's, and was evidently the acts of the same agency.

Another characteristic incident in the same vicinity, or on the Bell place, several years later, to which reputable gentlemen testify, is here presented.

Music of the Enchanted Spring

John A. Gunn and A. L. Bartlett testify that during the year 1866 they had occasion to cross Red River, and the stream having swollen too full for fording; they left their horses on the south, or Bell side of the river, and crossed over in a canoe. Returning late in the afternoon, they landed near the famous enchanted spring, designated by the spirit as the hiding place of the treasure trove. They did not land there, however, with any expectation of finding the treasure — oh no. They sought a cooling draught of limpid water to quench their burning thirst, so they say, which is evidently true. However, after refreshing themselves, they started up the hill, when a sweet strain of music pierced their ears like a volume of

THE BELL WITCH PROJECT

symphony vibrating the air.

They both in voluntarily stopped, and seated themselves on a moss covered stone, listening to the ravishing melody which continued some thirty minutes. It was unlike any music they had ever heard. The modulating sound was indescribable, and unsurpassingly sweet. It was utterly impossible to discover from whence it came, the whole atmosphere seemed thrilled with vibrating euphony, and the gentlemen were caught up, as it were, on wings of ecstasy.

Heartless people who have no conception of the mysterious, no ear for music, no eye for the beautiful and no taste for the sweets of this life, ascribe such manifestations as this to the imagination under a peculiar state of mind, and bewildering circumstances. But not so in this case. These gentlemen were then in the vigor of young manhood, and had crossed the river that day in defiance of wind and wave to spend a joyous Sabbath with their best girls. Evidently they did not return with their hearts attuned to a heavenly sonnet, for neither of them married on the north side of the river, nor did they ever cross again on the same mission, and therefore could not have experienced the passionate throbbings that calls forth such an euphonious dulcet.

The writer can bear testimony to some remarkable experiences in crossing the same stream near the charmed spring, and it is under altogether different circumstances and state of mind that ones imaginations take flight, catching sweet intonations from the rippling waves, and chasing billows, bringing the cadence into diapason with the melody of the birds, and the chant of the sylph, forming a transporting consonance that carries the soul beyond that blessed abode where the ordinary mortal is willing to stop. These gentlemen had no such experience; in truth they sought a draught of lethe in all possible haste — a spring known to all lovers of that section as the gushing stream of oblivion, and he who drinks may depart in forgetfulness. Kate the spirit, is ever present to administer to the comfort of' a despairing swain.

There was no circumstance attending this incident that could have possibly exercised the imagination. The gentlemen were tired and had no imagination, and there could not have been any illusion or delusion, in the melodious sound that pierced their ears. It was no other than Kate, the witch, who always put in just at the right time and place unexpectedly and most mysteriously, and no doubt that the sweet strains of music was very helpful to their fatigued feelings.

Be this as it may, they are men of veracity and testify to the truth of this incident. They were then fresh from the field of battle, familiar with the sound of rattling musketry and roaring cannon, and were not easily frightened or deceived. Kate was a musical witch, and the circumstance is characteristic of the acts performed years before.

The writer has information of two incidents which occurred in 1872, a few miles from the Bell place, that were of the same nature and character of the disturbances that annoyed the Bell family so much, and unmistakably emanated from the same source or agency. These demonstrations were witnessed by two young ladies who could not have been mistaken. But, for proper and prudent reasons, they request that the circumstances and details be omitted in this publication, and in deference to their wishes they are not recorded. However, these incidents are sufficient to enable the author to trace the operations, of the agency known as the "Bell Witch" from 1817 to 1872, a period of fifty-five years, and he leaves readers to form their own conclusion as to the nature and authorship of the demonstrations. The testimony presented is given on the authority and statements of the very best people of the country, men and women who would not tend their names and influence for the purpose of making up a story of fiction, and altogether goes to establish, beyond question or doubt the existence for fifty-five years of the greatest mystery and wonder that the world has any account of.

The writer has only to say in conclusion, that if it was the work of human agency, the author was a shrewd devil, of great age and wonderful cunning, to have escaped detection during so long a reign terrorizing the fears of timid people, continuing still at large undiscovered and unknown, in a country of sharp detectives, set to catch evil doers of every description. Conceding that it is possible for a person or persons, through any kind of mechanism, skill or human genius, to inaugurate such a mystifying terror, continuing over a half century undiscovered, is to admit that the present century of Christian civilization has progressed far beyond any other age in developing deviltry in human nature.

END OF THE ORIGINAL BOOK

Continued >

THE BELL WITCH PROJECT

THE BELL WITCH PROJECT

The Mississippi Bell Witch Legend

Bell Witch legends are almost as prevalent in Mississippi as they are in Tennessee. This is due to the fact that the families of two of John Bell's children, Jesse Bell and Esther Bell Porter, moved to Mississippi in the 1830's.

Also, late in life, Betsy Bell Powell removed to Yalobusha County MS where she died in 1888.

The noted folklorist, Arthur Palmer Hudson (1892-1978), was instrumental in preserving two of these legends for posterity.

FIRST VERSION

In 1928, while a Professor of English at the University of Mississippi, Hudson published a book entitled SPECIMENS OF MISSISSIPPI FOLKLORE under the auspices of the Mississippi Folklore Society. At pages 157-160 of this book is found a version of the Bell Witch Legend which differs significantly from the Tennessee legends and which I have appended as follows:

THE BELL "WITCH"

For some time I have known of the existence of the story of the Bell "witch." Miss Lois Womble, of Water Valley, first told me about it. She knew only of its general outlines — a family by the name of Bell pursued from Illinois (as she heard the story) to Mississippi by a sort of larva familiae which its members called a witch, and which exerted its malign powers in various ways, from rough practical jokes terrifying in their effects to serious harm.

Last summer I asked Miss Ethel Lewellen, who was then living in Panola County, the home of one branch of the Bell family, whether she had ever heard of the Bell "witch." She replied that she had, but beyond mentioning that she had

THE BELL WITCH PROJECT

heard of a book on the subject she was able to contribute little to what I had heard from Miss Womble. She promised, however, to make inquiries and to transmit to me whatever she discovered. To her I owe most of the facts, presented in her own language below.

One other informant, Mr. Fonnie Black Ladd, who formerly resided at Oakland, Mississippi, and who is now a student in the University, added a few details of the story which Miss Lewellen's account lacked.

The details from both accounts do not, I am sure, tell the whole story of the Bell "witch." It is probable that not even the book referred to tells it all, for the story, like all stories that become the property of the folk, apparently has many mutations, and has undoubtedly been growing since the book was published (as the testimony indicates to be a fact). Lacking the book, which I hope eventually to see, I set down the details in the order which they seem to sustain to one another.

Miss Lewellen writes as follows in a letter transmitting her account of the story:

"Bauxite, Arkansas, March 28, 1928.

"Mr. A. P. Hudson, University, Miss.

"Dear Mr. Hudson:

"So far, the book containing the Bell Witch story has not been located; but if I can ever find it, I shall be glad to send it to you.

"I am enclosing some of the stories that the older members of our community could remember about the Witch - or rather the Wizard. I am told that the family of Bells who believed so implicitly in this 'Witch' moved to Mississippi in the hope of ridding themselves of its presence.

"I am glad to send you this for I think it pictures some of the beliefs of ignorant, superstitious, though probably good, people of earlier days.

Sincerely,

ETHEL LEWELLEN."

"To Panola County, about a half century ago," Miss Lewellen begins, "there moved with the Bell family a 'witch' that tormented one of the Bell girls and caused a great deal of suspicion to arise among the other members of the family and the community."

Mr. Fonnie Black Ladd, from recollections of the story as he heard it in his childhood at Oakland, adds some details about the circumstances in which the family moved to Mississippi. The Bells were living at Bell, Tennessee. Becoming dissatisfied, the father of the family expressed his desire to sell his farm and go somewhere else. The mother was opposed to going. One of the daughters agreed with her father and argued in favor of going to Mississippi. One night the lar familiaris of the family spoke to her and warned her against going. The daughter nevertheless persisted in her arguments and finally persuaded her father to sell out and move to Mississippi. Before the family left, the lar addressed her again and threatened to pursue her with its vengeance.

When they got to Mississippi, Miss Lewellen's account proceeds, "the members of the family talked of sending this girl away so that they might be free from the 'Witch's' awful presence. They also hoped that the girl might rid herself of the unspeakable torture which the 'Witch' visited upon her. 'There's no use for you to do this,' said a Voice, 'for no matter where she goes I will follow.'

"No one was ever able to see the 'Witch'; but often some member of the family would see food disappear as the 'Witch' carried it from the cupboard to 'his' mouth. 'His' favorite food was cream, and 'he' took it from every jar of milk. The Bells were never able to get any butter from the milk they churned.

"An old Negro woman once hid under a bed and tried to see the 'Witch' but ere she had long been there, something began to bite, scratch, and pinch her; and she was almost killed before she could get out.

"Although the 'Witch' treated the girl very cruelly, 'he' was not entirely inimical to other members of the family; on the contrary, 'he' proved very helpful on several occasions.

"One day Mr. Bell was talking of visiting a family in which every one was ill. 'I have just come from there,' said a Voice from nowhere, and proceeded to describe the physical condition of every member of the family, and also to tell what every member of the family was doing on that particular day. Investigation showed that the report of illness was false and proved the accuracy of every detail of the Voice's account of the state and activities of the family.

"On another occasion Mr. Bell was preparing to go for a doctor to attend one of his sick children. The Voice said, 'There's no need for you to go; I can get the doctor.' No one else went, but in due time the doctor came.

"One day the 'Witch' caused the wagon in which the Bells were going to church to stop on level ground. After vain efforts to get their horses to start the wagon again, the unseen hand of the 'Witch' lifted the wagon and horses off the road, transported it through the air a short distance, and set it down again without harming any one."

Mr. Ladd tells another story of the wagon which may be merely a variant of the foregoing, but which has some circumstances indicating that it is independent. To understand its proper connection beyond Miss Lewellen's remark that the "witch's" attentions to other members of the family were not always malignant but were sometimes benevolent, the reader will remember that Mrs. Bell, according to Mr. Ladd's account of the circumstances attending the removal of the family to Mississippi, opposed leaving the Tennessee home. Thus, according to Mr. Ladd, the "Witch" was always kind to the mother. Mr. Ladd's story runs like this:

One day the whole family was invited to attend a quilting bee. Mrs. Bell was ill; there was therefore some discussion about the propriety of leaving Mammy at home sick. As Daddy was invited too, the children all insisted on his going. There was a family row, the upshot of which was that everybody piled into the wagon and started, leaving Mammy at home sick. But before the happy party had proceeded far, the "Witch," champion of Mammy's rights, asserted himself. One of the wheels of the wagon flew off and let the axle down into the road with a bump. Not much disturbed by what seemed to be a mere accident, the boys and the old man piled out and replaced wheel and "tap." They had gone but a short distance when another wheel mysteriously flew off. Again they re placed the wheel and proceeded, somewhat sobered. Then one of the children saw a spectral hand pull another wheel off. When they had put it back in place, they held council, turned the team around and drove back home, going softly. On the way back not another wheel came off.

Another story by Mr. Ladd illustrates the puckish character which the Bell "Witch" sometimes assumed. On several occasions when the old man and the boys went out to catch the mules and horses in preparation for a day's work or a trip to town, the animals would resist bridling like mustangs, plunging around in the stable as if stung by invisible hornets or possessed of evil spirits. When finally harnessed or saddled, they would buck like broncos. These antics were always explained as the work of the Bell "Witch."

Miss Lewellen's account continues, showing that Mr. Bell had something of

THE BELL WITCH PROJECT

the scientific spirit:

"Mr. Bell was very curious about the 'Witch,' and finally persuaded 'him' to permit the familiarity of a handshake. He promised not to squeeze the hand. The hand that Mr. Bell shook was as small, soft, and chubby as a baby's. One day Mr. Bell raised a discussion of how the 'Witch' entered the house. 'I raise a certain corner of the house and come in,' said a Voice outside. 'Watch.' The house top was raised several inches and then let down.

"Other people of the community reported that they often met what appeared to be a riderless horse; but the horse would stop, and some one on his back would carry on a conversation with the person met.

To return to the girl, the devoted object of the "Witch's" vengeance. Mr. Ladd was unable to recall concrete details of the general statement that the "Witch" tormented her and tortured her. Miss Lewellen gives only one instance:

"One time the girl whom the 'Witch' tortured was getting ready to go to a party. As she was combing her hair, it suddenly became full of crockleburs. The 'Witch' explained, 'I put these in your hair; you have no business going to the party.' The men-folks came in and fired shots in the direction from which the voice came; but every shot was met by one from the invisible hand of the 'Witch,' and the engagement proved a draw.

Miss Lewellen concludes her account of the Bell "Witch" with the statement;

"The girl grieved her life away; and after her death the 'Witch' never returned either to torment or to comfort the Bells."

Mr. Fonnie Black Ladd supplies the final detail describing the funeral of the unhappy girl. The coffin containing the body was conveyed to the country graveyard in a farm wagon. As the little procession drove out of the yard of the homestead, some one looked up and saw a great black bird, something like a buzzard or the bird which the Negroes call a "Good God," with a bell around its neck slowly ringing, This great bird flew with miraculous slowness above and just ahead of the lumbering wagon all the way to the graveyard, and poised in air over the grave while the funeral service was being held. Then it flew away, the bell still slowly ringing. And the Bell "Witch" never visited the family again.

SECOND VERSION

In northern Mississippi, where descendants of the original family concerned

THE BELL WITCH PROJECT

still live, the legend survives in somewhat fragmentary but independent, orally traditional form. Of the considerable number of people who told it, or parts of it, to us, a few said that they had seen "The book" a long time ago, and most of the others had heard of a book; but we were unable to find a copy in Mississippi.

Our following version of the legend has been recovered exclusively from oral tradition in Mississippi, and was put together before we ever saw a printed version. Most of our sources know the main outlines but remember especially some particular episodes or motives. A few tell the whole substantially as we reproduce it. But there is great diversity in the details and motives. We have taken the main outline on which all agree and have sketched in, as consistently as possible, the minutiae from numerous Mississippi sources. The dialect used, the few simple figures of speech, and the folk locutions are genuine and are true to the speech of our informants.

Back in the days before the War there lived somewhere in old North Carolina a man by the name of John Bell. Bell was a planter and was well-fixed. He had a good-sized plantation and a dozen niggers of field-hand age, and mules and cows and hogs a-plenty. His family was made up of his wife, a daughter thirteen or fourteen years old they say was mighty pretty, and two or three young-uns that don't figure much in this story. Until he hired him an overseer, Bell got along fine.

The overseer was a Simon Legree sort of fellow, always at sixes and sevens with other folks, and especially with the niggers. He didn't even mind jawing with his boss. They say Mr. Bell was half a mind to fire the scoundrel and hire another one. But he tended to his business. He had a way with the womenfolks. Some say he had an eye open for Mary, the daughter. And Mrs. Bell stood up for him. So he stayed on for a good while, and the longer he stayed the uppiter he got. Whenever he and Bell had a row — and their rows got bigger and bitterer —the overseer went out and blacksnaked three or four niggers, for they were the only critters in the shape of man that he could abuse without a come-back. He was the worst kind of a bully, and a man of high temper, in fact, a regular overseer of the kind you hear about in Yankee stories.

Mr. Bell had a tall temper too, and the men did not spend a lot of time patting each other on the back and bragging about each other's good points. A stand-up fight was bound to come off.

It did. Some say it was about the way the overseer had beat up one of the niggers. Some say it was about something Mr. Bell heard and saw from behind a cotton-house one day when Mary rode through the field where the overseer was

THE BELL WITCH PROJECT

working a gang of niggers. Bell went away blowing smoke from his pistol barrel, and mumbling something about white trash. The overseer didn't go away at all.

Of course Bell was brought into court, but he plead self-defense, and the jury let him off. He went home, hired him another overseer, and allowed that everything was settled. But the truth was that everything was now plumb unsettled.

That year and the next and the next the crops on the Bell place were an out-and out failure: bumblebee cotton and scraggly tobacco and nubbin corn. His mules died of colic or some strange disease like it. His cows and hogs got sick of something the horse-doctor couldn't cure. He had to sell his niggers one by one, all except an old woman. Finally he went broke. He got what he could for his land — lock, stock, and barrel — and moved with his family to Tennessee. They say that where he settled down the town of Bell, Tennessee, was named for him. Any way, he bought him a house and a patch of land near the home of old Andy Jackson, who had knocked off from being President and was living in a big house called the Hermitage.

Not long after the move to Tennessee, strange things began to happen in the Bell home. The children got into the habit of tumbling, or being tumbled, out of bed at least once a week, and of waking up every morning with every stitch of the bed-clothes snatched off and their hair all tangled and mussed up. Now for young-uns to tumble out of bed and to wake up in the morning with their heads uncombed is a mighty strange thing, and the Bells realized it. The children couldn't explain this carrying-on, for they were always asleep till they hit the floor; and it was a peculiar fact that they were never tumbled out while awake.

The old nigger woman told them it was the ha'nt of the overseer Mr. Bell had killed that was pestering the children. She was as superstitious as any other nigger, and she said she had always felt jubous about what the ha'nt of a man like the overseer would do. But she had spunk, and one day she allowed she would find out whether she was right by spending the night under the young-uns' bed. In the middle of the night Mr. and Mrs. Bell were fetched out of their bed by a squall like a panther's. When they lit a lamp and ran into the room, they found the old nigger woman sprawled in the middle of the floor, dripping cold sweat like an ash-hopper, her face gray-blue as sugarcane peeling, and her eyes like saucers in a dishpan. She was stiff-jointed and tongue-tied. When they got her sitting up and her tongue loosened, she screeched: "It's him! It's him! For God, It's him! It pinched me all over, stuck pins in me, snatched de kinks outen ma haiuh, an' whup me, Lawd Gawd, how it whup me, whup me limber an' whup me stiff, whup me jes' lack him. Ain't goin back there no mo', ain't goin back there no mo'."

THE BELL WITCH PROJECT

The Bells were so scared they told some of the neighbors. Old Andy Jackson heard about it and decided to ride over. He didn't take any stock in ha'nts, and as he rode through the gate he spoke his mind out loud about tarnation fools that believed nigger tales about them. He hadn't got the words out of his mouth before something whaled him over the head and skipped his hat twenty or thirty yards back down the road. Old Andy didn't say any more. He motioned his nigger boy to hand him his hat, and he went away from there.

It seems like the Witch could get hungry like folks, and was satisfied with folks' grub. But it had to be the best. One day the old nigger woman came tearing into the front room where Mrs. Bell was quilting and said the Witch was back in the kitchen drinking up all the sweet milk.

Mrs. Bell was scared and said the old woman was lying. "Come see for yo'se'f, missus. Come see for yourself. Ah was back there a mixing up de biscuits, and ah reached ovah to get a cup of milk, and fo' Gawd, de cup was in de middle of de air, and de milk was a runnin' right outen hit — and hit wa'n't gwine nowhere, missus — hit wa'n't goin nowhere. Jes' run outen de cup, an' den Ah couldn't see hit no more." "You're just seeing things," said Mrs. Bell.

"Jes, whut Ah ain' doin' — ain' seein' de milk. Go on back in de kitchen efen you don' believe it. Go on back daub an' look fo' yo'self — No, ma'am, Ah hain' gwine back in dar place. No, ma'am, dat ha'nt kin guzzle an' bile up all de milk de cows ever give before Ah raise mah finger to stop hit."

Mrs. Bell went back into the kitchen and looked. There was a cup there that had had milk in it, and the milk was gone, sure as shootin'. She was now as scared as the old nigger woman, and sent right away for her husband to come out of the field.

They couldn't figure out how a ghost could drink milk, or what becomes of the milk if he does. Does the milk dry up into the ghost of itself? If not, where does it go when the ghost swallows it? Ghosts can't be seen. At least, this one couldn't. They could see through where it was. If they could see through it, why couldn't they see the milk as plain when it was inside the ghost as when it was outside? The old nigger woman said the milk was running out of the cup, but it "wa'n't goin nowhere." An old Holy Roller preacher from down in Tallahatchie bottom who rode over to talk about it argued that, if the old woman's tale was true, milk must be of a higher class than folks. When it turns into the soul of itself, it leaves nothing behind; but folks leave behind a corpse that must be covered up with dirt right away. Folks argued about it on front galleries in the summer time and around the fire in winter — but they didn't argue about it on the Bells' front gallery or by the Bells' fire. And the preachers preached about it at camp meetings.

But the Witch didn't let up on the Bells' grub. No one ever saw it; but lots of times some member of the family would see something to eat dive out of the cupboard or pop out of the safe. The Witch's favorite was cream, and he got to skimming it from every pan in the spring-house. The Bells were never able to get any butter from the churning.

Mr. Bell might have stood for having his young-uns' rest disturbed and his old nigger woman all tore up this way, but he couldn't stand for letting the ghost eat him out of house and home. So he called the family together and allowed he would move again — this time to Mississippi, where land was rich and cheap. Mrs. Bell raised up.

"Pa," said she, "it seems like to me we have been getting along tolerable well here. I don't see any use moving away. What would be to keep the Witch from following us down there?"

"Nothing in the world," spoke up a hide-bottomed chair from a corner of the room. "I'll follow you wherever you go," the Chair went on. "And I'll tell you what: if you stay on here, I won't bother you much; but if you go traipsing off to Mississippi — well, you'll wish you hadn't."

Mr. Bell was scared and bothered, but he studied a while and screwed up his courage enough to ask the Witch why he couldn't live where he pleased. But there was no answer. He asked some more questions. But the Chair had lapsed into the habit of silence that chairs have.

Mary, Mr. Bell's daughter, was now old enough to argue with the old folks about things. She was pretty as a spotted puppy, they say, and had lots of spunk and took after her pa. She sided with him. Girls always like to be moving. So when the family got over its scare about the Chair they argued back and forth. But finally Mrs. Bell and what they remembered about the Witch got the upper hand. Mr. Bell and Mary gave up the idea of moving to Mississippi, for a while anyway.

And for a while the Witch eased up on them. It even did some good turns. One day Mr. Bell was talking of visiting a family across the creek where he had heard everybody was sick. "I have just come from there," said a Voice from the eight-day clock, and went on to tell how well everybody was and what everybody was doing. Later Mr. Bell met up with a member of the family and learned that everything the Witch said was so.

THE BELL WITCH PROJECT

Maybe because she had taken side with him in the argument about going to Mississippi, the Witch was partial to Mrs. Bell. The old nigger woman said the ha'nt sided with her because she had stood up for the overseer when Mr. Bell wanted to fire him in North Carolina.

One Christmas time the family was invited to a taffy-pulling. Mrs. Bell was sick and couldn't go. They talked about whether they ought to go off and leave their mammy feeling poorly. Mr. Bell was invited too, and they needed him to do the driving; so Mary and the children begged him to take them. Mrs. Bell told them to go ahead, she didn't need them and could make out all right. So they all piled into the wagon and started.

But before they got far one of the wagon wheels flew off and let the axle down into the road with a bump. It looked like a common accident, and the old man climbed down and put the wheel back on the axle and stuck the linchpin in. He looked at all the other linchpins and saw they were on all right. Before long another wheel flew off. They looked on the ground for the linchpin but couldn't find it there. Mr. Bell whittled a new one, and when he went to put the wheel back on he found the old one in place. He fixed the wheel and drove off again, telling all of the children to watch all of the wheels. Soon they saw something like a streak of moonshine dart around the wagon, and all four wheels flew off, and the wagon dropped kersplash into a mud-hole. They put them back on, turned round, and drove back home, going quiet and easy, like sitting on eggs.

When they got there, they found their mammy sitting up by the Christmas tree eating a plate of fresh strawberries, and feeling lots better.

Other pranks were laid to the Witch. Often when the old man and the boys would go to the stable to catch the horses and mules for the day's plowing or a trip to town, the critters would back their ears and rare and kick and stomp like hornets or yellow-jackets were after them. Some morning they would be puny as chickens with the pip, and caked with sweat and mud, and their manes and tails tangled in witch-locks. The neighbors said that off and on they met an unbridled and bare backed horse, and the horse would stop, and something on his back that they couldn't see would talk to them — but not long — they had business the other way.

Maybe because Mary had sided with her pa against her mammy and the Witch, the Witch was harder on her after the argument than on anybody else. She would wake up in the middle of the night, screaming and crying that something cold and heavy had been sitting on her breast, sucking her breath and pressing

THE BELL WITCH PROJECT

the life out of her.

One time she was getting ready to go to a play-party. Some of the young sprouts were waiting for her in the front room. While she was combing her long, black hair, it suddenly was full of cockleburs. She tugged and pulled and broke the comb to untangle it, and when she couldn't, she leaned on the bureau and cried.

"I put them in your hair," said the Witch from the looking-glass. "You've got no business going to the party. Stay here with me. I can say sweet things to you."

She screamed, and the young fellows rushed in the room, and when she told them about the Voice they shot at the glass with their pistols. But the glass didn't break. And the Witch caught every bullet and pitched it into their vest pockets and laughed. So they called it a draw and went out of there. And Mary stayed at home.

Mary was now mighty near grown. She had turned out to be a beautiful woman. She had lots of beaux. But whenever one of them screwed himself up to the point of popping the question he always found that the words stuck in his throat and his face and ears burned. For young fellows these were strange signs. But it was always that way. And none of them seemed to be able to ask Mary the question. They laid it on the Witch, and finally quit hitching their horses to the Bell fence.

All but one. His name was Gardner. He was a catch for any girl, smart as a briar, good-looking, easy-going and open-hearted, and the owner of rich bottom land, a passel of niggers, and a home as big as the courthouse, with columns as tall and white. He got all wrapped up in Mary, and they say Mary was leaning to him.

The way of the Witch with him was different, more businesslike. Maybe it was because the Witch realized this was the man Mary was setting her heart on. One night when Gardner was walking up the row of cedars in the Bell yard to see Mary, something he couldn't see reached out from a big cedar and touched him on the shoulder, and a voice said, "Wait a minute." Gardner was afraid to wait, but he was more afraid to run. So he waited.

"You might as well understand, here and now, that you are not going to have Mary Bell."

"Why not?" Gardner asked.

THE BELL WITCH PROJECT

"You might have guessed from all that's happened round here. I'm in love with her myself. It's going to be hard to get her consent, and it may be harder to get the old man's. But she's not going to marry you. I'll see to that. If you open your mouth about it tonight, you'll be dead as a doornail before morning."

Gardner studied a while and said, "If you'd only come out like a man."

The cedar tree stepped out and snatched his hat off and stomped it.

"Well, I reckon I'll have to lay off for a while," says Gardner. "But I do love her, and I'd go to the end of the world for …. "

"Well, you don't have to go that far, and it wouldn't do you any good if you did, and if you love her the only way you can keep her out of hell is to get out yourself. If you keep on hanging round here, I'll make it hell for you. Now this is how far you go. Pack up your traps and get out of the country, hide and hair. Go any place you think the Bells won't hear tell of you — and go before breakfast. If you slip out quiet without raising any ruckus I'll never pester you again. What's more, on the day you get married I'll give you a pair of new boots you'll be proud of all your life."

Gardner couldn't see why the Witch's promise of a pair of wedding boots was in the same class as the threat of death before breakfast, but he didn't split hairs, and he didn't argue any more. He picked up his hat, sneaked back to his horse, and rode off.

He never said or wrote a thing to the Bells about what had happened, part because he was scared, but more because he was ashamed of being scared. He left the neighborhood before sunup and moved to the western part of the state. He got somebody else to sell out for him. They say the town of Gardner, where he settled, was named after him when he got old and respected.

After he had been there a while he fell in love with a girl and got engaged to her. And they say that when he was dressing for the wedding he couldn't find his boots. He looked high and low, every place a pair of boots was liable to be and lots of places where they couldn't possibly be, but no boots could he find. He was about to give up and go to his wedding in his sock feet, when a Voice told him to crawl out from under the bed and look in the bed. And there between the sheets he found a pair of shiny new boots. He put them on and went his way rejoicing and thinking of how well a ghost kept his word, and wondering if the boots would ever wear out and if they were like the Seven-League boots he had read about in old McGuffey.

THE BELL WITCH PROJECT

But they looked like natural boots. He told some of his friends how he had got them. They thought he was a liar. But they had to own up they were wrong. One day Gardner's houseboy made a mistake and carried them instead of another pair to a cobbler. The cobbler said they were in perfect shape; they were not made by mortal hands; and the soles were sewed on in a way that no man or man-made machine could have stitched them. And there is a lady in this neighborhood who has seen the boots.

While Gardner's mind was getting mossed over about Mary, Mr. Bell decided again to move to Mississippi. It looked like his move from North Carolina was jumping from the frying pan into the fire, but he figured maybe the skillet wouldn't be any hotter. Gardner's break-up with Mary and Mary not marrying hung heavy on his mind. Mrs. Bell raised up again, telling him about rolling stones. And the Witch homed in. By this time the family got used to the Witch and would talk free with him, but respectful. Every time the question came up there was a row between Mr. Bell and Mary on one side and Mrs. Bell and the Witch on the other. The old nigger woman told Mr. Bell the ha'nt didn't want him to move because he was afraid of witch hunters in Mississippi. She said there were powerful ones down there.

And so one winter after the crops had petered out on him again, he sold his place dirt cheap. But the old nigger woman told him to wait till spring to start. She said Easter was early that year and there would be plenty of time to pitch a crop. Good Friday would be a good day to leave, she said, for the ha'nt would have to go back to his grave and stay three days under the ground and would be puny-like several days more. While he was in good working order he could be in two or three places at once and be in any of them in the bat of an eye, but then he would have to lie low, and that would give them plenty of start. So Mr. Bell early on Good Friday stacked his furniture and duds in a couple of wagons, climbed into the front one with Mary, put the old nigger woman and his biggest boy into the hind one, and told Mrs. Bell, "Get in with old Patsy if you're a-comin', and don't forget the young-uns."

And that was the way the Bell family came to Mississippi. Mr. Bell bought him a little place in Panola County, ten miles east of Batesville on the Oxford road. He was all ready to begin life over again without supernatural interference.

But the Witch made a quick come-back, not before the family got there, but before they moved into their new home.

When Mr. Bell first got to Batesville, or Panola as they called it then, he left

THE BELL WITCH PROJECT

the family there and went out to look at the land he aimed to buy. When he got a place that suited him, he went back to town for his family and stuff. There was some sort of hitch, and the wagons did not get started till late in the evening. As the wagons moved slowly out of town, dark clouds began to roll up in the south and west, and before they had gone three miles the storm broke. Dark came on earlier than usual, for the clouds hid the sun. The rain beat down on the wagon covers. Every now and then the lightning flashes lit up the swaying trees on each side of the road, the draggle-tailed horses, and the road itself, — a long, muddy creek, — and then it was dark as a stack of black cats. The folks all stopped talking. There was nothing to listen to but the beating rain and the thunder and the suck of the horses' feet and the wheels in the mud.

All at once the hind wagon, with the family in it, slid to the side of the road and sunk into the mud up to the bed. Mr. Bell saw it in a lightning flash and came back. It couldn't be moved; the horses had no purchase and the wheels were in too deep. And then the Witch took a hand.

"If you'll go back to your wagon and stop your cussin'," said the empty dark beside the wagon, "I'll get you out. Hump it back to your wagon now — light a shuck!"

Mr. Bell waded back and crawled in.

And then the horses and the wagon and the furniture and the family and the dog under the wagon and the calf tied behind and everything else but the mud on the wheels rose up about eight feet high and floated down the road till they were just behind the front wagon, and then they settled down easy and went on home without any trouble.

The family got settled down in their two-story double-log house amongst the cedars on the Oxford road.

A few nights later, the Witch spoke up from one of the andirons and told Mr. and Mrs. Bell he was in love with Mary. He said he wanted to marry her. Mr. Bell was shocked and surprised. He explained, respectful but emphatic like, that he could never dream of letting a daughter of his marry a ghost, not even so noble a ghost like the one he was talking with.

"I got a claim on you, John Bell," said the Witch. "I got a claim on you and on yours. I got a claim." And his voice was deep and hollow-like.

This was a point Mr. Bell maybe didn't want to hear any more about. So he

THE BELL WITCH PROJECT

said, "Have you spoken to Mary?"

"No, not spoken."

"Well, how do you know she would have you?"

"I don't. But I haven't got any reason to believe she wouldn't love me. She's never seen me. She doesn't know whether she would or not. Maybe she would consider it an honor to be married to a ghost. Not many girls are, you know. Why, it would make her famous."

"I don't want any daughter of mine getting famous that way. And besides, what if you were to have children? What in the world do you reckon they'd be like? Like you or her? Maybe half good human meat and bone, and the other half sight unseen. Or maybe, they'd be the vanishing kind and going round here and raising hell invisible. Do you think I want a passel of soap suds young-uns floating round here and popping up into puffs of wind every time I pointed to the stove wood pile or sprouts on a ditch bank? Not on your life. I reckon plain flesh and blood's good enough for Mary."

"But, John Bell, I love Mary. And remember. Remember."

"So do I, and that's why I'm not going to let you marry her. Why, when she got old and hard-favored I reckon you'd quit her for some young hussy. You could do it easy enough. Mary'd have a hard time keeping up with a stack of wind and a voice, and I'd have a hard time tracking down and shooting a low-down, no-count dust devil. When Mary marries, she marries a man that's solid and alive in body."

"I gather, John Bell, that you're opposed to me courting your daughter. But she's the one to say, and I'm going to talk to her about it. You'll be my father-in-law yet, or you'll be a-mourning, a-mourning."

"But what kind of wedding would it be like?" Mrs. Bell put in. "Think of it. Mary standing in front of the preacher and the preacher saying, 'Do you take this woman?' to a vase of flowers. And the ring floating down to Mary from the hanging-lamp maybe, or rising up from under a bench. I won't stand for it. I've stood for a lot of things, and you can't say I haven't been a friend to you. But I won't stand for Mary being a laughing-stock and disgrace to the family."

"If we're a-going to add to this family," Mr. Bell took up, "we're a-going to be able to see what we're adding. I don't even know what shape you've got, if any."

THE BELL WITCH PROJECT

"Oh, I can give you some idea what shape I have. I'll let you shake hands with me. But you must promise not to squeeze. We're very delicate, especially when we touch folks. Here, hold out your hand, and I'll put mine in it."

Mr. Bell held out his hand, felt something, and grabbed it. It was, he said later, the hand of a newborn baby — soft and crinkly and warm and just about the size of a newborn baby's hand. "How big are you all over?" he asked.

"I can't tell you that."

"Well, there's one other thing I want to know. How do you get into this house any time you want to when every window and door is locked and barred? Do you ooze through the walls?"

"No. It's a lot easier than that. If you'll watch the corner of the ceiling up there, you'll see."

And all the rest of his life Mr. Bell swore to trustworthy witnesses that he saw the corner of the ceiling raised a good three feet and then let down again—all without the slightest racket.

"Do you mean to tell me that anything with a hand like that can lift the top off of the house that way?"

"Sure," came the answer. "But — about Mary. I'm going to talk to her right off."

"Don't," said Mr. Bell. "Do you want to drive her crazy?"

But the meeting was over, for there was no answer. And the fire had died down, and the andiron looked glum.

The story is kind of skimpy here. Nobody seems to know what the Witch said to Mary or what Mary said to the Witch.

But the family noticed next day that she was drooping and wasn't minding what was going on around her. For days she wandered about the house and up and down the yard under the gloomy old cedars, like somebody sleepwalking. And the color left her face, and deep in her wide-open black eyes was a faraway look, like she was trying to see something that ought to be but wasn't there. Every day she got up later and went to bed earlier.

THE BELL WITCH PROJECT

And finally there came a day when she didn't get up at all. In the evening a screech-owl hollered in a cedar right by the gallery.

That night her fever was high, and by midnight she was raving. "We've put off seeing a doctor too long," said Mrs. Bell.

"The roads like they are, it'll take me two hours going and him and me two hours coming," said Mr. Bell. "It'll be might' nigh daylight before we get back. But I reckon you're right, and I'll go as quick as I can saddle a horse."

"No use," said a Voice. "All the doctors and medicines in the world won't cure her. But if you want one, I'll get him, and get him a lot quicker than you can."

The doctor got there just as the old eight-day clock struck one. "I heard somebody hollering at my window about midnight, telling me to come out here right away. When I got to the door, nobody was there; but I thought I'd better come anyway." He was a young doctor just starting out. "Say, what kind of road overseer and gang do you fellows have out this way? Last time I came over this road, about Christmas, it was the worst I ever saw. Why, I picked up a Stetson hat in the middle of a mud-hole near the four-mile board, and by George there was a man under it. 'You're in the middle of a bad fix, old man,' I said. 'Hell,' he said, 'that ain't nothin' to the fix this mule's in under me.' I had to lift up my feet half the way to keep them from dragging in the mud by the horse's belly. But tonight my horse skimmed over it in an hour. Well, who's sick out here?"

"It's her mind and nerves," he told them after he had questioned them and examined Mary. "I won't conceal from you, she's in pretty bad shape. And medicine won't do her any good. You've just got to be gentle and careful with her. Humor her and be patient with her. I'll give her something to put her to sleep when she gets like this. Watch her close and don't let her get lonesome. She's young and strong and ought to come round in time."

But she never did. For a month she lay there on the bed, looking at nothing and yet straining to see something, something too far off. At night her pa and ma took turns sitting up. They didn't want the neighbors in. They called the doctor back a few times, but he shook his head and said he couldn't do any more. So they would watch and wait, wanting to do something, but helpless.

One night her ma was sitting there, holding Mary's hand and stroking the dark hair back from her forehead. Suddenly Mary pushed her mother away and sat up and looked across the foot of the bed, as if somebody was standing there.

THE BELL WITCH PROJECT

"Mamma," she whispered, "Mamma, I see him at last. And I think, I think I'm going to love him."

And she died with the only expression of happiness they had seen on her face in months.

Some folks have tried to explain Mary's strange death. A few say the Witch tortured her continually and kept her in such constant terror that her mind was affected. Others have heard that a schoolteacher ventriloquist that was jealous of Gardner played tricks on her and the family, and then, when she wouldn't have him, tormented and frightened her to death. Some believe she was in love with the overseer from the first, and then when he was killed she was in love with the Witch and didn't want to live because she knew she would never be happy with him until she too became a ghost.

But she died, just the same. And they say that on the day of the funeral, when the coffin was carried from the house to a wagon a great black bird flew down from the sky and hung in the air just above the wagon. And around its neck was a bell that tolled in the most mournful tone ever heard by the ear of man. And when the funeral procession began to move, the great bird floated just in front of it all the way to the graveyard and circled round and round the grave during the burial, the bell tolling all the while. And when the mound was rounded up, the bird swung high up in the air and flew away to the west and finally became just a little speck above the treetops and disappeared. But long after it was gone the mourning notes of the bell floated back to those who stood and watched.

SPOOKS, GHOSTS AND TELEPATHIC HALLUCINATIONS

Do you believe in Ghosts? Most educated men nowadays, it may be anticipated, would answer, No. A majority, or at lowest, a substantial minority of educated Europeans, at any date within the last two hundred years, would probably have given a similar answer had the question been put to them. But by the greater number of the human race at the present day, and by learned and unlearned, civilized and uncivilized alike, at any previous period in the world's history, an answer would unhesitatingly have been returned in the affirmative. In fact the belief in ghosts has been so widespread that it may almost be claimed as universal. The very conception of a future life is intimately bound up with the belief: it has left its traces on all the religions in the world.

The elaborate arrangements for embalming the dead amongst the Egyptians, the offerings to the dead which formed part of the funeral ceremonies in early civilizations, and are still found throughout a great part of the world at the present day, are obviously associated with the belief or at least the hope of the survival of a quasi-material soul a soul having form and substance, appetites and desires. Among the Egyptians the soul which was weighed in the balance and found wanting was doomed to be devoured by the Eater of the Dead. The Homeric ghosts were thin squeaking shadows, anaemic extracts of the heroes whose names they once bore, thronging to the smell of blood. We find the same idea in the once general terror of vampires, and in the part traditionally played by freshly shed blood in the ceremonials of black magic. Plato makes Socrates, in this no doubt reflecting the current belief of his day, speak of the soul of the sensual man as prowling in visible shape about tombs and sepulchres. Milton testifies to the same belief in his day.

" Such are those thick and gloomy shadows dank

Oft seen in charnel vaults and sepulchres,

Lingering and sitting by a new made grave

As loath to leave the body that it loved."

The Scotch alchemist, Maxwell, adopts the same belief and essays a scientific explanation of the facts. In mediaeval art the soul is constantly represented as a mistlike semi-transparent figure in the shape of the body, which issues from the mouth of the dying man to hover over the corpse, until it is borne away to its appointed place. A similar conception of the soul as having Bodily form runs through all poetical speculations on the after life, from Dante to Tennyson.

If we consider existing beliefs amongst the more primitive races we find the same conception. The Australian cuts off the right thumb of his dead enemy that he may be unable to throw a spear in the Spirit world; the Congo Negroes refrain from sweeping the house after death lest the dust should injure the ghost. The souls of his departed friends visit the savage in dreams. His conception of a future life is mainly, perhaps wholly, based on these dream visitations. We, the inhabitants of educated Europe, have learnt under the guidance of science to look upon dreams as simply the creations of our own imaginations. We no longer, in the popular phrase, "believe in dreams." But both savage and civilized men from the earliest historical times down to the present have professed, and still profess occasionally, to see figures of their dead friends, not in dreams but in waking life, with their own eyes open. It is these daylight apparitions for which the name of " ghosts " is now commonly reserved, and in view of the important part played by them in religious belief, from the earliest times down even to the present day, the enquiry into their nature and significance must needs be of serious interest.

THE BELL WITCH PROJECT

But before we ask what ghosts are we must endeavor to find an answer to the previous question whether in fact there are ghosts. We must first ascertain the facts. To most persons no doubt a ghost is like a sea serpent something which somebody hears that somebody else has seen, or thinks that he has seen, a long way off or a long time ago. We distrust the tales of the sea serpent, because they proceed for the most part from an uneducated and proverbially credulous class; because we rarely get them from the actual witness; because when the incident is told at first hand we generally find that it happened many years ago. But apart from the defects in the evidence, which may or may not be accidental, there is one special reason for distrusting these stories. The sea serpent is a familiar figure in folklore and mythology ; he has come down to us from the childhood of the world. As Dragon, Kraken or Behemoth, he is indelibly painted on the imagination of the race. From old travelers we hear of him guarding his horrid den in untrodden recesses of the Alps; in old maps we may see him corkscrewing his scaly folds through the wastes of uncharted seas. We suspect, therefore, and are probably justified in suspecting an hereditary pre-disposition on the part of our ignorant sailor to interpret floating driftwood, a basking whale or a string of porpoises, into the likeness of the traditional monster. To justify belief in the sea serpent demands evidence of quality so unexceptionable as to over-ride the adverse presumption derived from this innate tendency.

The most instructive sea serpent story which I have come across was told by a well-known literary man in a letter to the Times, 6th June, 1893. The writer had received in 1851 a description of the monster from a lady who had watched it disporting itself in a small bay on the coast of Sutherlandshire. But the writer had something more to tell. He himself searched the rocks and found some of the serpent's scales, as big as scallop shells. For many years he preserved these unique relics; but, alas, when he wanted to exhibit them to Sir Richard Owen,

"They were gone as the dew of the morning, They were lost as the dream of the day!"

Now all that can be urged, a priori, against the belief in the sea serpent can be urged against the belief in ghosts and much more. There is, as we have seen, no belief which is more deeply rooted in the past life of the race; there is no belief which appeals more surely to the popular imagination. The ' new ' journalist in search of a sensation finds nothing better suited to his purpose than a traditional ghost story brought up-to-date, and furnished with a local habitation. And ghost stories appeal further, jas we have seen, to the inherited religious instincts. Many for whom the merely marvelous would count for little seek in these narratives confirmation of a belief in personal immortality.

THE BELL WITCH PROJECT

If we are justified, then, in our suspicion of the sea serpent, we are doubly justified in the reluctant hearing which we yield to ghost stories. Man, as has been said by someone, is not naturally a veridical animal. It is not in fact an easy thing to tell the truth. It is the most difficult of all arts, and one of the latest acquirements of the most civilized races. There are in the first place defects and excesses in narration caused by self interest, or by the dramatic instinct, the love of telling a good story. But defects of this kind are generally recognized and proportionately easy to guard against. The real danger is more subtle. Not only our memory but our very acts of perception are shaped by our preconceptions and prejudices. To put it crudely, what we see and what we remember is not what actually happened, but what we think ought to have happened or what was likely to have happened. The retina supplies us with an imperfect photograph a crude sensation. But this imperfect photograph is not "perceived" until it has been telegraphed up to higher brain centers, and it is the business of these higher centers to touch up the photograph, to fill in the lacunae, to select what seem the more salient and notable features, and to color the whole with the emotion appropriate to the situation. It is likely that in most cases something is added to improve the picture. The result is no longer a photograph but a finished work of art, which contains at once more and less than the photograph the original sensation. This process of selection and embellishment may be carried still further in the memory, until at last the finished picture may come to bear no essential resemblance to the original retinal photograph.

In matters of every day life the picture, no doubt, generally serves the purpose as well as the photograph; better in fact, for the brain artist, if he has done his duty, has selected only those features which are needed for retention, and blotted out the rest. But where the emotions and prejudices are deeply concerned, another principle of selection is introduced. The sedulous artist works to please his patron—our noble self—and he is apt to produce a picture intended less for instruction than for edification. This is something more than a parable. It is an honest, though of course extremely crude and inadequate, attempt to express in psychological terms our actual mental procedure. The whole process is of course an automatic one, and could be alternatively expressed in terms of stimuli and nerve reactions. But the essential features of the process are no doubt easier to grasp if expressed in the language which is to most of us more familiar.

Now in this question of ghost stories, it is hardly necessary to say again that there are potent influences ceaselessly operating to guide the process of brain selection in other words to pervert testimony, or to warp it to predestined ends. We are bound, therefore, to apply the most stringent tests to the tales of ghostly apparitions. To begin with, we shall require that every ghost story must be told at

THE BELL WITCH PROJECT

first hand. If the man who saw the ghost is dead, and has left no written record behind him, so much the worse his ghost, for all evidential purposes, has perished with him. Nor can we in matters of this kind be content to rely upon a single memory. If a man tells us that he saw a ghost, we must have some evidence that he thought it of sufficient importance to mention it at the time to someone else. Again, whilst not rejecting the evidence of peasants and un-educated persons, we shall by preference seek for testimony amongst the educated classes, as having for the most part achieved greater proficiency in the difficult art of telling the truth. Again, in order to give the memory as little opportunity as may be for adding its finishing touches to the picture, we shall give the preference, ceteris paribus, to narratives committed to writing within a short period of the event related; and we shall value above all other testimony that of diaries and contemporary letters.

Such are the main principles which must guide us in our search for evidence of ghosts. Other principles will be made clearer as the discussion proceeds. But there is one other point which should be emphasized at the outset. The stories of sea serpents are comparatively speaking few in number. That of course constitutes a further serious defect in the case. In seeking evidence for any unusual phenomenon we must have regard to quantity as well as quality. Even a good witness may be mistaken, or there may be some unsuspected cause to give rise to a false belief. But the more witnesses of competence and good character are multiplied, the more improbable it becomes that they could all have been mistaken, or that the circumstances which may have deceived them will have escaped recognition.

It is important, therefore, for the reader to bear in mind that the narratives cited in this book are only samples, chosen from a much larger number, and that in making the choice I have necessarily been guided by the desire, not only to find good evidence, but also evidence which has not been staled by frequent repetition. Most of the stories printed in the book will, I trust, be new to the reader; and he can find some hundreds of others equally well attested in the publications of the Society for Psychical Research and other sources upon which I have drawn.

Here then are a few of what may be provisionally called "Ghost Stories." The first account comes from a lady who has had two or three similar experiences.

THE BELL WITCH PROJECT

From Miss Gollin.

130 Lafayette Avenue,

Brooklyn,

March 2nd, 1905.

"During the year 1896 I was employed in the office of a certain newspaper in this city. On Saturday, the 25th of January, 1896, at about 12:30 p.m., while attending to my work, all at once I felt conscious of a presence near me. In fact, it was just the same feeling one has when some one is intently looking at you, and you feel an inclination to turn to see who it is. This feeling was so strong that I turned almost involuntarily, and there at the back of my chair, but a little to one side, I saw the full figure of a young man with whom I was well acquainted; in fact, engaged to marry. (I wish to state here that this young man had never been in this office.) The figure was very distinct. In fact, it was all so plain that I felt the young woman sitting next to me must see it also, and though very much overcome and not understanding it at the time, I turned to her and asked, 'Did you see any one just now standing back of my chair?' She replied, 'No,' and, of course, wondered why I asked. I did not explain my reason to her at the time as, though she knew this person from hearsay, she had no acquaintance, and I felt she might think me foolish. However the incident is perfectly clear in her mind even to this day, and if necessary I can furnish her name and address. In fact, it is her husband who prevailed on me to make this communication to you.

"On the previous Sunday to this incident I had been at church with this young man, and he was, apparently, in very good health, though previously he had been ailing somewhat, we thought from overstudy, as he was just completing a college course. That evening after our return from church he made an engagement to see me the middle of the week. Instead of seeing me, received a letter from his sister saying he had a cold and might not come to see me until the end of the week, but that it was nothing serious. I wrote back, saying that as the weather was so bad he had probably better not try to come to see me until the Sunday following. (That week we had a great deal of wet weather.) I heard nothing further from any member of the family and fully expected to see him on Sunday.

"On reaching home on Saturday, January 25th, 1896, I found a telegram waiting for me, which read : ' If you wish to see W. come at once.' I did not reach home until about 2 p.m. I hurried to his home, and on arriving was told he had died about 12:30. It was a case of typhoid fever."

THE BELL WITCH PROJECT

In a later letter Miss Gollin explains that the figure appeared "fully dressed in a black suit of clothes."

Mrs. Burrows, the friend referred to, corroborates as follows :

179 Prospect Park W.,

Brooklyn, N. Y.,

29th March, 1905.

"I do not remember the exact date of the occurrence she mentions. I remember distinctly, however, that we were sitting together working in the office of the Evening Post, where we were both employed. Miss Gollin's chair was placed at right angles to mine, so that anyone approaching her chair would have been plainly visible to me. I remember her asking me if I had noticed a man standing back of her chair. As she said this she was in the act of looking behind her, as if expecting to find someone standing there, or as if she were conscious that someone had just been standing there. I saw nothing whatever myself, and am sure that no one in the flesh did approach her chair at that time. I told her I had seen no one, and thus the incident closed for the moment.

"I did not see her again for several days, when she told me, that on arriving home she had found a telegram stating that her fiance was dead. Later she learned the hour of his death corresponded exactly with that of the apparition which she had seen while at work."

In the next two cases the apparition, which was seen some hours after death, conforms more nearly to the orthodox conception of a " ghost " a discarnate spirit. The first case was originally narrated verbally to the late F. W. H. Myers by Lady Gore Booth, who afterwards wrote to him the letter of which an extract is given below, and at a later date sent the two subjoined accounts from her daughter, who was aged fifteen at the time of the incident, and her son, then a schoolboy of ten.

The above are a few samples of the testimony which is held by some in the present day to warrant belief in "ghosts." In the next chapter an attempt will be made to analyze the evidence and interpret its significance.

THE BELL WITCH PROJECT

GHOSTS AS HALLUCINATIONS

In the preceding chapter we have given a few examples, selected from many hundreds of similar narratives communicated to the Society for Psychical Research within the last thirty years. From the mere quantity alone the case for the ghost would seem to be much better than the case for the sea serpent. But if we examine the quality of the evidence, we find its superiority still more marked. Here we have to do, not with credulous and irresponsible sailors, but with well-educated men and women; and men and women who feel their responsibility in the matter sufficiently to allow their names to appear in attestation of their reports. Their testimony is given soberly and deliberately; it is impossible to doubt at any rate the sincerity of the witnesses. They may have been mistaken ; and in any particular case it is perhaps not difficult to suggest a plausible explanation, on normal lines, of the supposed apparition. Mr. Tandy may have mistaken some outside object bird or tree branch for the face of his friend looking in at the window; Mrs. McAlpine may have seen a fellow guest standing in the doorway of Mr. Bryce Douglas' sitting-room; Mr. Gore Booth may have caught a hasty glimpse of the new hallboy ; Frau Rieken may simply have been dreaming, and so on. But when these or similar explanations have to be applied to hundreds of stories, they are seen to be a little thin. It becomes more reasonable to believe that something out of the way was really seen in many of these cases a figure, but not a figure of flesh and blood.

Was this figure then a ghost? Are the dreams of men of old, the fancies of mediaeval poetry and art, justified by the facts? Is there really in each of us a quasi-material form having all the limbs and due proportions of the body which can leave the body for a time during life, which must leave it permanently at death, and which can under favorable conditions make itself visible to mortal eyes ? It may no doubt be said that there is nothing in our present knowledge of the constitution of the material world to forbid such an hypothesis. There may be, as one eminent physicist suggested in the last generation, intercalary vortex atoms ; there may be interstitial ether ; there may be space of four dimensions. We know too little to say absolutely that such an ethereal or psychical body could not exist. But it cannot be too clearly understood that there is no evidence of its existence. These apparitions have never yet been weighed or photographed, nor have they furnished any other proof of their kinship with matter.

But if it be admitted that in a universe which lies even yet for the most part in darkness or twilight, there may be room for ghosts as well as for ethereal vibrations, the ghost-theory, at any rate as applied to these apparitions, will still be found to present almost insuperable difficulties. Let us suppose that it was an ethereal or psychical counterpart of a human being which appeared to the several witnesses whose testimony was cited in the last chapter. The ghosts, it will have been observed, always appeared clothed. Have clothes also ethereal counterparts? Such was and is the belief of many early races of mankind, who leave clothes, food, and weapons in the graves of the dead, or burn them on the funeral pile, that their friends may have all they require in the spirit world. But are we prepared to accept this view ? And again, these ghosts commonly appear, not in the clothes which they were wearing at death for most deaths take place in bed but in some others, as will be seen from an examination of the stories already cited. Are we to suppose the ethereal body going to its wardrobe to clothe its nakedness withal ? or that, as in the case of Ensign Cavalcante's appearance to Frau Rieken, the ghost will actually take off the ethereal clothes it wore at death and replace them with others ? It is scarcely necessary to pursue the subject. The difficulties and contradictions involved in adapting it to explain the clothes must prove fatal to the ghost-theory.

There have, of course, been numerous claims on the part of Spiritualists and other latter day occultists to photograph spirits, and also the nerve emanations or perisprit of the living body; also on occasion to weigh so-called spiriti. But I am not acquainted with a single experiment of the kind which would justify any modification of the statement in the text.

Whatever else they may be, it seems clear that these apparitions are not ghosts in the old-fashioned sense. And yet, unless we are to distrust human testimony altogether, they are something. It is only within the last three or four generations that science has been in a position to explain what in fact these apparitions are. It is now generally agreed that they are of the stuff which dreams are made of; they are, in fact, waking dreams, or in technical phraseology, sensory hallucinations. There are in the brain, it has been estimated, some three thousand million nerve cells. In these cells are registered all sensory impressions; everything that we see, hear, feel, makes some kind of impression in some of these brain cells, and when the particular cells are again set in action the original sensation is reproduced, but in a fainter degree we remember what we saw, heard, or felt. The brain cells are variously and extensively connected with each other, so that when we are awake, the impressions made on one group of cells are continually touching off other associated groups ; and our main stream of thought is accompanied by currents of further images. In waking life these random chains of side association pass almost unregarded. But in sleep, when there is no continuous main stream of thought, any slight disturbance, within the body or without, may set going a chain of cells, each cell as it discharges itself touching off the next like a battery of Leyden jars and we have as a result a dream. The things seen in a dream are only memory images, or combinations of memory images; but the,y seem often as vivid as actual present sensations, because there is no present sensation to compare them with.

Now a hallucination is also a combination of memory images, but from some causes as yet very imperfectly understood it takes on momentarily the strength of an actual sensation is in fact an actual sensation. For psychologically there is no means of distinguishing between a memory image and a sensation image except by their relative strength. And if a man says he sees even when there is nothing there to be seen we must take his word for it. He is the only person who can possibly know. In other words, a typical hallucination is indistinguishable from a sense perception. To understand how this can be we must realize that in most, if not all, so-called acts of sense perception we perceive a great many details which may never have made an impression on the ear or eyes. This is especially noticeable when we are trying to see something in a dim light, or straining our ears to catch a faint sound. Everybody recognizes that in such a case we misinterpret by adding mental images to sensory data, until in the result we may really see or hear something entirely different from the object which turns out to have been actually present we may hear carriage wheels in the rustle of dead leaves on the drive, or a footstep in the creaking stair, or may see a threatening figure in an old tree outlined against the twilight sky. But even the normal processes of perception contain such memory images raised by association to the sensory level; or, as Taine has put it, "every perception is a true hallucination; as every hallucination is a false perception." A sensory hallucination therefore is simply an abnormal result from a normal process; it is, so to speak, a malformed perception, or an hypertrophied memory image.

We find a good illustration of the latter class of hallucinations, the pure memory image, in a recent record by M. Ernest Naville of his personal experience. The distinguished writer, now in his ninety-third year, is visited by numerous visual hallucinations. Amongst these hallucinations was one of a crowd of women wearing those enormous starched white coifs (cornettes) so common in France.

Searching for the origin of this vision, he finds it in an experience of his youth. Sixty-two years ago, in 1846, M. Naville was staying at the baths of Salins. In the church on Sunday was a large crowd of peasant women in huge coifs, who, tired with their week's work, fell asleep during the sermon. M. Naville still recalls the quaint sight presented by all these coifs violently agitated when the Cure interrupted his sermon to cry, *"He!! Que de dormeuses, mon Dieu."*

("Hey! What sleepers! My God!")

THE BELL WITCH PROJECT

Some years back there was much discussion on the question whether hallucinations were always started from without, either by the misinterpretation of some actual sensation, or by some defect in the sensory organ, or whether they could ever be centrally initiated, from the brain itself. Such questions have now been practically settled by the study of hypnotism. For in hypnotism it is unquestionable that true sensory hallucinations can be engendered by the mere suggestion of the hypnotist. These post-hypnotic hallucinations, indeed, are some of the most valuable and interesting results from the study of the induced trance. I have seen an educated lady, a nursing Sister, on waking from the trance pick out one of several blank cards. In accordance with a suggestion given during the trance, she saw on the blank card a photograph of one of the persons present. The card was given to her; she thanked the donor, congratulated him on the excellent likeness, and put the sham photograph in her pocket. As I afterwards learnt from her, when she found the card in her pocket on her return home an hour or two later, it had returned to its original blankness. But the force of suggestion will go further than this. It is not difficult to make a good subject see the figure of a person not actually present. Professor Bernheim relates that he suggested to a soldier in the trance that on a certain day he, the soldier, should come to Bernheim's study, where he would meet the President of the French Republic, who would bestow a decoration. On the appointed day the soldier entered the study, saluted low, and returned thanks for the imaginary decoration.

The late Edmund Gurney made a few successful experiments of the kind upon a particularly suggestible subject, Zillah, a maid-servant in the employment of Mrs. Ellis, then of 40 Keppel Street, Russell Square. In the third trial the suggestion was given to the girl when in the trance on the evening of July 13th, 1887, that she should see an apparition of Mr. Gurney on the following day at 3.0. p.m. Mrs. Ellis was not forewarned of the experiment. On the 14th July she wrote:

"As I suppose you gave Zillah a post-hypnotic hallucination, probably you will wish to hear of it. I will give you the story in her own words, as I jotted them down immediately afterwards, saying nothing to her, of course, of my doing so. She said : ' I was in the kitchen washing up, and had just looked at the clock, and was startled to see how late it was five minutes to three when I heard footsteps coming down the stairs rather a quick, light step and I thought it was Mr. Sleep (the dentist whose rooms are in the house), ' but as I turned around, with a dish mop in one hand and a plate in the other, I saw someone with a hat on, who had to stoop as he came down the last step, and there was Mr. Gurney! He was dressed just as I saw him last night, black coat and grey trousers, his hat on, and a roll of paper, like manuscript, in his hand, and he said, 'Oh, good afternoon.' And then he glanced all round the kitchen, and he glared at me with an awful look, as if he was going to murder me, and said, ' Warm afternoon, isn't it ?' and then, 'Good afternoon' or 'Good day,' I'm not sure which, and turned and went up the stairs again, and after standing thunderstruck a minute, I ran to the foot of the stairs, and saw like a boot just disappearing on the top step.' She said, ' I think I must be going crazy. Why should I always see something at three o'clock each day after the seance? But I am not nearly so frightened as I was at seeing Mr. Smith.' She seemed particularly impressed by the awful look Mr Gurney gave her. I presume this was the hallucination you gave her."

AMELIA A. ELLIS.

Here, it will be seen, was a first-class ghost evoked in broad daylight by a mere suggestion given to the percipient some eighteen hours previously. But there is no need to multiply instances. Post-hypnotic hallucinations of this kind are amongst the accepted facts of science. And it has yet to be shown that these artificially produced hallucinations differ in any respect from the "ghosts" of which specimens are cited above. In default of any such evidence, we are entitled to treat these ghosts as simply hallucinations; the creation in each case of the percipient's brain. That solution avoids the great clothes difficulty, and simplifies the problem in other ways. But it leaves the question unanswered: If these apparitions are simply hallucinations—waking dreams with no substantial reality behind them—how is it that they should so often make their appearance when the person whom they resemble is seriously ill or dying ; or if, as sometimes happens, the figure is unrecognized, how does it come about that the same figure is often seen by others, either simultaneously, or at different times in the same house? Now if we accept the broad facts, that is, if we believe that not only in the five or six cases quoted in the last chapter, but in the hundreds of other equally well-attested cases published of recent years, there was an hallucinatory figure seen, and that the vision really came within a short time of a death or illness, or was really repeated within the experience of some other person or persons if we accept this statement of the case, there are obviously only two explanations. Either hallucinations of this kind are so common that we might reasonably expect to find such a number of coincidences, or there is some common cause for the coincidences. If we find two persons in the same neighborhood reading a book by Miss Marie Corelli, we shall probably be justified in attributing the coincidence to chance, the mere caprice of Mudie's agent. But if we find the two persons reading Basil Valentine, his Triumphal Chariot of Antimony, we can hardly suppose the coincidence to be accidental.

The question which we have to determine is whether hallucinations arerelatively as common as novels by Marie Corelli, or relatively as rare as mediaeval works on Alchemy. That is a question of fact, and can only be answered by actual statistics.

But even if we find that hallucinations are of sufficiently rare occurrence to make the coincidence of a hallucination with a death or any other event extremely improbable, it may be urged that there is not sufficient ground for inferring a causal connection between the two events. The mere fact that most persons who have experienced these hallucinations believe in such a connection has not really much to say in the matter. For most persons have been used to thinking of these apparitions as ghosts, and we have seen that they are not ghosts. But we should not be deterred from seeking for a causal connection between the two events because it is not immediately obvious. Our ancestors saw no connection between imperfect drainage and typhoid fever; and the connection, in the last generation, between the rare visits of a steamer to St. Kilda and an epidemic of catarrh on the island was for long a matter of popular observation before it was accepted by medical science.

But the search for a cause may well be deferred until we have some reasonable grounds for thinking that any cause is indicated other than the fallacy of human testimony. In a scientific enquiry the first step is to ascertain the facts. It so happens that, whilst the hallucinations of madness and disease have for long attracted the attention of medical men, no serious study had, until recently, been made of hallucinations occurring in normal life. Indeed, by most persons, medical men and others, until a generation ago, the occurrence of a hallucination would in itself have been held to indicate serious disturbance of health. But the study of Hypnotism, and the work of the Society for Psychical Research, presently to be described, have shown us that such is not the case. A hallucination is no doubt in the strictest sense a pathological event, but it is no more serious, if somewhat rarer, than a toothache or such a mild attack of cramp as most persons occasionally experience. It has indeed been aptly defined as a cramp of the mind.

In 1887 the late Professor Sidgwick, at the instance of the Congress of Experimental Psychology, which met in Paris in that year, undertook to institute an enquiry into the nature and distribution of spontaneous hallucinations of the sane. He was assisted by a committee of the Society for Psychical Research and a large staff of voluntary workers, who were all carefully instructed in their duties. By these means the following question was put to 17,000 persons, mostly residents of the United Kingdom ' Have you ever, when believing yourself to be completely awake, had a vivid impression of seeing or being touched by a living being or an inanimate object, or of hearing a voice, which impression, so far as you could discover, was not due to any external physical cause?"

THE BELL WITCH PROJECT

The results showed that 655 out of 8,372 men, and 1,029 out of 8,628 women 9.9 per cent out of the whole number had experienced a sensory hallucination at some time in their lives, many more than once. Of the total number of hallucinations, about two-thirds affected the sense of sight.

It will be noted that the great majority of the visual hallucinations take the form of realistic human figures ; in fact, other forms are so few as to be almost negligible. The most important point, evidentially, to be deduced from the table is that these hallucinations, impressive though they no doubt were at the time, tend to be soon forgotten. The apparitions during the first year are more numerous than in any previous year. There is a drop in the second year, and a still greater drop in the other years of the decade, but a distinct rise in the fifth and tenth year. This rise is, again, an indication that the figures are not wholly trustworthy " five years ago " and " ten years ago " have no doubt been given as round numbers. Once more, the average age of the percipients was forty, and they were asked for accounts of all experiences since the age of ten. If all hallucinations were remembered the figures in the column "more than ten years ago" ought therefore to be double those in the previous column. In fact, they are only 15 per cent higher. After a careful consideration of all the circumstances, the Committee estimated that, to arrive at the actual total of visual hallucinations experienced by this group of 17,000 persons during the period in question, the numbers in the table should be multiplied by four.

We have now to consider whether hallucinations of this kind are sufficiently frequent to justify the assumption that their coincidence say with a death, being a unique event in each man's experience is due to chance alone.

If in the table we take only the recognized and realistic apparitions of the human figure, and subtract all doubtful cases, i.e., cases where it seems possible that the figure seen may have been that of a real man or woman, and all cases where the percipient had had more than one similar experience, we find that we have 322 cases to deal with. Multiplied by 4, these amount to 1,288, or in round numbers 1,300.

But of the 322 we find 62 are reported to have coincided with a death, i.e, to have occurred within twelve hours, on one side or other, of the death of the person represented. Now of the 62 death coincidences, 11 are reported as occurring in the previous ten years, and 51 before that date. The average age of the narrators of death coincidences is forty-six (that of our informants generally being only forty), so that, as experiences under ten years of age are excluded, there are twenty-six years included in the remoter period. If 11 experiences occur in 10 years, we should look for 29 at most in the remaining 26 years we find 51! So far from being forgotten, the hallucinations coinciding with death appear to be remembered too well. It is clear that, as the experience recedes into the past, the closeness of thje coincidence is apt to be magnified, or the narrative in some other way unconsciously improved. After making liberal allowance for this unconscious exaggeration, and for another disturbing cause the possible influence of selection on the results! the probable number of death coincidences is reduced by the Committee to 30.

We have, then, 30 coincidences with death in 1,300 apparitions. But the death rate for the last completed decade (1881-1890) of the period under review was 19.15, i.e., the probability that any person taken at random would die within any given 24 hours was 19.15 in 365,000= about 1 in 19,000. If there is no causal connection between the hallucination and the death, we should find but 1 coincidence in 19,000 we actually find 1 in 43.

If we accept the Committee's estimates we must, it will be seen, dismiss the explanation of chance coincidence. But the Committee's estimates may be at fault in two ways. On the one hand they may not have allowed enough for forgetfulness in ordinary cases. It is scarcely conceivable, however, the margin being so wide, that any error in this direction would appreciably affect the results. If we multiplied the total of 322 by ten, or by a hundred, we should still find the non-coincidental hallucinations too few.

But, on the other hand, we have seen that the death coincidences have been improved and exaggerated, and it may be urged that this process of embellishment may have gone to far greater lengths than is allowed for in the estimate. To adopt that explanation of the results is no doubt to assume grave inaccuracies on the part not only of the original informants, but of their friends who have furnished corroborative testimony. And we have to assume these inaccuracies in connection with an event which of all others is most calculated to leave a permanent impress on the memory. Moreover, in some cases the reports of the apparitions are supported by entries in diaries, or contemporary letters. The assumption of wholesale inaccuracy in the reports is therefore a violent and improbable one. But since we have good reason for holding that some at least of the reports are inaccurate, we cannot summarily dismiss the objection. For the present writer, indeed, it has considerable weight; it seems difficult to place any limit on the untrustworthiness of human testimony, especially in cases where the emotions are involved, or where there is occasion for edification. And if the hallucinations alleged to coincide with death were isolated phenomena standing altogether alone in human experience, we should probably quote a hasty utterance of the Hebrew

THE BELL WITCH PROJECT

Psalmist and pass on. But since, as will be shown in later chapters, they do not stand alone, but appear to fit into a larger scheme, the reader is asked for the present to hold his judgment in suspense, until he shall have the whole of the facts before him.

TELEPATHY

So far, we have seen reason to believe that apparitions occasionally occur at the time of a death, that these apparitions are not ghosts but hallucinations, and that they occur so frequently as to render it, if not practically certain, at least a matter of high probability that they are in some way connected with the death.

Now a hallucination being a product of thought, a kind of waking dream, we have next to enquire how a dying, or perhaps a dead man, can affect another man's thought and make him dream a dream. On this point science has no explanation to offer. The facts already cited, and other kindred facts which will be considered in a later chapter, clearly indicate such a possibility, and the hypothetical process has been named Thought Transference or Telepathy (from Greek tele, at a distance, and pathos, feeling). But the name is not explanatory ; it is, like Gravitation, a name for an observed or presumed process of which no clear conception has yet been formed.

The theory of gravitation simply expresses the observed fact, that all bodies in the Universe exercise a certain pull upon each other, or rather act as if they exercised such a pull. Newton measured the pull, but did not explain it.

The theory of Telepathy simply collects into one generalization a number of observations, tending to show that under certain conditions not yet understood a human mind or brain can act upon another mind or brain by means of which we are as yet ignorant. Just as there are theories which essay to explain the action of gravitation in accordance with what we know or guess of the physical construction of the Universe, so it has been suggested that the action of Telepathy may consist in the transfer of molecular disturbance from one brain to another by means of ethereal vibrations. We know, or perhaps it should rather be said, we infer, that there are molecular changes in brain cells corresponding to all acts of thinking or feeling ; we know, too, that there are gaps in the scale of ethereal vibrations; and there is nothing to forbid the supposition that one or other of these gaps may hereafter be found to be filled by undulations competent to convey intelligence from one brain to another.

But beyond this there are no facts to go upon; the theory of Telepathy is as much in the air as the theory of gravitation itself, and it need scarcely be said, is immensely inferior to it in the breadth and security of its basis. Even with this qualification, to compare Telepathy, a humble postulant for scientific recognition, with the great generalization which is the chief glory of modern science may seem almost an impertinence; but, in fact, the two theories are closely related, though Telepathy, it must be admitted, figures at present as a very poor relation.

For the conception of an inexplicable force linking the stars together, and the conception of an inexplicable force linking men and women to each other are in their origin but different aspects of the same primitive idea. Both alike proceed from astrology; the Chaldean astronomers, gazing at the stars from their Babel-towers, conceived the idea of a subtle influence binding together all the heavenly bodies and directing their wanderings. It was but a short step to suppose that these same influences which radiated from star to star affected also the dwellers upon earth. The belief in these starry influences as affecting the affairs of men persisted through the Middle Ages and almost into modern times. Van Helmont, one of the most distinguished physicians and chemists of his day, whose life over-lapped by a year or two that of Sir Isaac Newton, took the facts of astrology as beyond controversy. "Ye grant," he says in one of his polemical writings, " that material nature doth daily draw down Forces by its magnetism from the superior orbs, and much desire the favour of the celestial bodies, and that the Heavens do in exchange invisibly allure something from the inferior bodies, that there may be a free and mutual passage and a harmonious concord of the members with the whole Universe."

And some even of Van Helmont's successors found specific illustrations of this reciprocal influence between all things in the universe in the relation between physican and patient, between disease and health-giving drugs, and between witch and victim. As star could influence star across the void, so herbs and gems could heal disease at a distance. The wise physician could read the thoughts of his patient from afar, and the witch, a kind of malefic star, could project his or her baleful influence on her fellows. By like means spirits could read the thoughts of those who questioned them, and in this power to read thoughts the Mediaeval Church found the surest test of the presence of a demon in the patient.

In a word, this belief in unseen mental influences is probably as old as the earliest civilization of which we have any records. At the present day the belief in similar processes, whether of reading the thoughts of other men, or of obtaining information from direct communion with the natural world, or of inflicting disease or death by the mere act of will, is found in many uncivilized races. The person exercising the power usually passes into a kind of self-induced trance or delirium, apparently like that of the Pythian priestess, who chanted oracles to the ancient

THE BELL WITCH PROJECT

Greeks. Two or three instances may be cited.

The first point which will strike the critical reader in all these accounts is the great variety in the figures seen. The popular conception of a ghost is of a figure appearing in a definite shape and with a definite purpose. But the popular conception is by no means borne out by the majority of the well-attested first hand records.

But there is another point worthy of notice. The ghostly visions were in each case preceded by inexplicable noises, interpreted in some cases as footsteps. In some accounts especially stress is laid by the narrators on the alarm excited by these unexplained sounds. But it is clear in tother cases that the noises caused, if not actual alarm, at least uneasiness and anxiety. In this respect also these stories may be accepted as typical. In most authentic ghost stories, it may be said, the appearance of the ghostly figure is preceded by mysterious noises. Sometimes, as in the case of a "haunted house," the haunting may be said to consist exclusively of mysterious sounds. It has been shown that the house was found by a careful observer to be exceptionally noisy. This is not so clearly established in other cases, though it should be mentioned that in one case there was a railway embankment not far off. There seems good reason for thinking that at any rate in the first two cases the mysterious sounds which first excited and alarmed the occupants were misinterpretations or imaginative exaggerations of real sounds. We have then the following sequence of events. First: loud and mysterious sounds probably due to normal causes. Second: a state of uneasiness and apprehension, amounting in some cases to actual panic, in the occupants. Third: the appearance of manifold ghostly figures, sometimes of a terrifying character.

The sequence is repeated again and again in the best authenticated narratives, those in which the incidents are recorded near the date of their happening, and it seems permissible to suggest that the sequence is a causal one that real sounds, exaggerated and misinterpreted, induced in nervous persons a state of uneasy expectancy, and that this nervous state in its turn gave rise to hallucinations.

We find a somewhat similar state of nervous expectancy with concomitant hallucinations at some Spiritualist seances. But the subject, it must be admitted, requires further investigation. At any rate we have here a possible explanation of at least nine tenths of what pass for ghost stories.

But the explanation, itself only tentative, does not cover all the admitted facts. In case cited above, it seems clear that Miss J. A. A., at the time when she

THE BELL WITCH PROJECT

saw the figure of a child, had not heard that a similar figure had been seen in the house by others. In another case, Miss Blencowe, who apparently had heard no details of Miss S.'s experience, saw a similar figure standing in the same spot. The same feature occurs in a few other cases the appearance of a figure frequently bearing a resemblance to a figure previously seen, to a person who had been kept in ignorance of the previous apparitions. It is true that people may in the course of years forget what they have been told. But apart from the improbability of forgetting such an exciting incident as a real ghost seen by a friend, there is the further consideration that in many cases the original percipient would be unlikely to let her story be widely circulated, for fear of alarming the other inmates, especially servants.

On the whole it seems reasonable to suppose that the accounts given may be in the main correct; and that a similar type of hallucination may, without any verbal suggestion, recur in the same locality.

Again, as in the case of the apparitions previously discussed, we are driven back upon the hypothesis of mental suggestion. But it need scarcely be pointed out that the vague purposeless nature of the phantasm lends no support to the view that the suggestion emanates from the mind of the dead. The figure seen is as lifeless and unreal, for the most part, as a magic-lantern picture. It is dreamlike, anyway, and common sense points to its source in the dreams of the living whom we know, rather than in the imagined dreams of the unknown dead.

It will be seen that the facts when closely investigated lend tittle support to the popular conception of a ghost. The spirit of the sensual man, still hovering near the scene of his earthly joys, the repentant monk, the murderer still doomed in nightly penance to re-enact his crime, the soul in the torture of purgatory who comes for comfort and absolution all these are, it would seem, but figments of popular superstition. The real ghost, as we have learnt to know him, is but a painted shadow, without life or meaning or purpose the baseless fabric of a dream.

But the investigation of these curious phenomena is by no means complete; and though they should prove to be wholly born of earth, these ghosts of the living and of the dead assuredly illustrate in a striking manner the mysterious workings of the human mind, and the unsuspected influence of soul on soul. They are meteors which throw strange gleams of light upon the structure of the Cosmos of which they form a hitherto neglected part. Once more we see the justification of the scientific maxim, to study residual phenomena.

THE END?

THE BELL WITCH PROJECT

THEY ARE NOT LIKE YOU AND ME...THEY DEFINITELY ARE NOT ORDINARY FOLKS

—THEY ARE—

VERY STRANGE PEOPLE

All New!

"MAD" MOLLIE FANCHER
THE BROOKLYN ENIGMA

Religious Miracle Worker?

Or Supernatural Phenomenon?

After suffering near-fatal accidents, "Mad" Mollie – the "Brooklyn Enigma – took to her bed and did not rise for 51 years. She steadfastly refused any food and was regarded as a saint, drawing thousands to observe her apparent sacred ability to live in defiance of the laws of nature.

But "Mad" Mollie possessed many supernatural traits making her popular with the spiritualist and psychic communities. These abilities included:

She was said to have slept for days at a time and never got up even to walk around the room. It was claimed that she lost several of her senses – those of smell, taste and sight. Despite this she could accurately tell time just by listening to the ticking of a clock that was out of normal hearing range. She created elaborate embroidered pieces though she apparently lacked mobility and certainly had no devices at her disposal to produce them; in fact, it was said she was pretty much paralyzed. She was oblivious to pain and was able to read a book or paper simply by holding it in her hands.

Here are also other strange paranormal happenings centered around women at approximately the same time. ** – A potbelly stove in Italy that began to speak, uttering demonic curses, while two young female mediums served as a conduit for "spirit paintings" created by artists from the world of the dead. ** – In another case, spooky faces began to appear on the tiles of a family home. The faces could not be destroyed even when the floor was dug up.

An amazing account about an amazing lady – Good Golly Miss Mollie had it all!

Order "MAD" MOLLIE – THE BROOKLYN ENIGMA - $20.00

Large Format —242 pages—ISBN: 1606111884

ORDER FROM:
Timothy Green Beckley · Box 753 · New Brunswick, NJ 08903

THE BELL WITCH PROJECT

Just Released!

THE BELL WITCH PROJECT

Poltergeist – Ghosts – Exorcisms And The Supernatural

In Early American History

**

– Here are America's earliest and most frightening tales of the paranormal – with a new overview of the scariest poltergeist case of all time ... THE BELL WITCH! .

You've seen the various Hollywood horror movie variations of this horrifying American poltergeist case– but these cinematic efforts have never done justice to what really happened in Tennessee back in 1817 that created mass hysteria and even caused a soon to be president – General Andrew Jackson – to feel the wrath of this horrid specter from beyond the grave. The Bells were an upright farming family said to have incurred the ire of one Kate Batts, who put a deathbed curse on the Bells that defies all rational understanding.

REVEALED IN THIS VOLUME!

Super psychic Shawn Robbins, a protege of the late ghost hunter, Dr. Hans Holzer. was able to "revisit" the scene of the Bell Witch haunting and gain new insight into the nearly two hundred years old case. The highly respected paranormal expert, Paul Eno, recounts stories of vampires in New England in the 18th and 19th centuries and also tells the little-known story of an invasion of demonic specter "hooligans." Journey with Tim Beckley to the historically haunted locales of Jerome, Arizona, and Sleepy Hollow, New York, where ghostly spirits and disembodied voices seem to have established a haven and interact frequently with visitors.

Acclaimed writer Sean Casteel contributes accounts of phantoms and monsters as well as a synopsis of a case of demonic possession that occurred in another New England clergyman's home some 20 years before the trials in Salem made everyone vulnerable to the charge. Also, read about the lesser known Salem witch trial of 1878, in which one Christian Scientist sued another over the "mind crime" of Malicious Animal Magnetism. And let us not forget the stories of swamp women – flying creatures – and specters and phantoms and things that go bump in the night and continue to scare us all to this very day.

Order: The Bell Witch Project - $20.00 — Large Format — ISBN: 1606111892

Timothy Green Beckley · Box 753 · New Brunswick, NJ 08903

THE BELL WITCH PROJECT
Updated Edition!

SECRETS OF THE REAL DOCTOR FRANKENSTEIN
Mad Scientist Andrew Crosse – Monster Maker

Did he create the building blocks of life in his laboratory? Or was he delusional? Or perhaps even a total fraud? His contemporaries in the scientific community were puzzled by the very nature of his experiments. And while the eye does not deceive, they were unable to duplicate his findings and reproduce under controlled conditions the striking life forms that were plainly visible and clearly moving around Crosse's laboratory table.

To the farmers living in the area surrounding Crosse's palatial Fyne Court, he quickly became recognized as a heretic dabbling in dark areas that led him to be on the receiving end of a significant number of irate letters from God-fearing folk who summarily and loudly accused him of blasphemy, or even trying to replace their God as the ultimate creator.

The contentions of the nearby country folk were only compounded by Andrew Crosse's ability to seemingly capture bolts of lightning and direct them through a mile long coil of copper wire that was suspended from poles and trees all around his estate. Events reached a boiling point when Crosse began to receive anonymous death threats. There were those who firmly blamed him for a failure in the year's wheat-crop; and there was even a demand that an exorcism of the whole area be undertaken in the surrounding green hills. It is said that the author of Frankenstein, Marry Shelly, got her inspiration from Crosse's "demented" laboratory experiments.

Order: Secrets of Dr Frankenstein – $22.00

Large Format – 350 Pages—ISBN: 16061111906

SPECIAL – BOTH BOOKS—*The Bell Witch Project and Secrets Of The Real Doctor Frankenstein— $37.50 + $5.00 S/H*

Timothy Green Beckley Box 753 • New Brunswick, NJ 08903

THE BELL WITCH PROJECT

Best Seller! Pop Culture-Quirky Topic

PIONEERS OF SPACE — LOST BOOK OF GEORGE ADAMSKI

My Trip To The Moon, Mars And Venus

Were His Astounding Claims Fact Or Fiction? Did He Really Ride In A Space Ship To The Moon And Beyond? Or was his best seller Flying Saucers Have Landed It All Merely A Rewrite Of A Work of Science Fiction Published Some Years Before, in the late 1940s?

Copies of this initial work — *PIONEERS OF SPACE: A TRIP TO THE MOON, MARS AND VENUS* — have been almost impossible to obtain so that researchers could check the similarities for themselves. A few copies recently turned up on the internet where they were being offered for over $700.00.

Our limited reprint of this volume is an exact reproduction of this rarity - truth or fiction. Included in this reproduction is some even earlier writings involving a metaphysical society Adamski called The Royal Order Of Tibet, and a 1951 article from Fate magazine detailing an event in which UFOs posed for his telescope in front of numerous witnesses THAT CANNOT BE DENIED!

Order: PIONEERS OF SPACE—$29.95—318 Pages – Large Format—ISBN 1606110357

REALITY OF THE INNER EARTH — RETURN TO THE CAVERNS WITH RICHARD SHAVER

Shaver claims to have visited an underground civilization populated by a sun starved race of soulless, mutated, beings known as the Dero. The Dero kidnap humans and take them to their subterranean cities for sadastic purposes and often to eat their flesh. Shaver says UFOs are piloted by an ancient race who are in touch with these demented creatures who are responsible for mind controlled murders, accidents and wars worldwide.

Here are: Ancient Death Ray Machines That Are Aimed At Surface Dwellers Constantly In An Attempt To Create Havoc Among The Population. Holographic Projections That Create False Illusions And Are Responsible For Unexplained Appearances of Many UFOs. The Existence Of Numerous Underground Races Including The "Good Guys" Known as the Tero, The Ancient Race Of Titans, And Atlantean Giants.

Order REALITY OF THE INNER EARTH—$15.00—150 Pages—Large Format —ISBN: 1892062925

Wild Claims Department!

OMNEC ONEC – AMBASSADOR FROM VENUS and VIVENUS STARCHILD

The late Dr. Frank E. Stranges said he once met a man inside the Pentagon who was from another world and could read minds. The visiting stranger had no fingerprints because there was no crime on his home planet nor any wars. A college professor once told me how he had witnessed the landing of a spaceship and saw its alien crew emerge and drive off in an American-made automobile, only to see one of them standing in a supermarket line shortly thereafter.

These unique works are the personal accounts of living human beings who, with their full consent and active cooperation, were transported to Earth in a spacecraft from another planet. Both arrived after being carefully prepared and conditioned to live here and grow in the physical society of the native life-wave of our own planet. And the remarkable thing is that Omnec Onec is still here, perhaps getting ready to reemerge from hiding once more as our planet's people go through tough times yet again. On the other hand, ViVenus has vanished – perhaps to go back to her home planet?

Order: OMNEC ONEC—$24.00—Large Format—282 Pages—ISBN: 1606110519

Order: VIVENUS STARCHILD—(Bonus: Flying Saucer Revelations, Included)—$16.00—162 Pages—Large Format—ISBN: 160611106X

SUPER DUPER SPECIAL – ALL 6 BOOKS ON THESE THREE PAGES JUST $99.00 + $10.00 S/H WITH BONUS TV INTERVIEW WITH VENUSIAN LADY

Just ask for the Very Strange People Series (Please give us your street address for delivery) Timothy G. Beckley, Box 753, New Brunswick, NJ 08903

www.ingramcontent.com/pod-product-compliance
Lightning Source LLC
Chambersburg PA
CBHW080358170426
43193CB00016B/2752